PEACE
THROUGH CHRIST

RADIO MESSAGES BROADCAST IN

THE SEVENTH LUTHERAN HOUR

By

WALTER A. MAIER, PH. D.

Professor of the Old Testament
Concordia Theological Seminary
St. Louis, Mo.

O send out Thy light and
Thy truth! — Psalm 43:3

St. Louis, Mo.
CONCORDIA PUBLISHING HOUSE
1940

FOREWORD

THE past months have afforded radio its first opportunity to broadcast coast-to-coast messages of Christian truth during widespread international warfare. Hearts have been heavy in this country since the outbreak of the European struggle. Added to the fear that our nation may become involved in this conflict is the pressure of personal perplexities, the economic problems confronting millions in the United States. Government reports indicate that every sixth American is supported by public relief funds. Social investigation reveals that half the children of our cities grow up in surroundings that do not permit a decent standard of living. Children in the rural districts fare no better. At the same time the menace of atheistic Communism has increased; the prevalence of crime continues to alarm even public officials; American education often applauds irreligion; and, worst of all, unbelief has gained mastery in many churches. Spiritual ignorance marks both the high (literary experts, in a question-and-answer broadcast, know the first sentence in the Declaration of Independence but not the opening verse of the Bible) and the low (50,000 youngsters from New York sidewalks vote that President Roosevelt means more to them than God). Under the financial pressure of the last decade churches have retrenched and restricted their expansion.

During these disquieted days our mission of the air has therefore followed one supreme purpose — to bring the masses tuned to our broadcast the promise of peace through Christ, the soul-rest established on Calvary through the redeeming death of God's Son. Nothing else can comfort and sustain human hearts, convicted of their own sin and impressed with the futility of finding human agencies that can quiet the conscience and restore the joy of life. Consequently we have steadfastly sought to emphasize the inerrancy of the Scriptures, Christ's deity, His full, free, and final atonement, the blessing of His resurrection, justification by faith, and the life everlasting.

Because these foundation doctrines are systematically assailed, it was necessary, as far as the radio code permitted, to repel the attacks on revealed truth and the encroachments on Christian liberty. This required, for example, a declaration setting forth the dangers involved in sending a presidential representative to the Vatican. To counteract the anti-Biblical tendencies in certain newspapers and publications, it was expedient to mention specific, flagrant instances of this enmity. Repeatedly we warned against the subtle propaganda designed to draw this country into the overseas conflict. We were determined, however, that the center of each message, the source of every comfort, the strength of all hope, should be Christ crucified, resurrected, eternally victorious. By finding soul-peace in Him, our appeal emphasized, even during these days of racial hatred and class opposition, men could be moved by thoughts of love toward all mankind.

How were these Christ-centered broadcasts received? Had the Lutheran Hour's audience grown weary of the Gospel after six years of our radio preaching? Has our "Bringing-Christ-to-the-nation" endeavor been overshadowed by the religious programs of large churches or powerful councils?

At the conclusion of no previous broadcasting season have we had as abundant reason to thank God Almighty for the sustained outpouring of His blessings as now, at the end of the Seventh Lutheran Hour. While each successive year has brought added evidence of His divine guidance, the present season has fairly overwhelmed us. Measured by every standard at our disposal, the 1939—1940 mission of the air is far in excess of any previous record.

In the first place, the number of stations in the present coast-to-coast network was increased over the Sixth Lutheran Hour from sixty-six to ninety-four. This extension was concentrated especially on the Southeast, Alabama, Tennessee, Kentucky, and North Carolina, a vast area previously untouched by our broadcast. New outlets were also added in other sections of the country not adequately served, notably the State of Michigan.

Of greater significance than the addition of twenty-eight new chain stations was the wide use of

electrical transcriptions. Valuable, strategically lo-
cated stations, not affiliated with national hook-ups,
were asked to accept our transcribed messages; and
the response was so wide-spread that during the course
of the six months no fewer than seventy-two stations
in the United States were thus added to our broadcasting system. Even a preliminary survey of the
returns from this form of radio is impossible at
present; yet the results during this first season prove
the value of transcriptional broadcasting beyond all
doubt. We are so convinced of its effectiveness that
this department will be notably increased for the
Eighth Lutheran Hour.

The most noteworthy achievement of the past
season, made possible largely by these transcriptions,
was the extension of our radio system into fields outside the United States. Three stations in Canada, one
in Panama (short- and long-wave), one in Porto
Rico, one in Ecuador, three in Colombia, one in
Venezuela, and one in Bolivia (short- and long-wave),
have been secured for our messages. Indications
abound that many more outlets will be made available
to us in South America, since the response from
station-owners in that continent is very gratifying.

Most of the South American broadcasts are in
Spanish. This necessitates the translation of Lutheran Hour addresses, the preparation of hymns
and announcements in that language. This department, with all the details of its correspondence, has

been conducted by three students at Concordia Seminary, Mr. Alfred Saez, Mr. Manuel Morales, and Mr. Samuel Assaf.

Perhaps the most penetrating of all our stations outside this country is KZRM in Manila, secured for us chiefly through the efforts of Chaplain Floyd Dreith, U. S. Navy. The messages broadcast from this oulet, the most powerful commercial station in the entire Orient, have brought letters from listeners throughout the Philippines, in China (as far as one thousand miles up the Yangtze River), Indo-China, Australia, New Zealand, New Guinea, and even India. Is it not evidence of divine guidance that God's Word can now be preached with this almost unbelievable spread?

Because of this remarkable increase in our broadcasting facilities we have enjoyed a parallel growth in our audience. The number of letters from listeners totaled 175,000. Almost 13,000 letters have come to headquarters during a single week, almost 3,500 in one day. With this volume of mail it can be understood why, at the season's height, it was necessary to employ a clerical force of twenty-five workers. This number does not include my own staff, engaged exclusively in answering personal and problem mail.

If this correspondence were catalogued, it would show, first of all, many letters from church-members. Representatives of practically every Christian denomination wrote us lines of encouragement. Contrary to the opinion of many, the greater part of the correspondence does not come from those affiliated with my Church. Investigation of some thirteen hundred letters received during a certain period at Station WCAE, Pittsburgh, revealed that only fifty-five were written by members of my communion.

The wide sweep of the Seventh Lutheran Hour may be visualized also in the polyglot character of this mail. Many of our listeners write in Spanish, German, Norwegian, Swedish, with other languages used in isolated instances. The extent of our correspondence in braille increased notably, and for their general assistance in our enlarged work among blind listeners we thank especially Mr. Frederick Graepp, Mr. David Ronecker, Mrs. Bertha Schroeder, Miss Adeline Ruenzi, and the Rev. O. C. Schroeder.

Christians throughout the country who love the Lord Jesus and want their creed to harmonize with all His teachings have been whole-hearted in their support of our work. Many regard our broadcast as the voice of conservative Biblical Christianity, pleading for the faith once given, emphasizing Christ's blood-bought salvation as the only hope of the race, indicting all attempts to minimize the Savior's deity and His atoning blood. The response from Protestants and Catholics shows a wide and deep love for the Gospel. While we did not go out of our way in these radio addresses to criticize every false doctrine within modern churches (particularly since the present Broadcasters' Code looks upon such procedure with disfavor), we did not side-step any condemnation of error suggested by the text.

Once again the radio demonstrated its value in bringing the message of the Cross to isolated localities. Listeners in Northern Ontario, forty miles from the nearest church and cut off during the winter months from all possibility of attendance, welcomed this Sunday afternoon service. Friends in New Guinea wrote that their closest white neighbors are thirty-five miles distant, across the open sea. A lighthouse-keeper on an island off the British Columbia coast enjoying little contact with the rest of the world except the infrequent visits of the supply-ship, joins our weekly assembly of the air. Southern high-landers, forest wardens, prospectors, Canadian mounted police, and others who, through occupation or natural barriers, are prevented from worshiping with their fellow-Christians, are regularly numbered in our audience. If the radio did nothing more than serve these people and reach the outposts of civilization, it would well repay its cost.

Among the most appreciative listeners are the sick and crippled who, whether at home, in hospitals, or public institutions, are otherwise unable to hear God's Word. They, together with the many sorrow-laden and impoverished, found comfort, soul-healing, and strength in Christ. A special department of our work deals with personal perplexities, the doubt and gloom overshadowing many lives. Among our most treasured letters are those from groping souls that have shared their troubles with us and have found peace by following Christ-centered direction.

We may be asked again whether it pays to broadcast the positive message of evangelical Christianity. This question becomes the more pointed when we realize that last year the Lutheran Laymen's League expended no less than $140,000 for the Lutheran Hour contributed by thousands of supporters in our Church and in many non-Lutheran groups. From an expenditure of this amount we may indeed expect noteworthy returns; and we are not disappointed. Hundreds of our own pastors, guided by a desire to practice careful stewardship in the Lord's work, write us that the broadcasts must continue and be expanded. The radio is one of the quickest and cheapest methods by which we can begin to fulfil our missionary instruction of preaching "the Gospel to every creature." As we stated in the only direct financial appeal we have ever made on the air: "Ten cents contributed to our Gospel broadcast brings the message of Christ to 200 people, a dollar to 2,000. Ten dollars will give the Gospel to a whole section of South America. One hundred dollars will cover Central America for several months. One thousand dollars — and what is a thousand dollars if only a single soul be won? — will keep the broadcast Gospel for an entire year in the Philippine Islands and large areas of South Japan, China, French Indo-China, Australia, New Zealand, the Malay Peninsula, even India and other countries." May the Holy Spirit move some who read these lines to help us with generous gifts! No salaries are paid the speaker, the announcer, the choirs, or their directors.

Despite the disadvantages under which the religious broadcaster speaks, since only a turn of the dial can remove his words, God has been good in permitting us to see many visible results of His blessing. Multitudes have been strengthened in their faith. The comfort of Christ has enriched unnumbered souls. Pastors and Christian workers have been fortified, missionaries encouraged, inquirers answered, children brought to our Christian day-schools. Above all, the Gospel has been preached to millions and the message of the Cross brought to thousands of localities in which our Church has never been represented. As definite evidence of God's benediction the statistician of our Church reports from incomplete returns that, for example, during the Sixth Lutheran Hour hundreds were won for Christ and thousands enlisted as missionary prospects. Almost daily, friends write us that only eternity will reveal the power with which the Holy Spirit has accompanied the broadcasts. Truly, His Word, even on the radio, will not return void.

Before us lies a veiled future, heavy with problems but challenging in its opportunities. We are firmly convinced that at least one hundred more stations throughout the world can be secured for the dissemination of the eternal Gospel; and we are concentrating on such international broadcasting. The Savior's command still directs us: "Go ye therefore and teach *all* nations."

Earnestly do we ask friends of the Lutheran Hour to remember our radio mission in their prayers. One of our workers who particularly watches the prayer references in the mail recently stated that in his opinion our mission of the air is "the most prayed-for enterprise in the entire Church." Certain it is that without the fervent and daily intercessions of many Christian hearts throughout the land this remarkable progress may not have been granted us. It is equally evident that the future will present multiplied obstacles. The powers of hell will redouble their determination to silence our testimony. Periodically efforts have been made within certain church groups to keep messages like ours off the air. These assaults must not prevail; and they cannot prevail if our intercessions constantly come before the Father in Jesus' name. So pray for our broadcast! Pray for its extension! Pray for the Spirit's blessing upon its words of warning and its appeal of grace!

Only God knows how much of the success of the Lutheran Hour, humanly speaking, must be ascribed to my coworkers. With deep gratitude I mention: Mr. Reinhold Janetzke, announcer for the last five years; the Lutheran Hour Chorus of Concordia Seminary, Ronald Ross, director; the St. Louis A-Cappella Society, Mr. Wm. B. Heyne, director; and the Markus Male Chorus, Mr. Alvin Burmeister, director. I acknowledge again the help extended by volunteers from the Lutheran Woman's League, Evening Division, who after their day's work came to the Seminary at night to assist in correspondence, filing, and mailing.

Special recognition is to be accorded the cooperation of Mr. T. G. Eggers, Executive Secretary of the Lutheran Laymen's League, Pastor Herman Gockel, Radio Secretary, Mr. Martin Daib, Field Secretary, the office force, and my personal staff. Credit should be given our advertising agency, Kelly, Stuhlman, Zahrndt, Inc., for publicizing the Lutheran Hour in the nation's newspapers. For their cooperation in placing bill-boards we are likewise indebted to the Outdoor Advertisers of America, for example, to men like Mr. Edward C. Donnelly, Jr., of Boston, whose organization helped us secure 100 large Lutheran Hour bill-boards in that city. To all, notably pastors and teachers, who in any way have stood at our side, in prayer, word, or deed, we say, "Thank you! God bless you!"

We praise the Lord also for permitting us to put the radio addresses, reedited and amplified, into more permanent form on the following pages. It has been a source of deep gratification to know that these volumes go to various sections of the globe, to be read in thousands of homes, and used even in churches and preaching-stations.

In issuing this volume, I enjoyed, besides the splendid courtesies of Concordia Publishing House, the assistance of Mr. Rudolph Bertermann, who each week prepared the final copy of the address, Miss Lucille Biehl assisting. Miss Harriet Schwenk gave painstaking care in the preparation of the manuscript. Dr. Wm. Arndt, Ph. D., D. D., again, for the seventh season, obligingly read the messages each week, offering invaluable suggestions. My wife, especially, lent generous assistance in every phase of the work. To this cooperation I owe much more than any printed acknowledgment of my thanks can express.

As we entrust these pages to the Spirit's power, may they help bring many distracted souls in this war-torn age to "peace through Christ"!

WALTER A. MAIER

Concordia Seminary
Saint Louis, Missouri
Ascension Day, 1940

TO

MR. AND MRS. CHARLES J. STAERKER

CONTENTS

PEACE — THROUGH CHRIST

"Being justified by faith, we have peace with God through our Lord Jesus Christ." — Romans 5:1.

Christ, who art our Peace:

M ercifully look down upon our war-torn world, and if it be Thy will, by the power of Thy Spirit, put an end to the slaughter of human lives! Forgive us our hatreds and prejudices! As we behold Thine example of compassion, teach us to love even our enemies! Grant us, above all, through faith in Thine atoning blood and life-giving death the peace with our heavenly Father, our conscience, and our fellow-men by which we can find rest and assurance in the toil of these overclouded days! To this end bless our broadcast in many hearts and lives! Make it a mighty testimony to Thy saving love! We ask this, precious Savior, humbly, yet confidently; for we pray in Thy holy name. Amen.

"O FATHER, if it be Thy will, preserve peace unto our nation! O Jesus, spare our United States the horror, the blood, the agony, of another war! O divine Spirit, break to pieces the unholy counsel of those who would hurl all civilization into the disaster of a second world conflict!" This, in effect, has been the plea of millions throughout the land during the nightmare of the past two months; this prayer, and much more, should be the heart appeal of American Christians during the even blacker months before us.

Despite the satanic schemes of some munitions-makers, armament agents, international bankers, who seek profit in traffic with human lives, — and may God have mercy on their greedy souls! — despite the lie that another world war will mean higher prices for you farmers, better wages for you factory workers, steadier employment for you on WPA projects; in the face of many falsehoods in the press, on the air, by which foreign and domestic propaganda seeks to mold the mind of America for international slaughter, this is the hour for those who call themselves Christ's to follow the Bible's plain command, *"Seek ye peace and pursue it."* This is the crisis in which the words of the Lord Jesus Himself, *"Blessed are the peacemakers,"* have a double appeal.

The consequences of our participation in Europe's battles may be terrifying for the Christians in our land. Hundreds of thousands of parents will mourn their sons, slain on Europe's battle-fields. Another world war will throw the churches into far greater financial difficulties than those which ten years ago this month (as a result of the last great struggle) helped to retard the spread of Christian missions. Another international conflict will further demoralize American youth through a new collapse of morality and the deadening unemployment of necessity following a world holocaust. The sword swinging wide swaths over the earth will muster new forms of atheism and tyranny to attack the Church and the Christian home; for — be clear about this! — whoever wins this war, Communism is destined to score new triumphs. In 1918, before the Red revolution, the Lutheran Church in Russia numbered 4,000,000 members. A year or two after the revolution this Church was completely wiped out as an organization, and hundreds of its pastors were shot down by Red firing squads. Don't say that the horrors of the U. S. S. R. cannot be repeated in the U. S. A.; for there may be a black-out of Christianity in the United States even in this generation, a nation-wide assault on American churches, and a gory triumph of atheism. Let us rather dedicate our efforts as citizens to guard our peace, but as children of God — and this is our emphasized appeal — to work and pray so that the reign of war's terror and the triumph of unbelief be kept far from our shores.

Yet human peace, the truce established by armies, diplomats, conferences, is often partial and unjust. Twenty-one years ago representatives of the world-powers signed a treaty that was to end all wars; but it sowed the seed perhaps for a century of bloodshed. It was to save the world for democracy, but it created a world order safe for the dictator, the atheistic destroyers. Who can help feeling that the peace which will follow this war, when one side or both collapse in complete exhaustion, will lay the foundation only for future bloodshed?

How we ought to thank God, then, on bended knees, in whole-hearted praise, that there is a perfect, permanent peace for each conflict of our souls, a never-ending tranquillity, that, passing all human understanding, can heal every strife-torn life! How can we better begin this seventh season of broadcasting than by bringing you the message of

Peace — through Christ

pledged to every true disciple of the Savior in the words of Romans 5:1, *"Being justified by faith, we have peace with God through our Lord Jesus Christ"*?

I

PEACE THROUGH FAITH IN CHRIST

To understand this promise of soul calm and heart quiet, we must know what Saint Paul means when he says, *"Being justified by faith."* This investigation reveals no sparkling tribute to human goodness, no pretty picture of virtue in your life and mine. On the contrary, it shows our race at war with God, petty, puny creatures in rebellion against the Almighty. It exposes men's heart, not filled with lofty impulses but as the centers of ugly depravity, cruel, lustful, envious, adulterous, hate-filled! We must push aside the modern, fashionable, upper-crust type of Christianity that continually prates about man's goodness; instead we must survey our own lives, examine our own hearts, and honestly admit, "How wicked, how treacherous, we are!" We must renounce all those convenient theories which cater to human vanity and picture the race steadily improving, gradually approaching perfection. Indeed, we must return to that teaching which much of twentieth-century theology has thrown overboard, the doctrine of our total depravity, the admission that original and acquired sin curses every man on the face of the earth.

Was it ever easier to demonstrate the failure of everything human than in this hour, when hundred millions of our fellow-men (in a world which but for greed would give more than plenty to every man, woman, and child) are diabolically trying to kill one another? Picture the horror of it — the best brains in England, Germany, France, inventing new means of slaughter by which masses of their fellow-men may be reduced to bleeding pulp, cities wiped out overnight, millions of non-combatants blockaded into scurvy, starvation, and death, ships torpedoed and thousands drowned in dark terror! Think of the youth in these countries, born only to die on the battle-fields of age-old hatred! As this nightmare rises before you, you need no further argument to convince yourself that the brutal rule of sin tyrannizes the world today, despite all culture, schools, libraries, in our much-vaunted civilization.

You and I are part and parcel of this sinful world. The same passions and hatreds that have slaughtered legions on Old-world battle-fields flare within our hearts. The same uncleanness and lust that last year helped to make almost a million young women in the United States

illegitimate mothers or prenatal murderesses, smolder within our souls. The same treachery and greed that sent
Federal judges and common thieves behind penitentiary
bars tempts us to dishonesty. For no matter how individuals
may differ in learning or ignorance, wealth or poverty,
respect or dishonor, achievement or failure, in the sight
of God all are on one common level — they are sinners,
men and women of unclean thoughts, wicked words, and
destructive acts.

Some of you, hearing this broadcast for the first time,
are doubtless saying to yourselves, "What a narrow, outworn, disappointing message he brings!" It would be a
hundred times more pleasant, humanly speaking, if we
could side-track the indictment of God's Word, *"All have
sinned and come short of the glory of God"* and speak to
you on the political, social, or international issues of our
day. A dozen different proposals have been made asking
our radio mission's support for political or secular movements. But six years ago we promised you — and today
we renew the pledge — that the goal toward which we will
direct every broadcast must be the saving message of the
crucified Christ.

Because you cannot understand Jesus, explain His cross,
know the power of His blood, until you have felt and
confessed the sin in your own life; because you cannot
realize what that blessed Son of God means to you unless
you know that your sin has separated you from your Father,
banished you from heaven, consigned you to eternal death,
this first broadcast asks you to lay your soul bare before
God, to remove all excuse and disguise, to confess yourselves sinful, helpless, lost, to join me in a nation-wide confession of our sins: "Almighty God, we bow ourselves
before Thee, not daring to lift up our eyes to Thine holiness, because we have continually sinned against Thee and

brought down upon ourselves Thy just punishment, the doom of death. We have no means of our own by which we can find pardon and peace, no strength by which we can resist the conquest of evil, no hope through our own ability of attaining to light, life, and salvation. O God, help us, we beseech Thee!"

If your heart has sincerely repeated this prayer, you are ready to be led into the riches promised by our text, *"Being justified by faith, we have peace with God."* Then, turning to the mercy of God, we learn that our heavenly Father, though we daily sin much, has not cast us off; that He has not asked us to discover any human pathway to forgiveness and life. For — O glorious truth! — we approach Jesus, the true Christ, the Christ of the Bible, the Christ of God — not merely Jesus the Man, Jesus the Example, Jesus the Teacher, and, despite our sin-stained hearts, we learn through faith that, though we have sinned, He as God's suffering Servant Himself bore our iniquities and carried our griefs. By the most sacred promise human ears have ever heard, *"If any man sin, we have an Advocate with the Father, Jesus Christ the Righteous,"* we draw near to His cross on Calvary to be assured that by His immeasurable love Jesus took our place before the judgment of God's holiness, removed the sins that drive us from His grace, bore them in His own holy body, and, as our Substitute, died to pay sin's wages.

Even this glorious message of compassion does not express God's entire love. In the climax of His divine tenderness He gives us the pledge of this pardon, not as a reward for our repentance, a payment for attempted good deeds, nor a compensation for protracted sufferings, but — thank God! — as the free gift of Christ's mercy. If you come to Christ and, raising contrite hearts to Him, say, "O Jesus, I know that Thou art the Redeemer of this wayward race, and especially the Savior of my soul; I believe with all my heart that Thy holy, precious blood has cleansed me from every sin, and I trust Thee, Jesus, Lover of my soul, through life and into death itself, since my hope is built on nothing less than on Thy blood and righteousness," — by this confidence in Christ you are made just and holy in the sight of God. You have been brought back to the waiting arms of your heavenly Father.

That is the justification by faith, and by faith alone, of which the Apostle speaks in our text, the central doctrine of Christianity, restored to the world four centuries ago through Martin Luther. Next Tuesday marks the anniversary of his Reformation, an occasion that should be observed throughout the country despite the noise of the Hallowe'en counter-celebration. When on the thirty-first of October in 1517 this intrepid, God-inspired monk, the greatest figure in modern history, nailed his Ninety-five Theses to the door of the Castle Church at Wittenberg, he not only inaugurated a new era, which paved the way for many of our highest American liberties, but through God he battered down the damnable error that salvation is achieved by our character, contributions, sacrifices, fastings, pilgrimages, sacred vows, by rituals, heaped prayers, repeated penances and charities; but he also valiantly exalted the sacred, supreme truth that we are saved only but surely through faith in Christ's atoning death and life-giving resurrection.

Four centuries have passed since Luther turned the tide of human events; but this sacred heritage has often been exchanged for the pottage of publicity, sacrificed to popular criticism, since people resent being told they are sinners. In how many churches do not groping souls, eager to learn the way from fear to faith, from death to life, seek in vain for that consolation and instead hear a moral talk or a political discussion!

As men turn from this saving truth, it becomes the more necessary to emphasize justification by faith as never before in this land. For, if we are not saved by the grace of God, through faith in Christ, we shall never be saved; but if we have Christ enthroned in our humble, trusting hearts, no army of men, no legion of devils, can tear us from the greatest joy of life.

What, then, must be our prime appeal in this season's broadcasting if not this, that in the name of the thousands of Christians whose missionary zeal has made this nation-wide hook-up possible; in the name of God-fearing parents, believing husbands and wives, who are praying that many of you be converted to God, or return to Christ; and, above all, in the merciful Savior's name we broadcast this appeal to the unconverted thousands from Maine to California: "Get right with your God! Come to Christ in trusting faith, and, loving Him who first loved us, assure yourself, even here on earth, of eternal life!"

The precious Savior's grace is extended to every one. A patriotic organization in our country closes its doors to a talented colored woman; but, my Negro friends, Jesus recognizes no color line. How I thrilled recently when in the city of Pittsburgh I stood before a colored mission-congregation where forty-three men and women of your race, won for Christ directly or indirectly through this broadcast, had been instructed and baptized in the Christian faith! In strife-torn Europe millions of Jewish nationals have been persecuted, plundered, segregated into Ghettos. Even in this country clerical voices are raised to fire the passions of class hatred. Yet the arms of Jesus are never spread wider than when they receive His own countrymen, to whom, first of all, He came. The poor who, as the Savior reminds us, are always with us, but who have never been more numerous than today (when, for

example, half the entire State of Oklahoma is on relief);
the aged, shelved by cruel competition; the imprisoned,
from whom the pharisaical element in modern society turns
in reproach — all these may suffer under handicaps and
injustice; but their Savior, who spent hours with the underprivileged for each minute He devoted to the smug and
self-satisfied, tenderly assures them, *"Him that cometh to
Me I will in no wise cast out."* Come, then, to this Savior
of free grace, who says, "Only believe!" to the Savior of
full grace, who loved the whole wide world, with no soul
too low, too vicious, for His benediction! Come to the
Savior of assured grace, whose cross leaves no doubt or
question, but whose Word is the eternal, unbreakable truth!
Come to the Christ of peace, the perfect, supreme, endless
peace for life and death itself!

II

PEACE — WITH LIFE'S HIGHEST BLESSING

That harmony between the human and the divine is
promised all believers by the assurance of our text, *"Being
justified by faith, we have peace with God through our
Lord Jesus Christ."* *"Peace with God!"* Life's highest
blessings cluster about this pledge! *"Peace with God"*
changes our lives, banishes our souls' fears. Luther tells
us that before the new light of justifying faith dawned in
the black terror of his heart, he trembled at the very mention of God or at the sight of a crucifix. He would have
welcomed death as an escape if only there were no eternity
in which he would be confronted by a just and holy God!

Today, too, notwithstanding the imposing parade of our
progress, men cower before the thought of death and the
Judgment. Thousands who have written us, and tens of
thousands more who could well unburden their souls, are
restless, fearsome, threatened by nervous disorders or even

collapse, their whole spiritual life overclouded by uncertainty. If only they would take God entirely at His word and thus have their mental slavery changed to spiritual freedom through the joy of Christ's salvation! Once you are *"justified by faith,"* so that Christ controls your heart, the spell of fear is broken; the voice of your conscience has been stilled; the wall that separates you from your God has been removed; you are a new creature in Christ.

Approach Jesus more closely, then, all you burdened with clutching terror concerning the next world, the surging questions that involve your soul and your sin; and as you turn with eyes of faith to the Savior, you will hear Him speak this comfort: *"Fear not, for I have redeemed thee; I have called thee by thy name; thou art Mine."* Blessed by this peace, you can come to God through Christ without any human intermediary or earthly credentials. You yourself can pray to your heavenly Father in unbounded confidence; without any saint or minister or practitioner required to introduce you or intercede on your behalf you can turn to Him in every unmarked path for guidance. Each moment you spend in His heavenly presence will enrich you with good counsel, draw the outline of the heavenly homeland more brightly, and bring you the ever-growing joy of reconciliation with the Father.

Under the benediction of this peace we can live every day of our lives in the quiet victory of faith. Do not misunderstand! Jesus never promised His followers the ease and comfort of frictionless existence. His ultimatum is still, *"Take up the cross and follow Me!"* These new creeds promising men a financially and socially successful career are destructive delusions, too often a source of profit only for the promoter. However, if the Christian's road is hard and up-hill, what a sacred compensation he finds in this *"peace with God"!* Every moment of his life is guarded

by the omnipotence behind this universe, by the love streaming from the cross. The more frequently some of God's
children suffer, the sweeter and the deeper is their peace;
for they believe that *"whom the Lord loveth He chast-
eneth,"* and they interpret every obstacle as a stepping-stone
to higher grace and the gateway to fuller glory. The deeper
the valley of the shadow may be or the higher the toilsome
summits, the more fervently they thank their God. Side
by side with them, unseen by human eyes, their Savior
walks, repeating this comfort, *"My peace I give unto you;
not as the world giveth, give I unto you. Let not your
heart be troubled."*

Our reason, of course, vainly seeks explanation for the
divine ways which are not our ways. Christians wonder,
for example, how God could permit a defective seventy-
five-cent radiator valve to suffocate five infants in a New
Jersey hospital. From these tragedies in smaller circles
they turn to the world today with its suicidal mania for
blood and ask how God can hear the cannon, see the
slaughter of battle, without rising up in His power. Yet
through Christ they can learn that, while every judgment
of God against those who reject the Savior is a punishment, every affliction in the Christian's life is a disguised
blessing, a strengthening, peace-bestowing evidence of
divine mercy.

If some of you protest, "I am a Christian, yet I have
no peace"; if you are still grieving over a loved one
snatched from your side all too early in your estimation;
if you complain that you are neglected, abused, hated, let
me ask you: Are you leaning entirely on Christ? Do you
daily pour out your heart in prayer to Him and daily seek
the counsel of His Word? Trouble, worry, discontent,
rage even within Christian hearts because the static of doubt
and self-reliance mars the reception of Christ's promises.

That *"peace of God"* helps give us peace with our fellow-men. As our faith deepens, this harmony with God can work with growing force in our homes. Too often hatred, distrust, suspicion, lodge under our roofs because the family has no time for the Prince of Peace. When the Savior's love constrains our thoughts and our actions, we can live amicably with our fellow-men; we can be at peace with those who are of another race, another color, another creed. We can — and this is the highest proof of Christ's power — love even our enemies, following Jesus, who, though He suffered rebuke and torture at the hands of those whom He had come to serve and save, nevertheless loved them and pleaded for them even in the agony of the cross.

These blessings, for which a war-torn age cries incessantly, our broadcasts, resumed in the name of Jesus Christ, seek to bring our nation. Will you not, since there is *"none other name under heaven given among men whereby we must be saved"* but the glorious name of Jesus Christ, pray with us and for us that the Holy Spirit may use this network to bring the peace of God into the hearts of untold millions by directing them to the Savior's cross? As the nations muster their forces for war, let this broadcast be a nation-wide mobilization call for Christ, — and that means for peace with God, our fellow-men, and ourselves.

Heavenly Father, who didst make this peace through the blood of Christ, grant us the benediction of a trusting, conquering faith, for His sake! Amen.

THE CALL FOR THIS CRISIS —
COME AND SEE JESUS!

> *"Then Jesus turned and saw them following and saith unto them, What seek ye? They said unto Him, . . . Master, where dwellest Thou? He saith unto them, Come and see. They came and saw."* — Saint John 1:38, 39.

Holy, Purifying Spirit of God:

If only a deep, personal sense of repentance, a triumphant faith in Jesus Christ, and an unwavering trust in His power to save to the uttermost would seize our souls and control our lives! Often we are too busy to follow the Savior's invitation, "Come unto Me!" too self-blinded to behold Jesus and believe that His love can solve every problem of our hearts and answer every question in this burdened age. Frequently — O God, forgive us for that Savior's sake! — we wilfully reject the eternal blessings of redeeming grace. Therefore, O quickening Spirit, enlighten thousands throughout the land, and as their Christ pleads with them, "Come and see," may they now have the faith to come just as they are and at the cross to behold the blood that was shed and the life that was given for them! Hear us and bless us for that Savior's sake! Amen.

"CHRISTIANITY has failed!" This taunting cry, which atheists and scoffers shouted over the roar of the first World War, is revived now that all Europe seems ready to spring into the suicide of a second slaughter. Yet, instead of arguing that the Christian faith has been found wanting in this trial, men should be honest to admit that the world has failed to give the Gospel a serious test. Not the Christian ideals of love and sacrifice that Jesus showed on the cross but the anti-Christian code of self and greed controls much of human affairs. The attacks on Christ are more wide-spread than in the persecutions of Nero, more violent than in the terror of the French Revolution, more deep-rooted than in the eighteenth-century hey-

[13]

day of European unbelief. One hundred years from now, if the world still stands, historians will refer to ours as the age of irreligion. Christianity a failure? How can it be when its message is not even heard by millions, its truth left unexamined, its blessing never investigated? Can you accuse a doctor of failure when his patient spurns the prescribed medicine and takes poison instead?

We grant that too much which parades as Christian has not met the requirements of this exalted name; for a merely human Christ, a Bible branded by ten- and twenty-thousand-dollars-a-year churchmen as a book filled with folk-lore and fairy-tales, the error of salvation by character instead of by grace through faith, the delusion of a social gospel rather than a saving Gospel, outward ritual in place of inward repentance, emotional moralizing instead of doctrinal preaching, worldly-minded, power-craving churches instead of Christ-minded, Spirit-craving churches, these cannot heal wounded souls. We admit, too, that many have lost their zeal for Christ. *The Missionary Review of the World,* a publication dedicated to the spread of the Gospel, suspended printing after almost half a century. Why? Because the publishers felt there was not enough interest to sustain this paper. "Christians" who refuse to live their faith, to whom suppers and socials mean more than sermons and Sacraments, the money-grabbing, pleasure-pursuing, success-worshiping church-members, must fail.

On the other hand we have this assurance from God Himself: The true Christian Church can never fail. Before one jot or tittle of any promise made by Jesus Christ, our Lord, can be removed, the vastness of our star-strewn universe will collapse into nothingness. Christianity — and we mean the glorious Gospel of a Savior slain on the cross for the sins of the world, the hope which looks only to Jesus — can never fail!

It follows, then, that all of us in this hate-saturated age, with its question-marks and signs of growing alarm, need, above men's money, advice, and help, the unfailing Savior. To show how Christ invites each one of us, we recall an incident in the Savior's early ministry, recorded in Saint John 1:38, 39: *"Then Jesus turned and saw them following and saith unto them, What seek ye? They said unto Him, . . . Master, where dwellest Thou? He saith unto them, Come and see. They came and saw."* These words show us

THE CALL FOR THIS CRISIS — COME AND SEE JESUS!

May God richly bless our meditation, so that every one who has ignored, denied, or betrayed Christ be led by the Spirit to find in Jesus the ever-blessed Redeemer!

I

A SERIOUS WARNING TO ALL UNBELIEVERS

On one of those unknown, undated days that mark mile-stones in the blessing of men, John the Baptist, probably in the midst of his busy ministry, was startled by the approach of an unusual personage, impressive in appearance, mysterious, superhuman in His bearing. No second glance was required to tell him that the Teacher his eyes beheld was none other than the Christ of God, whom he had baptized forty days before. Caught in the rapturous joy of greeting his God and his Savior, the Baptist pointed his audience to Christ and spoke the words that millions of Christians cherish as one of the highest of Scripture's golden promises: *"Behold the Lamb of God, which taketh away the sin of the world!"* On the next day Jesus again approached that fearless preacher of repentance, and the Baptist raised his voice to repeat, *"Behold the*

Lamb of God!" John had one supreme message: Christ was to him the sin-bearing, sin-atoning *"Lamb of God."* Oh, that the modern pulpit would find its model in this wilderness messenger and, instead of dismissing the power of the blood with a few condescending remarks, make the cross the climax of every sermon! The preaching that touches souls and gives the new birth is the unsparing stress on the damning consequences of sin and the stronger emphasis on the magnificence of the Savior's mercy. That appeal brings converts to Christ now, just as it did when men for the first time were directed to *"behold the Lamb of God."* Hardly had two of John's disciples, Andrew and a young man also called John (destined to become the author both of the gospel bearing his name and of four other New Testament books), heard their teacher acclaim Christ as the atoning *"Lamb of God,"* when they approached Jesus, requesting the privilege of discipleship. Then it was that our Lord spoke the pointed question *"What seek ye?"* just as today a person would say to those who keep following him, "What do you want?"

Before we go any farther, we should realize that the Savior's *"What seek ye?"* must be answered by every one who has heard that Christ is the *"Lamb of God."* Ten thousand other questions may remain unheeded. A legion of men may confront you with the demand "What do you want?" but whatever they do for or against you will never influence your soul. You may boast that you are neutral in the conflicts sweeping over large sections of the earth, but no one can maintain neutrality toward Christ. When people hear, as you have heard, that Jesus died for their sins, they either accept or reject that truth. They must choose between following the Savior or denying Him. They are unescapably placed before this alternative: Either Jesus is the Savior or an impostor; either He is the Light of the world or the darkness of delusion.

Ask yourself, then, this question, which involves your eternal destiny, "What do I want of Jesus?" Many in the twentieth-century rebellion against God and His Son seek to destroy Christ. There are in this country several major atheist movements, whose dastardly purpose is to ridicule Jesus and pour sarcasm on His redemption. Yet, can you enemies of the Cross who write us of your contempt for Christ offer anything of help and hope, now that the world moves into ever-deepening tragedy? One of our papers tells us that over in Hyde Park, London, where soap-box orators hold forth in open-air meetings, an atheist recently tried to argue publicly that there was no God and that Jesus Christ never existed. His blasphemies were interrupted by a young man who said: "May I ask a question? I want to know the address of an atheist hospital." A large number of the London hospitals had been founded by Christians, he explained; but "where," he demanded, "is there a hospital built by atheists?" No answer followed, and the young man continued: "Well, here's another question: Where is the atheist orphanage? Everybody knows Barnardo's and Spurgeon's and Muller's, and everybody knows that these men were great Christians. Is there any orphanage anywhere founded by a great atheist?" More silence. Then the courageous defender of the faith concluded: "Just one more question, please. Where is your association for uplifting backward races? Christians have them; 'missionary societies' they call them. . . . What are you atheists doing for the uplifting of the backward races?"

Similar unanswerable challenges can be hurled at every one arrayed against Christ. Ask the Modernists, the suave, polished, *élite* preachers in fashionable but Christ-denying churches, this question of our text, "'*What seek ye*' of Jesus?" and if their true purpose were revealed, they would admit: "We want a human, not a divine Christ; a natural-born and not a Virgin-born Jesus. We want our attainment instead of His atonement. We want a dead teacher instead of a living Savior." Yet we ask, Has Modernism ever produced one courageous leader who could forget high salaries and sacrifice himself for the masses? Can Modernism show a single missionary worthy to lace the shoes of men like David Livingstone, who asserted: "I will place no value on anything I may have or possess, except in relation to the kingdom of Christ. If anything I have will advance that kingdom, it shall be given or kept, as by giving or keeping it I shall best promote the glory of Him to whom I owe all my hopes for time and eternity."

Ask the Communists the question of our text, " 'What seek ye' of Christ?" and with a boldness strengthened by the Red flag's recent triumphs they will point to anti-God museums, wrecked churches, filthy effigies of the Lord Jesus; they will exhibit the dirtiest, vilest cartoons of the holy, stainless Son of God that diseased minds of degenerate men have ever produced; they will mutter, "We want to wipe the name of Christ off the face of the earth." Yet, when they take Jesus away, what can they give us in His place? The wife of a highly publicized American Liberal cut short her visit to Red Russia because she felt that she would go mad if she had to witness any longer the chaos of perpetual terror, the hell on earth, Communists substitute for Christian blessing. Underscore that, you working-men and -women, who, as Moscow plans, are to be the agents for the overthrow of the American Government and the American churches! Take care lest you be dragged in unwittingly to help destroy our national foundations!

Ask the teachers of our American youth, "What do you want with Christ?" and you fathers and mothers, anxiously concerned about sustaining your sons' and daughters' loyalty to Christ, will be shocked by the extent to which the ridicule of our faith has gained the mastery in many schools. What hope can these academic scoffers extend to souls in distress? Ask them, and they will answer: "Man is a developed animal. Life is only a series of chances. Our destiny is controlled by a tyrannical fate. Our end is as the end of the beast — destruction, decay and the darkness of death." With all their bitter, cut-throat attacks, many opponents of the Christian faith have never taken the time to become acquainted with Christ's truth. They have heard Jesus say, *"Come and see,"* but they have refused His invitation. David Hume, for example, one of the most aggressive eighteenth-century enemies of the Gospel in England, ruthlessly sought to destroy the Christian faith; but he was forced to admit that he had not read even half of the New Testament. Some enemies of Jesus Christ in the United States today have not a smattering knowledge of the true Savior and His Word. They often misquote and misapply the sacred Word. Jesus calls to them: *" 'Come and see!'* Come and examine the results of Christianity! See how it has changed the world and how it can change you," but in stolid indifference too many refuse.

From the first days of the Church, when Saint Paul saw Christ on the Damascus road, down to the present, unbelievers accepting Christ's invitation to *"come and see"* have been convinced of His deity and His redemptive power. Two titled Englishmen, Lord Lyttleton and Gilbert West, set out to show that the Gospel history was wrong; but when they came and saw Jesus at close range, their poisoned minds were purified by the Spirit. Their pens of hatred became instruments of praise, exalting our Lord's deity and His glorious redemption. Dr. Paul Elmer More, former editor of *The Nation,* Princeton professor, eminent

American philosopher, and thoroughgoing skeptic, shortly before his death came to this conclusion: "After all, any philosophy of God demands the incarnation." Finding God the Redeemer "suffering with man and for man," he turned from doubt to assurance, repeating with his own lips John's adoration *"O Christ, Thou Lamb of God, that takest away the sin of the world."*

Often adversity and opposition are required to help draw us toward our redemption. Mary Slessor, intrepid woman missionary to Calabar, admitted that she had never fully believed the story of Daniel in the lions' den "until," as she writes, "I had to take some of these awful marches" (through the jungles infested with lions), "and then I knew it was true and that it was written for my comfort. Many a time I walked along, praying, 'O God of Daniel, shut their mouths,' and He did." Perhaps some of you, the self-engrossed who think that you can live against Christ, must have your self-reliance broken before you will answer the call of Jesus. It will be a God-blessed adversity that will make you reflect on the questions of eternity and their answer in Calvary's cross.

"Come and see" — that is the invitation Jesus issues to every one of you; and woe to that man or woman who ignores Christ or deliberately rejects Him! You may laugh at the truth that He is your God; you may scoff at the power of His blood; you may ridicule the promise of His redemption and smile condescendingly at the pledge of His returning to judge the quick and the dead; indeed, you may question His very existence; but that ignorance or denial affects only you with its terrifying consequences. It does not touch the Lord Jesus. If the malice of His own countrymen could not remove Him; if the death on the cross did not destroy Him; if the sealed rock grave was not strong enough to restrain Him; if the legions of

Caesar's armies were unable to uproot Christianity and the heathen hatred in the far-flung mission-fields with their tens of thousands of Christian martyrs did not succeed in retarding the progress of the Gospel; if the mobilized brain-power of all infidels and heretics failed in discrediting the Biblical truth, who do you think you are when you boast that Christ means nothing to you and reject His plea even now as His words seek to wing their way into your hearts with the appeal, *"Come and see!"* If from this moment on you could do only one thing more in your life, I pray that it would be to approach the cross, study the love of Jesus Christ for your soul, and, with the Spirit's help, confess Him your God, your Savior, your King.

II
A BLESSED PROMISE TO ALL BELIEVERS

The two disciples in our text learned this most blessed of all lessons. When Jesus turned to them and said, *"What seek ye?"* one consuming thought expressed itself in their answer, *"Master,"* they inquired, *"where dwellest Thou?"* Without daring to clothe the hope in so many words, they wanted to visit Christ, to stay with Him, and learn the glorious truths which He, the divine Teacher, could impart. Although Jesus had no home of His own, He answered the two inquirers with the invitation, *"Come and see"*; and the text records, *"They came and saw."* In fact, they remained with Jesus the entire day.

The story itself here runs out into silence; yet how blessed the hours with Jesus must have been! I have always felt that this happy day under the Savior's personal teaching laid the foundation for two remarkable lives. For on the next morning Andrew, his heart still aflame with the instruction received from the Lord, hastened to tell his own brother, Simon Peter, *"We have found . . .*

the Christ," and to bring him to Jesus. Andrew lived and died for Christ; according to tradition he was crucified because of his fearless witnessing. The life of John, the other disciple who *"came and saw,"* seems to express even more intensely a consuming loyalty to Jesus. He died a natural death; yet he had to pay for his testimony to Christ with long years of opposition, persecution, and then exile on the lonely isle of Patmos. Those two disciples, the first to come to Christ, never, even in the pain of persecution, lost the impress of these hours with Jesus.

The same Savior, no longer homeless but now enthroned in majestic eternity, will answer your question, *"Master, where dwellest Thou?"* by pointing to the radiance of heaven and saying, *"Come and see."* May God give my words double power as I try to show the immeasurable glories prepared for those who find in Jesus the Savior of their souls! *"Come and see"* Christ for the most magnificent mercy of which even the all-knowing mind of God Himself could conceive! Accept His grace, offered for every sin, disloyalty, dishonor, crime, with which men disgrace themselves and drive their souls to hell! During the past six seasons of broadcasting I have received letters containing some of the most shocking confessions that men and women ever may have written. Yet, if these sins were a hundred times blacker than the horrible transgressions they are, Jesus, precious Savior that He is, would still tell those who trust His power to save to the uttermost: *"Though your sins be as scarlet, they shall be as white as snow; though they be red like crimson, they shall be as wool."* Are you burdened by a weight of iniquity that preys continually on your mind? We can help you! This radio mission is maintained especially for problem-weighted souls like yours. We have no political ambitions on this "Bringing-Christ-to-the-Nation" hook-up; we do not collect funds to build an earthly shrine; we conduct no antiracial programs. We broadcast for one and only one purpose: we ask you to *"come and see"* Christ and His full grace, Christ and His free grace, Christ and His assured grace.

"*'Come and see'* your Savior," we say to those who have lingered long on the pathway we call life and who now resentfully review their years of regret, failure, disappointment, "Oh, what peace they often forfeit!" when Jesus says, *"Come and see,"* they refuse to come and close their eyes to exclude Christ from their vision! It is bad enough, God knows, when a young man or woman refuses to accept the Savior's mercies; but it is much more shocking when aged men or women keep a sullen distance from Jesus. Their common sense ought to warn them that within a year or two death may summon them in their unholiness before a righteous God's judgment.

"*'Come and see'* Jesus," we say to you who are sick of body. The same compassionate Christ whose touch healed the afflicted can help your bodily ailments, and He will, if it is His good pleasure and for your eternal welfare. Often, as many of you can testify, even when specialists have pronounced the verdict of "hopeless," "incurable," the heavenly Physician has brought relief. We think particularly of a man in our audience who a year and a half ago was told by renowned surgeons at a leading hospital that the amputation of one of his limbs and possibly two would be the only means of saving his life. That man had faith in Christ; and while he was ready for the ordeal, he prayed to be spared this overwhelming sorrow if his Lord thought best. His pleading was answered, and after a divinely directed series of circumstances that brother was spared. He still has his limbs. Often, of course, the Savior permits His own to suffer amputations, cancer, tuberculosis, paralysis, and we would in no way minimize the blessings of sound medical treatment; but what comfort of soul is ours in knowing that whatever God ordains for His children is for their eternal good, that *"the sufferings of this present time are not worthy to be compared with the glory which shall be revealed in us"* when in eternity Jesus shows us that there is no more disease and deformity, no more suffering and agony!

" 'Come and see' Jesus," our text invites you who are haunted by phantoms of fear and sorrows yet to come. You wonder what this European war will mean to us, whether you will have to send your sons across the seas. You are worried about home-life, family conditions, money matters, and an endless chain of griefs that make you slaves to fear. If only you understood that Jesus can give you the victorious attitude toward life and its threatening dangers which enables you to walk calmly and confidently, your hand in His, through all possible terrors of life, even through death's darkness! Shakespeare's last will and testament closes with these words: "I commend my soul into the hands of God, my Creator, hoping and assuredly believing, through the merits of Jesus Christ, my Savior, to be made a partaker of life everlasting." Entrust yourself to Christ in this faith, and on the glorious day of your resurrection you, too, will experience the radiant fulfilment of His pledge, *"Where I am, there shall also My servant be."*

God grant you the strength, not to try Jesus by a see-what-happens, I-can't-lose-either-way faith, but to believe God by an I-know-that-Christ-is-true conviction! Then, as the Savior says, — and now He speaks to *you* directly, — *"Come and see,"* you can behold Him in His power as your God, your Savior, your King. Then you can help others *"come and see"* Christ by working and praying to keep the cross the highest glory in every Christian heart and life! God grant you that blessing for Jesus' sake! Amen.

A PERMANENT ARMISTICE ON HATRED

"Blessed are the peacemakers; for they shall be called the children of God." — Saint Matthew 5:9.

Christ, Thou Prince of Eternal Peace:

*F*orgive us the lovelessness of our cold hearts, the bitter hatreds of our sin-poisoned lives, and show us that by faith in Thine eternal blood-bought mercies these sins of soul-destroying malice are removed from us farther than the east is from the west! O Jesus, our Lord, our Savior, our King, send us Thy Holy Spirit, so that many may stop their warfare against God, Thy Father and our Father, and — for the joy of life here on earth as for their eternal salvation — accept that reconciliation and inner calm which comes through the assurance of our redemption! Grant us this peace, so that, walking in Thy footsteps, we, too, may be peacemakers and spread abroad the mercies of Thy love! Hear us, blessed Savior, as Thou hast promised! Amen.

TWENTY-ONE years ago yesterday — just time enough for another generation to grow up — the armistice was signed. Many of you will never forget the wild joy and delirious shouting which greeted the announcement that the "cease firing" order had silenced the din of death on Europe's battle-fields. Yet if the world had known then what it knows now, it would have realized that the little boy who mispronounced "Armistice Day" as "Our Mistake Day" unwittingly spoke the truth.

Can you picture to yourselves what that war cost? Three hundred and fifty billion, we are told by those who measure loss in dollars and cents. In reality, however, the total amount will be many times greater, and for years to come this burden will be heavy on the masses. Of course, some found bloated profit in bloodshed, the 21,000 American war millionaires; the Wall Street speculators in munitions stocks which sky-rocketed from $20 to $1,000 a share.

It is claimed that one international banking house through its tie-up with armament factories and arms merchants made more money in two bloody war years than its founder did during his entire lifetime. A Cleveland machine company dealt profitably in poison-gas shrapnel. But listen to this if you do not think that hate-filled, money-mad men can be worse than beasts — this concern advertised that the wounds caused by its shells meant "death with terrible agony within four hours if not attended to immediately. From what we are able to learn of conditions in the trenches," this statement continues, "it is not possible to get medical assistance to any one in time to prevent fatal results. It is necessary to cauterize the wounds immediately if in the body or head or to amputate if in the limbs." Yet blood-money can never bring blessing; and before urging participation in a second international conflict, the war-mongers in America should count the last war's cost in poverty, unemployment, and an increase of national debt so startling that we are now almost at the legal limit of our indebtedness.

But forget this monetary cost and think of the terrifying toll in human suffering and death! Eight million men — one out of every eight engaged in that war — lost their lives. Suppose these dead troops had begun to march yesterday in a spectral Armistice Day parade. If they had tramped twenty abreast in lines ten feet apart for ten hours every day at the rate of four miles an hour, almost a hundred days would have been required for this ghastly procession to pass any given point. Fifteen million civilians died from the starvation and disease that followed the war. In the same formation they would form a phantom column fifteen hundred miles long, reaching from Canada to beyond the Mexican border. Think of the twenty-one million bleeding, limping, broken bodies and shell-shocked minds, whose similar ranks would extend from the Atlantic to the Rocky Mountains. Add to these five million widows, nine million orphans, and you have a picture of war's staggering horror.

Now, if these myriads of the killed, mangled, crippled, starved, stunted, had sacrificed themselves for a new hateless, warless world; if out of these four years of gasping, moaning, shrieking, with their thundering cannon, whining shrapnel and droning bombers, there had come a hymn of international harmony and a symphony of love, even this appalling price would perhaps not have been too high for the benediction of peace. Yet with hardly two decades passed, we see the nations of Europe thrown into a conflict that may be far more disastrous than the first World War. Besides, we witness rankling hatred in the social struggle that pits class against class, in the economic conflict between employer and employee, the domestic hostilities that array husbands against wives, and at times even in the religious war between churches of different denominations.

Will you not agree with me, then, that this peace-robbed world needs

A Permanent Armistice on Hatred

for which Jesus promises His benediction in Saint Matthew 5:9, "*Blessed are the peacemakers; for they shall be called the children of God*"?

I

THE POWER BEHIND THIS ARMISTICE:
THE PURIFYING LOVE OF JESUS CHRIST

Make no mistake about this basic fact: When our Lord here speaks of "*peacemakers*," He has no thought of an age in which war will be completely outlawed. On the contrary, Jesus plainly teaches that until the end, yes, as an unmistakable sign of that end, there shall be *"wars and rumors of wars; ... for nation shall rise against nation ... and kingdom against kingdom."* In conformity with this verdict of Christ's truth we maintain, not only that the last twenty-five years, with more warfare than any similar period, show we are approaching closely to the end of time, when Jesus will Himself reappear to judge the quick and the dead, but also that as long as this world stands, we shall witness, despite all roseate wishes and Utopian hopes to the contrary, the bloody spectacle of men killing their fellow-men in the savagery of international warfare. As we survey the preaching in Protestant churches today, must we not pray God that many pulpits will drop their speculations concerning an earthly millennium of peace and power? So much time is often devoted to these issues, with preachers in the role of historical authorities labeling Hitler, Mussolini, Stalin the exact fulfilment of certain Old Testament passages that little time is left for the all-vital Gospel. Not a single sinner will ever be saved by preaching a millennium with a warless, hateless glamor. One supreme message must reecho throughout the pulpits of this land in crisis days like these — the appeal of Jesus Christ as the Son of the almighty God and the Son of the Virgin Mary, to find in Him peace with God and then to become one of His peacemakers, filled with love for our fellow-men. Jesus wants this peace. He came, lived, labored, suffered, died — all for that peace of soul and of mind. From the beginning of His ministry until after His glorious resurrection, by word and deed, He proved Himself the long-expected *"Prince of Peace,"* who wants His followers to be *"peacemakers."*

How, — and this is the pointed question many of you are asking, — how can we be *"peacemakers"* and help in establishing a permanent armistice on hatred? That in-

volves another question; for not until you and I have peace
in our hearts, can we exercise peace in our lives.   And
where — O searching question of the ages! — can we find
inner peace, calm and quiet for our souls?

I hope that none of you, disturbed by a restless spirit,
ashamed of your passions and hatreds, will look to yourselves or to the wisdom and power of your fellow-men for
this soul rest.   Few ages in history have had more drastic
demonstration of man's failure to maintain even outward
peace.   Think of the major treaties concluded within the
last twenty years that have now been ruthlessly discarded:
the Treaty of Versailles, 1919; the Treaty of Saint Ger-
main, 1919; the Treaty of Neuilly, 1919; the Treaty of
Trianon, 1920; the Treaty of Lausanne, 1923; the Treaty
of Locarno, 1925; the Convention of Munich, 1938 —
every one thrown aside contemptuously as scraps of paper.
If imposing treaties, signed and sealed by world-leaders,
libraries of international law, hundreds of peace movements
cannot keep nations from tearing at each other's throats
more viciously than jungle creatures, certainly no laws, no
resolutions, no education, can create peace for our unseen,
intangible, immeasurable souls.   You and I need something
inestimably more powerful than any human device to effect
within us that spiritual repose without which we cannot be
the blessed *"peacemakers"* of our text.

However, God, through His Holy Spirit, does what men
in their weakness can never do; and while human covenants
are often made only to be broken, hear this promise of your
God: *"The mountains shall depart and the hills be removed; but My kindness shall not depart from thee, neither
shall the covenant of My peace be removed."*   To be
blessed by that covenant, we must stand beneath the cross,
where the one central peace treaty of all ages and for all
men was completed when the Son of God finished forever

my redemption and yours. If these words by the Spirit's blessing now strike some heart at war with God and distrustful of itself, let me, in the inspired words of Saint Paul, point to that crucified Christ and promise, *"He is our Peace."* By the unsearchable riches of His mercy He ended forever the war between a stainless God and wicked men; He became your Substitute and mine, took our sins, the cause of all strife, hatred, and of death itself, suffered their punishment in His own holy body, and — O glorious love! — died for us His peace-bestowing death on Calvary's cross.

Let no one dismiss too lightly that struggle by which our peace was won! The terms of Golgotha's treaty were the hardest ever imposed. They condemned the Innocent for the guilty; they inflicted on the soul of Jesus an agony such as all the wounded and dying in a million wars could never suffer. That treaty required a death so agonizing and terrifying that no words of oratory, no brush of artistic skill, no powers of human analysis, can ever begin to picture or explain the fathomless suffering in Christ's last hours. Yet no peace treaty has ever brought a single blessing comparable with the outpouring of endless mercies that have come from this Calvary covenant of the precious blood. If you say that you cannot understand how God could bring the peace-sacrifice of His own Son, then, as we admit freely that it passes our powers of understanding, we ask you only to believe. If you object that you cannot explain why God chose you to receive these benefits, then we stand at your side with the same question, but we ask you to accept this mercy and build on it your hope for everlasting happiness.

Even more, we can show that Christ's peace is in our hearts by the power it exercises in our lives. When at the cross, through faith, the reign of sin is broken, the tyranny of envy and hatred is also destroyed; and we, reborn in the Spirit, new creatures in Christ Jesus, can become the *"peacemakers"* of whom our text speaks. Once our eyes of faith behold Christ as on the cross He prays not for Himself nor for His friends but for His enemies, we, too, through the new life in Jesus, can begin to spread peace and counteract the passions of hatred. From the very first days of the Church's history, when dying Stephen, his body bruised and broken by the jagged rocks of hatred, pleaded for his enemies, petitioning God, *"Lay not this sin to their charge";* from the years of the apostles, when Saint Paul, man-hunted and persecuted as few martyrs have ever been, wrote: *"Bless them which persecute you; bless, and curse not"; "If thine enemy hunger, feed him; if he thirst, give him drink,"* down through the conquests of Christian missions on the five continents, where savages have become saints, bloodthirsty cannibals devoted followers of Jesus, ruthless warriors humble builders of the Kingdom — throughout the ages this peace-bestowing power of Christ has mightily proved itself.

As we linger for a moment longer in the shadow of His cross, let us ask ourselves whether we have followed the peacemakers' pathway that Jesus blazed for us. This is the day of dictators and brutal militarism, the hour of propaganda and falsehood, when the flames of racial hatred are fanned to white heat, with labor trouble assuming formidable proportions and churches separated into opposing factions — a generation in which social workers and domestic courts can testify how cruelly love is supplanted by hatred even in the home. Above all, let none in this audience overlook in our own lives the flare-ups of anger, our easily wounded, oversensitive pride, our racial prejudices, our religious bigotries, our smoldering passions. Conscious of our many shortcomings, let us penitently come to Christ and to His peace-bestowing, hate-stifling Spirit!

You, the proud and self-confident, who have never confessed Him your Savior; you, the backsliders, who have fallen from His grace and cursed His holy name; you who brand the gentle, forgiving spirit of Jesus as effeminate weakness; every one nurturing secret or open hatreds, hear this verdict of Christ: *"Whosoever hateth his brother is a murderer!"* As we tell you by the authority of the Scriptures that hate can send you to destruction, kneel in spirit before Him who for you conquered hell and its malice! Sign this armistice against hatred and declare now: "O Christ, Thou Prince of peace and rest, this day as I look penitently to Thy love, forgive every word and action that springs from my sin-bound, hate-choked heart! Enrich me with Thy love, Thy self-denial, Thy willingness to sacrifice Thyself! Help me put into daily practice the spirit of humble devotion both to those beloved by me and to those even who hate me!"

If this armistice declaration is the earnest confession and plea of your soul, Jesus will not only answer, *"My peace I give unto you,"* but — glorious promise! — He will also use you as a *"peacemaker."* If you live in a divided house, a family separated by cruel self-love; if you husbands and wives, who ought to work together in the closest possible devotion, are suspicious, one of the other, or perhaps unfaithful to your marriage vows, and you want to be through with all this to secure help for your family, then believe that by the pardoning, cleansing Spirit of Christ you may be a peacemaker in your own home. You parents who have exiled or disinherited your children, you sons or daughters who have neglected your parents, by the promise of Jesus' word you can restore peace to your souls and to the aching, lonely hearts of your dear ones. Every one in enmity with his fellow-men can put the peace-bestowing power of Christ to work in a life of forgiveness and reconciliation.

Is not this the spirit our age needs? Should we not, in days doomed to perpetual warfare, so try to extend the Church of Christ and deepen our own faith that warfare and hatred, while not eliminated, will be restricted and God's mercies invoked upon our poor, bleeding, self-destroying world? God grant every one of you the desire and the resolution to become Christ's *"peacemakers"* for your home, your fellow-men, your world!

II

THE BLESSING OF THIS ARMISTICE:
PEACEMAKERS ARE CALLED CHILDREN OF GOD

How glorious that power is! As Christ told the congregation on the mount, so He strengthens all who believe Him with this pledge, *"Peacemakers . . . shall be called the children of God."* Jesus offers no earthly reward, no monetary compensation, for this peacemaking. New, highly publicized creeds today make their bids for disciples by dangling before the people worldly attractions, the ease of life, and the abundance of pleasure. Some religious leaders ride in cream-colored limousines, disport many and large diamonds, and actually boast that they have a lake of gold from which their followers, too, can draw the means of luxury and comfort; but the Christ of God — His life marked by poverty and persecution — sternly seeks to remove all craving for grandeur from the hearts of His disciples by warning, *"My kingdom is not of this world!"*

Yet to His *"peacemakers"* Christ has given a glory that outlasts any attraction men may know; for they, He promises, *"shall be called the children of God."* Who can declare the full magnificence of this distinction, — being called a child of God? Take any human title with which men may honor their fellow-men, the honorary degrees universities bestow upon prominent scholars, the ranks of nobility, the beribboned orders of knighthood and earldom, the Nobel prizes, and the scientific awards with which genius is recognized, the international medals and Congressional awards in war or peace; put them all together, and in the sight of the almighty Lord they are in no way to be compared with the preeminence of being *"called the children of God."*

As *"children of God"* we have an open approach to heaven. Through Christ we can come before the same God of unlimited power who made our globe as a tiny speck in the overpowering immensity of His universe, the same Lord of infinite wisdom who foresees the unformed events of tomorrow as clearly as though they were the history of the past, and we can say, "Thou art our Father, and we, praised be the mercy of Christ, are Thy children." What strength, what courage, what hope, lies in this new and blessed relation with your heavenly Father! Is it not worth a thousand times more than everything you may have to be fortified by this faith? Can you not see why our plea to you must always center in the appeal that you repent of your sins, accept Christ as your only Savior, and get right with God? Instead of sitting back in amused indifference, as you cultured scoffers do, when by the blood-bought grace of Christ, sonship with the Father is offered you; instead of arguing about the number of quails with which the Almighty could miraculously provide His people, as some of you self-sufficient skeptics do when you rehash the futile, outworn arguments against God's Book; instead of steeling your sorrow-swept, embittered souls against Christ and locking your homes against Him who says, *"Behold, I stand at the door and knock; if any man hear My voice and open the door, I will come in to him and sup with him and he with Me,"* will you not now ask God for the grace of true contrition, so that you may raise your hearts heavenward and say: "O God, I am not worthy to be called Thy child, for I have often sinned against Thee and daily offended Thy holiness. But by Thy Spirit help me to believe that on the cross Thy Son suffered for all the world, but especially for me, so that He might redeem me from the consequences of my iniquities! For the sake of His atoning death teach me, O God, that through this grace Thou art my Father and I am Thy child"?

Picture to yourselves the highest love an earthly father can show his children, self-sacrificing zeal for their happiness, ceaseless watchfulness over their lives, the intense desire to grant every helpful request; and then multiply this solicitous love of a human parent a thousand thousand times, and you are still far from understanding how blessed is the fatherhood of God and our sonship through Christ.

Try to realize in a practical way, however, what it means to say, "I am a child of my heavenly Father." This faith gives you the assurance that, whenever you pray to God in Christ's name and ask anything in accord with His will, you will be answered in God's time and His own way. During these perilous days when reliance on men reveals its utter folly, you and I need the sustaining power of true communion with the Father. Don't think for a moment that any kind of prayer will serve in this emergency; for though you plead by day and by night; though you shout your entreaties until your vocal cords are paralyzed; if your petitions do not flow from a believing heart; if you do not pray as a child of God who, forgiven by his Lord, readily forgives others, your supplications mean nothing more than the moaning of a passing wind. But treasure this comfort in your inmost heart: Whatever you ask in Jesus' name and for your own salvation will be answered though God move heaven and earth in granting His reply!

With God as our Father we have the deep-rooted conviction that despite all the opposition which may confront us, we live not a single moment without Heaven's guidance. Last week the Chancellor of Germany escaped death by eleven minutes, and the newspapers report that, commenting on his close call, he replied in a proverb, "A man must have luck." But Adolf Hitler will need far more than luck; nor can we be satisfied with a cold resignation to good fortune or bad, to a kind or a cruel fate. Give us God as our Father, so that all chance and luck are removed and, living our lives under His direction, each day brings us closer to our eternal good.

Sometimes parents must correct and punish their children, for the real test of true fatherhood is not indulgence that smiles at everything a child may do, right or wrong, but the love that reproves and chastises when necessary. In a much higher degree the great God above would not be the merciful Father that He is if He permitted His weak, self-engrossed children to rush on unrestrained in their self-destruction. To recall His own from the paths of wrong; to remove their thoughts from sensual pleasures and stay their minds on Him; to make them forget all tarnish, counterfeit, and tinsel as they concentrate on the pearl of great price, the kingdom of God, our all-loving Father permits sorrow, pain, money loss, family trouble, to visit His children. But underline this truth in your hearts! The same affliction that descends as a punishment on every one who rejects Christ's mercies comes to God's children as a disguised blessing from their heavenly Father, before whom they bow submissively to declare, *"He hath done all things well."* For Christians and the Church of Christ even the terrors of the present war will ultimately redound to their eternal peace.

To this never-ending joy the Savior's *"peacemakers"*

look continually. They have the pledge of His sacred
Word that, if they are God's children, they are His heirs
and, as the Scriptures emphasize, *"joint heirs with Christ."*
On earth this sonship with God finds scant recognition
among men; but what joy will be the peacemakers' when
the fulness of this inheritance is theirs, when they will be
face to face with Jesus! Eternal peace, with no more war
and hatred, as members of every race and kindred and tribe
are found among the ransomed souls in light! No more
religious quarrels and persecutions as from all denominations those who have accepted the Lord Jesus as their only
Savior are met there in heavenly array! No more class and
social hatred, even as God-fearing capitalists and Christ-
exalting laborers, as representatives of the upper class, middle class, lower class, unite in singing praise to Jesus! No
more family quarrels, ugly glances, and hateful words, as
husband and wife, parents and children, who have died in
the Lord, together with the whole family in heaven, live in
eternal peace!

Will you not — and once more we ask you in Christ's
name — come to Him for this calm of life and joyful
serenity in death? Will you not sign your name to this
perpetual armistice on hatred which checks your warfare
against Jesus, tears malice out of your life, makes you
a child of God and a peacemaker? Will not you whose
hearts Christ has cleansed help others in this war-torn,
hate-filled age to find peace with God and to live in love
toward their fellow-men?

May God, the Father of all who love the Lord Jesus,
guide you and grant you through His Son whatever of
material, earthly endowments His wisdom may see fit to
bestow; but first and forever uppermost, may He make
us all, — you in your individual lives and us in this radio
mission of the air — *"peacemakers"* with Christ, a blessing
to ourselves and to countless others! Amen.

THE MODERN MEANING
OF THE CROSS

*"The preaching of the Cross is to them that perish
foolishness; but unto us which are saved it is the
power of God."* — 1 Corinthians 1:18.

Enlightening Spirit of God:

We confess that too frequently we doubt when we should believe,
and too often we question the Cross when we should affirm its
grace. Forgive us these proud, vainglorious sins through the merits
of Jesus Christ, whose bleeding and dying purchased our pardon
and peace! Dwell in our hearts constantly, so that our faith may
increase, looking ever to Jesus for the pledge of soul-strength in
this life and the assurance of everlasting blessedness with Thee, the
Father, and our glorious Savior in heaven! Hold the radiance of
the cross before our eyes in every dark hour of sin, every night of
sorrow, especially in our last earthly moment! Hear us, O strengthening Spirit, and keep the imprint of saving grace forever on our
souls, for Jesus' sake! Amen.

AT last rabid atheism in America has dropped its friendly
mask and revealed its leering hatred of the Christian Church. Only recently the general secretary of the
Communist Party in the United States told the newspapers that a radical revolution within our boundaries
would bring a purge of religion, prohibit the teaching
of Christian doctrine, and remove most of our religious
leaders. After such open warning no doubt should remain
on this point: A Red victory in our country would mean the
hellish reality of closed, desecrated churches, and a de-
posed, persecuted clergy. If the Stars and Stripes are
pulled down to make way for the Hammer and Sickle,
we are assured, only a small group of preachers will be
spared. These favored few are not named, but we know

that they are the Modernists who heap scorn on God's Word and Christ's atonement, the skeptical, left-wing preachers, with their unmistakable communistic sympathies.

Now, instead of arguing that this campaign against the churches can never begin its destructive work on our shores, we should be far-sighted enough to realize that, if this country is drawn into Europe's slaughter, and if through the financial drain of long-drawn hostility the warring nations are thrown into bankruptcy, masses of laborers throughout the world, seething millions of unemployed, an army of disillusioned white-collar workers, will be ready to try Communism as a last resort and array themselves against Christ.

Nor is this Red nightmare the only threat confronting us. We have witnessed the fatal attacks of Fascism, the inroads of atheism on American education, the swelling crest of the crime wave. This, together with doctrinal indifference in some congregations and worldliness in the lives of their members, forms a far-flung offensive against the Savior's cross. While we know that the true Church will survive every brutal assault, Christian faith and power can help mightily in defeating God's enemies. The day has dawned when all groups which accept the Bible as Heaven's errorless revelation and which, in whatever denomination they may be found, acclaim Jesus their Lord and only Savior, should come together more closely. First, they should examine the doctrinal differences that have separated Christ's followers into dozens of opposing camps. Then they should learn just what God's Word teaches in these disputed issues; and on the basis of clear loyalty to this truth the Christian churches should be completely realined with an unswerving unity of faith and a determination to protect their creed against the cancer of infidelity in high church places. The cry in this disturbed hour must be: Back to God and His Bible! Back to Christ and His Cross!

In the mean time, until it please the Lord to give us a stronger outward Church, absolutely united on the whole Scripture, let us work and pray that the message of the saving blood be proclaimed with far greater power. Because Calvary's redemption, the one supreme Fact for which the Church exists, is violently attacked as a veil of dark ignorance and wilful misunderstanding conceals its radiance, we want to discuss with you

The Modern Meaning of the Cross

and show how true are both statements of our text (1 Corinthians 1:18), *"The preaching of the Cross is to them that perish foolishness; but unto us which are saved it is the power of God."*

I

THE CROSS IS STILL FOOLISHNESS TO THEM THAT PERISH

In Corinth, where Saint Paul had proclaimed the message of the Cross, the contrast between everything which Christ taught and all that the grasping, sensual world demanded was expressed as in few other places. Here was a city dotted with high-pillared marble temples, shrines filled with scores of gods and goddesses; and there, atop an ugly hill near despised Jerusalem, a blood-soaked cross on which Jesus of Nazareth had died as a criminal. In the Greek metropolis one could choose a favorite among the many gods, but at Calvary men were told to seek salvation only through Christ. In Corinth, a place described by a Church Father as "most licentious of all" cities "that are or ever have been," horrifying lewdness held undisputed sway. The very temples featured the shameful service of

Aphrodite, goddess of love. More than a thousand prostitutes were dedicated to her in a single Corinthian sanctuary. No wonder people thought Paul's message *"foolishness"* when he preached a Savior who denounced lusts of the flesh and warned, *"They which do such things shall not inherit the kingdom of God."* In that city of sin, one of the world's leading commercial centers, extreme wealth and lavish luxury led men to worship money. How could there be any love for Christ's Cross among Corinthian capitalists when Jesus had lived penniless, denounced ill-gotten and ill-used riches, and died a pauper? Especially were the educated classes immovably set in their opposition to the Savior. They listened to the philosophers discoursing on the enjoyment of life. They traveled to Athens, hardly forty-five miles away, to hear orators deny the possibility of a life to come. The wonder of it all is that Paul found any one, even among the 400,000 slaves in the city, who would accept Christ. Only the Spirit of God could overcome the deep-rooted hostility to the Cross.

Today, too, only the Holy Spirit can defeat the widespread hatred of Jesus which rules the world. While nineteen centuries of remarkable history and millions of twice-born men and women demonstrate Christ's power to remake men's hearts and lives, the preaching of the Cross is still *"foolishness"* to millions.

Ask the educated infidel why he brands our creed as *"foolishness,"* and in the spirit of Corinthian unbelief he will declare that Christianity is out of line with modern thought, that science must supplant the Bible. Perhaps this objection has caused some of you deep concern, and you waver in your allegiance to Christ. But why is it that many profound thinkers have been humble believers? A few days ago, from the press of Princeton University, came a large volume embodying the philosophies of

Dr. Archibald Allen Bowman, Glasgow University. Half-way through the book that eminent author pauses to say, "In my own view . . . the doctrine of the incarnation of God in the man Jesus is the only possible solution for the tragedy of the world that has lost itself." Tell this to any high-school teacher of sophomore physics who insists that the Bible is out of date and Christian faith an anti-quated superstition! Besides, the scientific pronouncements, supposed to take the place of revealed Scriptural truth, have too often proved completely erroneous. You on the farm will be interested to be told that two renowned thinkers, Cuvier and Huxley, are on record as declaring, against plain barnyard evidence, that the hog is a cud-chewer. Another widely applauded scientist, Sir John Herschel, taught that living creatures, spindle-shaped monsters, existed on the surface of the sun, an opinion no modern scientist would endorse. A committee of the celebrated French Academy investigated the lowly soup-bone and returned an utterly incorrect report. In these and a hundred other mistakes made, not by bungling amateurs, but by scientific leaders, we find repeated warn-ings against believing the theories advanced to discredit Scripture. We like the answer which Sir Isaac Newton, leader among scientists of all times, gave to a skeptic: "I am always glad to hear you when you speak about astronomy or other parts of mathematics because that is a subject which you have studied and well understand; but you should not talk of Christianity, for you have not studied it. I have, and I am certain that you know nothing of the matter."

Others are not troubled by so-called scientific contradic-tions. They blandly assert that the Cross is opposed to common sense and human reason. Ask the smooth cynic why the Gospel is *"foolishness"* to him, and he will answer: "You can't expect me to believe anything I can't understand. How could Christ, the Son of God, be born of a virgin? How could He die for my sins? How can His blood cleanse me? How can I, when this body decays, be resurrected into life?" — What unfairness those of you show who thus reject Christianity because you cannot account for it! Every part of your body, every moment of your existence, every inch of your world, is crowded with unexplainable wonders, universally accepted as every-day facts, which no highly equipped laboratory and no corps of scientists can begin to analyze. How utterly inconsistent you are when every day of your lives you take for granted a thousand different wonders, the force of which you see, feel, and hear; yet, when it comes to the mysteries of the soul and the marvels of God's love, you obstinately raise your voices in protest! How blessed, on the contrary, as Christ Himself reminds us, are they who *"have not seen and yet have believed"*!

Still others point to the Cross as a monument to *"foolishness"* for another reason. Ask many of our modern thinkers why they have arrayed themselves against the Christian hope, and they will answer, as they point to those who have been doomed to lifelong agony of body and disturbance of mind: "How can God be the Lord of love? How can there be a God of grace in the heavens above if He makes His children suffer as they do?" But this is a hasty, short-sighted objection. It misunderstands the purpose of pain. Looking aside entirely from those who are punished in consequences of their folly, this indictment of God's love does not recognize that there is a heavenly compensation for all woes and griefs and that, though we must suffer here, we shall be exalted with Christ in eternity, where we shall understand that anguish and reverses, even a lifetime of the worst sickness, disappointment, loneliness, infirmity, are *"not worthy to be compared with the glory which shall be revealed in us"* there in the heavenly home-land. Those of you who blindly accuse God of permitting men and women to endure pain have never understood that the sorrows and conflicts of life, through Christ, are purifying, uplifting, strength-imparting benedictions, re-markable evidences of God's mercy, through which be-lievers like Saint Paul can exult, *"I rejoice in mine in-firmities"* and actually thank God for their afflictions.

Some present-day attacks on Christ never confronted the early Christians; for instance, the charge that the Church works against the poor and oppressed. Ask the Communist why he wants to overthrow our faith, and he will charge that the Cross of Jesus Christ is *"foolishness"* to him because our creed is capitalistic and has no interest in the laborers and downtrodden masses. Much has been done, it is admitted regretfully, to encourage this error. If a hungry, unemployed man daily passes pretentious sanctuaries that have no room for the shabbily dressed; if he beholds limousines rolling up to cathedral-like build-ings used only once a week, sees middle- and upper-class congregations which turn away from the problems of fam-ilies on relief, you can understand why a distracted man can easily be led to insist that the churches must be opposed and destroyed. If a Negro finds that congregational members are eager to do business with him and take his money, but are unconcerned about his soul and refuse to have spiritual contact with him, it may be easy for radicals to gain his support as they promise him absolute equality and complete fellowship. The true Scriptural faith which some fashionable groups have forgotten or neglected is the best ally the working-man ever knew, the most ardent champion the colored race can have. What ennobled labor and exalted the working-man, lifting the various trades and professions from their low level? Not Communism, but the example and power of Christ, Himself a laboring man. What freed the slaves and liberated the black man? Not Communism, but the sacrifice and devotion of Christian men and women moved by the power of Christ's new commandment *"that ye love one another."* Lest this charge of capitalistic spirit be hurled with even more hatred against Christianity, churches must keep in touch with the restless, discontented masses. Particularly in years like these they must avoid the display of wealth. Their first concern must not be attractive and expensive buildings, costlier robes, more pretentious choirs, but a larger missionary policy that will bring the Gospel to multitudes still in ignorance of Christ's saving grace. The churches must recapture the service to the poor, sick, unemployed, which has been lost to community agencies, civic groups, and the state itself. The best way to counteract the radical claims that churches are tools of capitalism is to make them what Christ the Lord wants them to be, havens of refuge for all the oppressed, temples of the living God for all men.

Most of the opposition that brands Christ's Gospel as *"foolishness"* comes from the same love of sin that arrayed Corinth in hatred against Jesus. Because the cross on which the Savior died denounces dishonesty and perverted men want to lie, cheat, and steal; because Calvary thunders God's accusations against adultery and all sins of the flesh, while our lustful age laughs at faithfulness in marriage and seeks to spread debauch; because Golgotha indicts the sins of the tongue, perjury, falsehood, slander, while people today delight in malicious scandal-mongering and openly flaunt false witness before the courts — the Christless world still brands the Savior's message as the supreme folly. At the same time unbelief seeks to take away the terror of sin. Self-confident men laugh at the idea of punishment and retribution in the hereafter, laugh until confronted with death; and then their bravery turns into chattering fear. Our age has even glorified sin. Certain lecturers tell our young people that they promote their health and are up to date, enlightened, when they break the commandment of premarital chastity and follow their desire. Teachers applauded as authorities exalt — and this is just what the late, widely heralded Freud did in his last, error-laden book — as the ideals of modern marriage and home life the reign of lust which marked the family's collapse in Red Russia. The spreading of poisonous propaganda is acclaimed as patriotism. The nation is set above God Almighty and blasphemy paraded as though it were a shining virtue.

In protest the Cross still shines forth against the gloom of human error to tell our sophisticated, self-reliant generation that sin brings terrifying soul-destruction, and we can be saved from it only by the indescribable mercy with which the sinless Son of God gave Himself into death for the sinner. Calvary reminds us that our transgressions have marked us, every one of us, with a deep stain of guilt, from which we can be cleansed solely by the purifying power of His precious blood.

After you have heard this message of the Savior's cross, will you dare behold your Lord, His holy arms hitherto raised only in benediction, now stretched wide in the crucifixion agony; His feet, which otherwise bore Him swiftly to help the sorrowful and suffering, now pierced with cruel iron nails; His countenance, which could encourage sinners to approach His mercy, now blanched and spattered with blood — can you see this Christ, your Substitute, your Redeemer, and still say: "It is all 'foolishness'"? O God, prevent that! As we thank Thy holy mercy that Thou dost not strike down every scoffer who dares blaspheme Thy holy Son, we pray Thee, send Thy Spirit now to invade those hearts which heretofore have been fortresses of unbelief, centers of pride! Bring many to their knees, humble, penitent, believing, before this Christ of the cross, their only Hope for this life and the world to come! If I may now speak directly to you whom God has placed squarely before these issues of salvation and eternity, let me remind you: Our text says that the Gospel is *"foolishness"* only to those who — now comes the hardest word in the Bible — *"perish"*! Without Christ and against Christ — as hard as it may be for some of you to believe this, and it is much harder for me to say it — you are doomed! Education will not help you; and we think of a state university president, convicted on serious charges, seeking, despite his culture, to end it all in suicide. Money will not exempt you; and we recall the self-destruction of a millionaire's son who with the many contacts his riches gave him could not face the problems of life. Nothing but faith can save you. No pious prayers of your parents, no pleas of your husband or wife, no holiness of any saints, can deliver you if, beholding Christ's cross, you sneer, *"Foolishness!"*

The ancient city of Corinth is long destroyed, for past earthquakes have brought its haughty pride low; and perhaps divine justice is punishing you through the sorrows that surround you. Yet if you have escaped thus far; if you boast that you can succeed without God; if you think yourself prosperous and powerful enough to defy the Almighty, look at this word *"perish"* once more. It means that there is an inevitable justice before which you, whoever you are, must face your Maker; and if you persist in ridiculing the Cross, not even the holy and just God can have mercy on your soul. Then you are barred forever from a blessed eternity with Christ. You will exist, but it will be a living death, banished from God, separated from heaven's glory, beauty, love; doomed — oh, how we shudder at this word! — doomed to the hell which many modern churches have vainly sought to remove from the Bible and explain out of existence!

II

THE CROSS IS STILL THE POWER OF GOD TO EVERY ONE THAT BELIEVETH

Let us hasten, however, to the glorious promise of our text, Saint Paul's assurance that *"the preaching of the Cross . . . is the power of God"* to them that believe. Stunted minds may besmirch the Cross, vicious hatred seek to destroy it, sin-loving men try to forget it; but here it is, the Apostle declares as he points us to Calvary, *"the power of God"* — eternal, immovable, almighty!

First of all, of course, it is *"the power of God"* to forgive sin — every transgression, including the deep-grooved iniquities that cause many of you sleepless nights and restless days. You write that you are living with a man who is not your husband or that your daughter will soon be an unmarried mother; you send desperate pleas concerning your personal weaknesses and secret, degrading sins. Now, let nothing that we say minimize in your mind the heinousness of these transgressions; but let everything we say bring you penitently to Christ for pardon and peace. Because the message of the Savior's death is *"the power of God,"* it must be a perfect energy, with mercy and forgiveness in overabundance. It must offer complete remission, which asks for nothing more than your faith in Christ, believing that He, the ever-blessed Redeemer, paid the entire price, went the whole way, earned the full pardon.

More! The Cross strengthens us by *"the power of*

God" to combat sin, overcome our temptations, and lead a God-pleasing life. At Calvary, through faith and the rebirth in the Spirit, we become new creatures, with a blessed desire to walk in the footsteps of the Lord Jesus. We never reach perfection, it is true; but God's power sustains us. If some of you are burdened by besetting sins; if, for example, there is within you the tugging, clutching desire which may lead to drunkenness and its bestiality — fight that vice, above all, by keeping the cross ever before your eyes. Medical authorities and psychologists may give you different prescriptions; but the most potent influence for good and the most serious check on evil is the living consciousness of Jesus' love. The reason many of you are losing the battle against your pet sins and personal weaknesses is this, that you have relied on your own might instead of looking to the Lord Jesus and this *"power of God."*

How I pray that in the struggle for clean, honest lives, you young folks especially will realize and use this strength radiating from the cross! When you are Christ's, you can have Him at your side constantly to direct you; you have His Word to uphold you in those hard moments when heart and flesh want to surrender. You have baptismal grace, strength-imparting Holy Communion, and the promise of prayer, which can invoke God's omnipotence for your help. As Samuel Taylor Coleridge wrote to his nephew: "Believe me, to pray with all your heart and strength, with the reason and the will, to believe vividly that God will listen to your voice through Christ, and verily do the thing that pleaseth Him at last — this is the greatest achievement of the Christian's welfare on earth."

All this, however, does not exhaust the influence of the Cross; for it is *"the power of God"* to help us overcome the hostile world. Today more than ever before men ought to face the future not with drugged optimism or blind confidence. Christians, above others, realizing that the signs of the last times are being fulfilled before our eyes, should understand the perilous days ahead in which the forces of iniquity will attack the Church with redoubled force. Yet faith riveted to the Cross knows that the legions of hell and the regiments of an unbelieving world, multiplied to overwhelming proportions, cannot remove God's eternal truth. Give us churches which, without fear or favor, proclaim — and now I am quoting from the confessions of my Church —: "The first and chief article is this, that Jesus Christ, our God and Lord, died for our sins and was raised for our justification. . . . All have sinned and are justified . . . by His grace. . . . It is clear and certain that faith alone justifies us"; give these churches preachers with the perseverance of Judson in far-off Burma, who, when urged to return to the comforts of America, replied, "Were a vessel lying there in the harbor ready to convey me to any part of the world that I might choose, and that with the entire approbation of all my Christian friends, I should prefer dying to embarking"; send us missionaries with the zeal of John Eliot, who wrote, "I have not been dry day or night from the third day of the week unto the sixth, but so traveled, and at night pull off my boots, wring my stockings, and on with them again, and so continue"; give us a laity with the faith that moved Daniel Webster to declare: "I believe Jesus Christ to be the Son of God. The miracles which He wrought, in my mind, establish His personal authority and render it proper for me to believe whatever He asserts. . . . And I believe that there is no other way of salvation than through the merits of His atonement"; give the Cross its right place in Christian hearts and homes, and the armies of atheism will not keep us from the truth in Jesus Christ!

The Cross also offers an inexpressible comfort to you who need support for your burdens. Calvary shows us *"the power of God"* as a help in meeting life's adversities. Beholding the crucified Savior obedient to His Father's will, we see that, as the cross was preliminary to the crown and Christ's lowliness and suffering was followed by His glorious exaltation, so in our own lives implicit obedience brings light into the darkness of any troubled hour. After a long siege of sickness Colonel Gordon, the courageous Christian soldier, wrote, "I am glad to say that this disease has brought me back to my Savior, and I trust in the future to be a better Christian than I have been heretofore." In the same way the Cross changes affliction to advantage, grief to joy, bodily sickness to spiritual health, earthly loss to heavenly profit. How I thank God that every week in the many thousand letters which pour in on us, your living testimonies to the victory in Christ tell us how you, the paralyzed, crippled, incapacitated, incurable ill, know *"the power of God"* with unmistakable conviction!

Turn to Christ, then, all of you, and be fortified by these divine dynamics. Keep Christ, you, His disciples in faith, so that the crown of life may not be taken from you. Preach Christ, we ask you, called to be His ministers, and in an unbelieving, perverse world let your voices call the world to repentance and blessing! Use the power of the Cross and put its divine strength to work in our own beloved country for the growth of that righteousness which alone exalts a nation! For, through the constant impress of the Lord Jesus and the inner blessings of personal faith, you, I, millions in our country and in our world, can find *"the power of God"* for soul, mind, and body. Our heavenly Father grant every one of us that divine energy through faith in the Savior! Amen.

PRAY, AMERICA, PRAY!

"I pray before Thee now, day and night, for the children of Israel, Thy servants, and confess the sins of the children of Israel. . . . Both I and my father's house have sinned." — Nehemiah 1:6.

"And the king granted me, according to the good hand of my God." — Nehemiah 2:8.

O Christ, in whom alone we can find salvation:

Show us the power of prayer which pleads in Thy name and teach us that because of Thy cross and its death-bought redemption Thou art close to us in all our needs, if only we believe Thy mercy and do not reject Thy promise of pardon! By Thine eternal love for this sin-bound world forgive us our neglect of prayer, our half-heartedness, and sometimes irreverence in approaching Thee, our blessed Savior! Remove all our lukewarmness and indifference; send us Thy Spirit, so that for every weak moment we can find forgiveness and strength in penitent, yet confident communion with Thee! Hear us, O Jesus, and from Thy mighty throne in the eternal heavens answer us as Thou hast promised! Amen.

HOW remarkably penitential prayer has helped America in crisis moments! Three years after the Pilgrims landed at Plymouth, a severe drought burned the grass brown and threatened to destroy the crops. The stock of food was exhausted, and no longer could the colonists depend on supplies from England. In that dark hour, when all expected to die of hunger, the Pilgrim Fathers took refuge in God. For almost nine hours, on a day of humiliation and prayer, they pleaded with the Almighty, and the Lord heard them. Before evening, rain began to fall; the refreshing showers continued so long that the parched vegetation was revived and the harvest spared. The Plymouth Colony was saved by prayer.

Similarly, a century later, in 1746, when the French in Nova Scotia equipped forty warships to destroy New England, the churches in that territory set aside a fast-day, on which they most fervently besought divine help. While the colonists were praying, a wind suddenly arose. Under continued entreaty that God would use this wind to save the country, the storm became almost a hurricane. The French fleet was wrecked off the Nova Scotia coast; the Duke d'Anville, in command of that armada, and his second officer both committed suicide; hundreds were drowned, and others died of disease and exposure. Once more prayer had brought deliverance.

Again, in the devastating winter of 1777 prayer prevailed. The American struggle for independence seemed lost, when, at Valley Forge, the ragged Continentals hungry, ill-clothed, ill-shod, unpaid, disorganized, stained the Pennsylvania snows with their life-blood, while not far away, in Philadelphia and New York, the Tories enjoyed a smart social season and the atheist Tom Paine wrote vicious attacks on George Washington's character. In these gloomy hours Washington, according to an eye-witness, knelt down, as thousands of Christians knelt in their churches during that crisis, and pleaded with God to sustain the American cause. Light and hope dawned on the darkest hours in our war for freedom, and from that time on the prospects for victory constantly brightened.

Prayer likewise helped save our country early in 1863, when the Confederate troops not only defeated the Union army in the South but even advanced far into northern territory. In that time of testing Abraham Lincoln proclaimed a day of prayer and penance, requesting the nation to ask of God "pardon for our national sins and the restoration of our now divided and suffering country to its former condition of unity and peace." That plea, too, was answered; for within hardly two months the battle of Gettysburg had been won and the Union saved.

You see, then, that in the past, distress has brought America to its knees in supplication. But do you know that not once in the last ten troubled years, with their overwhelming problems, have our people observed a day of humiliation and prayer? We have some compensation for this neglect, however, since according to ancient custom, Christians have set aside this Sunday, the last in the church-year, for pleading with God; and though this occasion will not be generally observed because of pride and self-sufficiency, the pointed appeal of this problem-weighted hour is:

PRAY, AMERICA, PRAY!

The spirit of the prayer you, I, and the 130,000,000 of our fellow-countrymen need is found in Nehemiah 1:6 and 2:8, where the great patriot declares: *"I pray before Thee now, day and night, for the children of Israel, Thy servants, and confess the sins of the children of Israel. . . . Both I and my father's house have sinned." "And the king granted me, according to the good hand of my God."*

I

PRAY PENITENTLY!

Nehemiah's age shows remarkable similarity to ours. It was a time of reconstruction, a new era for Israel. A few who had returned from the Babylonian Exile were rich and oppressive; the masses were poor, and loudly did they complain of debts and heavy mortgages. Many were hungry and unemployed; particularly unhappy was the lot of the young people, often sold into slavery because business and commerce were paralyzed. From without, enemies threatened to overrun the country; but the danger from within was even greater. Ignorant of God's Word, the people no longer kept the Sabbath nor taught the Law to their children. Instead, family life was corrupt; as the Israelites intermarried with the heathen, the reverence of God vanished from their homes. In that emergency it was Nehemiah in far-off Persia who rose to the need of the hour. He did not create a board of investigation nor establish a trade commission; he did not institute a committee to survey social conditions. He fell on his knees in prayer!

Nehemiah was a layman — not a priest, professionally obliged to pray. In his high position at the Persian court he readily risked everything for his country and his Church. Can you not feel the challenge that today asks the laity's deep and personal interest in helping this nation remember its God? Too many feel that these spiritual duties rest chiefly on the conscience of the clergy, when in fact our difficulties are so formidable and overpowering that the plea, "Pray, America, pray! Turn to Christ in repentance and faith!" asks particularly for the petitions of you business men, public officials, executives, instructors, physicians, attorneys, professional men, who seldom raise your voices in the intense supplication that marked Nehemiah's faith.

Examine the multiplied dangers surrounding us. We face organized and well-financed efforts to coax our country into a war that can hang crepes on the doors of a million American homes, bring a financial collapse far worse than that of 1929, and sow the seeds of discontent for a harvest of disaster. Don't say that the masses in this country hate war and cannot be drawn in! At the beginning of 1917 the American people hated war, and still they were drawn in. Rather pray, Christians of America, pray, so that we may be spared this bloodshed and our youth may live!

Firmly intrenched against the American and the Christian way of living is the menace of revolution promoted by the Communists. Do you know that there are more than 600 of these anti-American and antichristian organizations in our country, more than 640 Communist and pro-Communist publications? Do you realize that within less than two years the membership in the Young Communist League, revolutionary youth organization, has doubled, and that within seven years the regular, paid membership in the Communist party has increased 500 per cent? During the last year for which figures are available, Communists in Chicago contributed an average of $26.96 for the overthrow of democracy and the churches' destruction—a figure in excess of the average Chicago Christian's gift to Christ's kingdom. When the present war is over, regardless of how much the victor may seem to have won, Communism alone may record unmistakable triumphs. Instead of saying, "Well, this can't happen here," the cry must be: "Pray, America, pray! Turn to Christ and ask His help!" so that divine omnipotence may form a wall around us which atheistic regiments cannot pass.

Other difficulties beset us: the increasing drain on our national treasuries; continued impoverization of the many poor and enrichment of the few wealthy; the studied efforts to give our youth a godless training that makes our boys and girls clever but leaves them without character and without helpful life foundation; the immorality and crime, the endless transgressing of God's law and man's, which, even with lenient justice, despite political influence and legal loopholes, has overcrowded the prisons of the land; the breakdown of many American homes with their wilful, sinful childlessness, the quick and easy divorce, which lightly dissolves a union that should hold husband and wife together until death do them part; the unconditional surrender of many churches to the menace and mistake of Modernism — these are the formidable foes arrayed against our God-blessed nation, enemies, we believe, even more dangerous than the Plymouth hunger, the French fleet against New England, Valley Forge, and the tragedies in the War of Brothers.

Nehemiah turned to God; and in whom else, we ask, is our refuge? The Lord wants us to use our brains and devise the best human programs, of course; but sometimes our choicest efforts are inadequate, and our problems lie too deep for human help. During the last ten years we believed that our difficulties could be solved by financial arrangements, and so we looked to economists, only to hear authorities like Dr. Stephen Leacock, former dean of the economics department at McGill University, assert: We are "lost in the jungle of economics; at a time when the world is in danger of collapse from the dilemma of want and wealth, the economist can shed no light, or rather only . . . fireworks, elaborate and meaningless." Instead of being a lighthouse, this authority claims, our money theories have sometimes become "wreckers' signals."

We have turned to laws and ambitious legislative programs; but despite the multiplied legal statutes, the spent billions, the mobilized brain-power, it is a fact, conceding the many commendable changes and necessary improvements, not only that the basic problems remain — unemployment, poverty, and (except for war profits) restricted industry — but that, in addition, other dangers have increased at an alarming rate. Never before has this appeal, "Pray, America, pray!" been more needed than now, when millions lull themselves into a sense of false security.

Nehemiah's prayer was a penitential plea for pardon. It voiced a contrite confession of sins. Instead of demanding recognition from God, it interceded with Him for

mercy. We, too, must have that spirit. The United
States likes to think itself morally superior to other nations.
We look down on the cruel Nazi treatment of the Jews;
yet how pharisaical this often is in the light of our own
attitude toward the American Indian and our unfair discriminations against the Negro! Who in this audience,
with the strong undercurrent of anti-Semitic agitation in
our country and its support even from radio preachers, will
deny that the flames of racial hatred can flare up within
our own boundaries? We shake our heads at the atheism
in Russia, but right here, often in schools maintained by
public funds, we permit intellectual atheists to instruct the
college youth. We deplore the barbarities and the wholesale slaughter that mark the conquest of China, but who
supports this destruction if not particularly the American
blood profiteers and our own laws which legalize the
exportation of their implements of death? We pride ourselves that our homes are larger, better, more efficiently
equipped than other nations'; but we forget that we have
more divorces than any other civilized country with the
exception of Red Russia itself. We congratulate ourselves
that we enjoy progress, wealth, education, as no other
people on earth; but we ought to lament the fact that
ours is the most crime-ridden country in modern civilization.
We sit back in self-satisfied pleasure to recall that we have
more automobiles, telephones, radios, luxuries, jewelry, than
can be found elsewhere on the earth; but we ought to
ask ourselves why we have proportionately more labor
trouble, theft and robbery, slander and perjury.

The time has come for a day of national humiliation
and prayer. Far more vital than a Democratic or Repub-
lican program, much more essential than all money theories,
trade arrangements, labor legislation, as helpful as these
may be, is the appeal, "Pray, America, pray!" by which

the people of our country are asked to humble themselves before God. Besides two national anthems that neither concede a single fault nor admit one wrong, we need a hymn that brings this nation before the throne of the Almighty with a contrite admission that we have sinned often, grievously, ungratefully. In addition to singing "God Bless America!" we should plead, "God Forgive America!" Instead of hysterical flag-waving we need heart-praying people; instead of superpatriots who shout, "My country, right or wrong!" give us Christians who ask, "O God, forgive us our wrongs and make us right!" Instead of party-blinded politicians give us statesmen whose eyes are directed to the eternal truth that *"righteousness exalteth a nation, but sin is a reproach to any people."*

If that contrition over our sins is to have force and value, it must be spoken by every one of us; for we have individually contributed to the total of our nation's iniquity. How excellent is Nehemiah's attitude in this respect! He not only makes the easier admission of Israel's wrong but, pointing to himself and his family, declares, *"Both I and my father's house have sinned."* It is easy enough, of course, to pick up a newspaper and with a "God-I-thank-Thee-that-I-am-not-as-other-men-are" attitude point out the murderers, embezzlers, adulterers, thugs, suicides, degenerates. It requires no heroic courage for disgruntled laborers to enumerate the sins of capitalists. But to stand before God Almighty, as Nehemiah did, and admit our personal, private sins; to confess, not daring to lift our heads to the holy Lord, that by our own hatred, lust, covetousness, by the impurity, dishonesty, and falsehood in our lives, we have offended God, injured our fellow-men and brought harm upon ourselves — that admission of individual guilt, without excuse or reservation, is one of the hardest confessions to pass over our lips. Yet may the Holy Spirit give us strength for that complete contrition!

II
PRAY CONFIDENTLY!

Nehemiah prayed confidently, and the Lord heard him. The Spirit of God opened the Persian king's heart, and Nehemiah records, "*And the king granted me, according to the good hand of my God.*"

Today we can have double assurance that our pleas for a better nation will be answered if, following the Savior's repeated prayer direction, we ask in His name and approach the throne of mercy not as we are in our sins but as we are in His grace. When you kneel before the cross to learn that He was wounded for your transgressions, that He died so that you might live; when you stand at the open grave where Jesus kept His life-bestowing promise, you know that He not only restored you to the heavenly Father's loving arms, but that Jesus Himself also stands before the Father to intercede for you. No matter how often, how persistently, how grievously, how blasphemously, how ungratefully, you have sinned against God, the love that spared not His own Son shows itself by hearing every prayer raised in the Savior's name and asked "according to His will."

What if unbelief sneers: "God cannot answer prayer!"? You know that the Creator and Sustainer of this vast universe has the power to fulfil your requests; you believe that the Lord of truth and purity hears all who call on Him in faith; you can point to many divine answers. What if modern enlightenment seeks to ridicule prayer! Cite great leaders in scientific thought who have been men of prayer! Michael Faraday, electrical genius, thought so much of prayer that once after captivating a scientific audience by his remarkable lecture on magnetism, he hastened to his village church without waiting to receive the compliments of royalty; he would not be late for the privileges of entreaty and worship. The daughter of Sir David Brewster, a scientist whose discoveries in the field of light are epochal, said that every morning her father prayed with such fervor that his petitions could be heard in the room above. James Clerk Maxwell, one of the outstanding figures in nineteenth-century science, took time every night, even when confronted by deep-rooted problems, to conduct evening devotions with his family, guests, and servants. Sir James Y. Simpson, renowned physician who openly declared that his greatest discovery was the fact that Christ was his Savior, constantly directed his students to the power of prayer and reliance on God. So did Adam Sedgwick, geologist, who started his classes with the words, "Let prayer be the beginning and end of our studies." So did Louis Agassiz, noted Harvard naturalist, who began and closed each of his lectures in the marine laboratory at Buzzard's Bay with a simple outpouring of his heart to God. Louis Pasteur, world-famed bacteriologist, openly admitted: "I pray while I am engaged in my work in the laboratory." Samuel F. B. Morse, inventor of the telegraph, believed Congress had refused to vote the funds necessary for his startling experiment and left the capitol at Washington disheartened; yet, despite his disappointment, he knelt for long and earnest prayer to God. Edward Emerson Barnard, astronomer at the Yerkes Observatory, discoverer of sixteen comets, was accustomed, visitors or no visitors, to attend prayer-meetings and to urge his guests to accompany him.— If great minds have not been ashamed of Jesus, you, too, taking God at His word, trusting His promises, beholding the multiplied examples of answered petition, can find help and strength for yourself, your family, your Church, your country through this blessed intercession. You, too, can have Nehemiah's assurance that your requests will be granted *"according to the good hand"* of your God.

The more urgent prayer becomes in days of trouble like ours, the more sophisticated unbelief seeks to discredit its power. In the midst of this lamentable war, atheism finds new ammunition for its attacks by declaring that both sides in the European conflict are appealing to God for victory, though only one can be answered. Our attention is directed to the fact that, while King George of England confidently asserted, "We can only reverently commit our cause to God; . . . with God's help we shall prevail," about the same time Chancellor Hitler, imploring divine help, stated, "The Lord God, who has always given grace to him who is determined to help himself, will stand by us."

Remember, however, that God does not promise to answer every prayer, and the reason many petitions remain unheard lies not in Him but in the wrong, sometimes destructive, prayers. Our heavenly Father will not hear you if you try to come before Him with sin on your hands, on your lips, and in your heart. These iniquities must be washed away. You must be reborn in His holiness if you would approach Him. Before you can pray with promise, you must know Christ as your Savior.

The Lord will not hear our requests for any gift or grant that might injure our body or soul, weaken our faith, increase our pride or self-reliance, and coax us from His mercies. To the contrary, He loves us so much that He permits life's reverses and sorrows in order to humble us and show the power of true Christian entreaty in His school of affliction. Indeed, if we learn to pray, as Jesus prayed, *"Thy will be done,"* and submit ourselves wholly to God's good and gracious guidance, we shall experience, even through shattered hopes and deep-cut grief, that God answers every prayer directed to His honor, the welfare of our fellow-men, and our own growth in grace.

He may not answer when we expect it. Nehemiah tells us he prayed *"day and night."* How many of us have acquired that persistency and learned, with Paul, to *"pray without ceasing"?* How many of us have ever faintly followed the holy example of Jesus, who repeatedly spent the whole night in prayer? How we wish the spirit of Nehemiah would be revived! A major trouble in America today is this, that masses neither fear nor love God enough, urgently, protractedly, to seek Him in prayer. Even half the Christians in the United States have probably not prayed — outside their church — personally and persistently for peace. Only a fraction of our citizenry is so convinced of God's power and so deeply concerned with the world's welfare that they have earnestly and continually asked God to preserve us in honorable peace. A nation on its knees, pleading in Christ's name, can help solve the problems of the day's conflict when all the enactments of legislative bodies and the theories of so-called social scientists may fail.

We have time for everything else, but so little time for God! If for only one minute each day the Christian world would pause in prayer, and Christians — wherever they are in the five continents and on the seven seas, on the Maginot or Siegfried lines of Europe's terrifying war, on submarines, dreadnaughts, airplanes, in business, manufacturing, commerce, in schools and homes — would drop everything and plead, "O God, in the name of Jesus Christ, our only Savior, we plead with Thee to forgive us our sins of hatred and to fill our hearts with love for our fellowmen, yes, Father, even for our enemies! Stop the horrors of this war, if it be Thy will, and grant us a peace that can make for mutual understanding, for cooperation between nations instead of competition, for harmony instead of hatred. Hear us, O Father, for Jesus' sake!" don't you believe that this one short minute — and how many hours people waste each day! — could help bring marked blessings on our strife-torn world? Are you not convinced, as you hear the holy, sinless Jesus promise, *"Whatsoever ye shall ask the Father in My name, He will give it you,"* that, if the Christian workers of America, instead of listening to the siren songs of radical agitators, and the Christian employers of America, instead of rigidly insisting on their rights, would spend a few moments every day in silent but mass prayer to God Almighty, beseeching Him for Jesus' sake to stop the disheartening conflict between C. I. O. and A. F. L.; open shop, closed shop; company union, trade union, the apalling loss and enmity could be checked? Because Jesus Himself promises, *"All things, whatsoever ye shall ask in prayer, believing, ye shall receive,"* the family altar in prayer-filled homes could eliminate much of the rancor and the domestic trouble that have made marriage a mockery in many houses.

Oh, why will so many of you live dark, depressed, sin-bound, hate-filled lives as you refuse to "carry everything to God in prayer"? No one who despises the Savior's offer to find peace in prayer can be truly happy; but all who have accepted His pledges can discover a divine power to strengthen their souls, a heavenly aid to the welfare and happiness of their fellow-countrymen.

May the God who can hear our pleas before they are spoken, strengthen every one of us to live and die in trusting communion with Him, so that now, in our humiliation and prayer service across this continent, a mighty host of blood-bought, Spirit-born men and women may repeat the disciples' plea, *"Lord, teach us to pray,"* dedicate themselves to a penitent prayer-life, and daily realize what privilege, what power, what blessing, is theirs in prayer! So pray, America, come to Christ and pray penitently! Pray confidently! Pray constantly! Pray in the name of Jesus Christ, Son of God and Son of man, our Savior and Substitute, our Prophet, Priest, and King, our Lord and our God! Amen.

CHRIST FIRST — FOR THE HOME!

"Learn first to show piety at home." — 1 Timothy 5:4

God, our Father:

By the power of Thy Spirit show us that, if we have Christ first in our families, with all our hearts acclaiming Him the Pardon for our transgressions and the Peace for our troubled souls, the blessed Savior will purify, comfort, and sustain our homes even in dark, strife-torn days! Bless us all, parents and children, with His forgiving love and help us believe that, no matter what our needs, sorrows, sins, and weaknesses may be, Jesus, our glorious Advent King, seeks to approach us with the answer to distracting questions, the solution for each perplexity, the lightening of every burden, the ransom for all wrong! Oh, send the Lord Jesus to be our Guest, our Peace, our Blessing! Amen.

AMONG the most distinguished jurists ever to occupy the United States Supreme Court bench was John McLean of Ohio, remembered particularly because of his courageous antislavery ballot in the Dred Scott case. Justice McLean had been indifferent to the claims of Christ during his earlier life; but one day, after hearing a message on the blessed meaning of Jesus' death, he learned to love the Savior. Before that day of his new birth closed, he rushed home, announcing, "I have just found that Jesus died on the cross for me. Let us go to the drawing-room and pray together." Although a group of attorneys waited in that room to consult him, he declared, "I have given myself to Jesus, and now I propose to invite Him to my house." Addressing the lawyers, he continued, "You may do as you please, stay or go; but I want Christ in this home, and now I am to make my first prayer in my own house." They remained, and from that day Justice McLean lived in the positive, unshrinking faith that kept Christ first for his family. God grant that many of you who hear this appeal for repentance, trust in Christ, and the new life will be led by His Spirit to find in the ever-living, ever-loving Lord your Savior, and as the first-fruits of your faith make Christ the Head of your home!

A deep reliance on Jesus' blood-bought mercies always gives the Savior the principal place in the family circle. When the jailer at Philippi, his heart pierced by penetrating sorrow over his sins, cried, as I pray God you have, *"What must I do to be saved?"* and then received this pledge of full, free redemption, *"Believe on the Lord Jesus Christ, and thou shalt be saved,"* this new disciple rose from his despair and — so we like to picture the scene — in the first act of his reborn life helped bring his wife, children, relatives, servants, to Baptism, so that Christ would rule over his entire household.

Martin Luther had hardly started the titanic task of restoring the Christian faith when he sought to win the home for Jesus. Not many years after he began writing the magnificent treatises which have provoked the admiration of friend and foe alike, he prepared, especially for fathers, a short summary of the saving truth, so that they could teach their children the way to heaven. He knew that Christ had to be First in the family.

Last year when we broadcast a message of the Savior's grace, a man in Minneapolis was brought by the Spirit to accept Jesus. Immediately after the broadcast he hurried to a pastor's house, requesting help in bringing his loved ones to the Lord. Having accepted the Savior, he knew, Christ must be First in his house.

You see, then, that people in various stations of life, when they find themselves saved by grace, want the husband or the wife, their parents and their children, to have the same exalted faith that is theirs. Intensely do they long to meet their own in heaven; and to secure these blessings they know that Jesus must reign supreme in their earthly dwelling. As we declare from shore to shore — in the spirit of our message for today —

CHRIST FIRST — FOR THE FAMILY!

this is no mere personal plea. It is rather the instruction of God Himself (1 Timothy 5:4), where Saint Paul writes: *"Learn first to show piety at home."*

I

CHRIST FIRST FOR THE CLEANSING OF THE HOME!

This appeal is addressed by the Apostle to children bereft of their fathers. In the world of that day, much more than now, a widow could exist only under heavy handicaps; and Saint Paul reminds Christian children in such families that they must *"learn first to show piety at home,"* love their widowed mothers, support them, and in general follow Christ's teachings. No one who understands the emphasis which both the Old and the New Testament lay on the blessedness of keeping Christ in our every-day domestic life will take it amiss when we say that today the plea, *"Learn first to show piety at home!"* may be regarded as addressing itself to all children and to all parents, earnestly pleading that in their family life Jesus "reign supreme and reign alone."

Many modern experts on the home, of course, often have no thought whatever of Christ. They are interested in architecture, but they do not realize that one cannot successfully build the permanently happy home without Jesus. Specialists write pretty books about furnishings and interior decorations, but they push aside the soul beauty that Jesus alone can give. Family financiers speak knowingly of expenditures, budgets, and economies, but with how

little attention they sometimes regard the price Jesus paid
for their soul's redemption! Domestic doctors discuss
education as an aid for the better life, and though they
may write many commendable prescriptions, we ought to
realize that not public instruction in matters of sex but
home-training in the spirit of Christ should be our watchword. American houses need roof and wall insulation
against zero weather but more than that Christ's heart- and
soul-protection against the blasts of many destructive
theories. Before Federal housing aid, millions in our
country should have Heaven's family aid.

As long as sin rules unchecked in any home, the forces
of evil that many of you know only too well seek to
banish peace by promoting selfishness, lust, hatred, and
a dozen other vices. Without Christ people often seem to
live in a certain kind of harmony; yet be sure of this:
if the Savior is not accepted and acknowledged in our
earthly homes, we shall never be acknowledged and
accepted in the heavenly mansions.

With the blessings Jesus offers: the complete forgiveness of purple vice and scarlet sin; the free approach to
this mercy by grace through faith; the new heart and the
right spirit by which temptation's lure may be restrained
and fleshly lusts rejected; His constant companionship for
guidance, strength, hope; His invitation, *"Come unto Me"*;
His assurance, *"Thy sins are forgiven thee"*; His pledge
of heaven, *"Because I live, ye shall live also"*; with all
these promises, the love of Christ should be eagerly accepted
by every soul throughout the world as the most magnificent
mercy that even the power and love of Heaven combined
could grant sinful man. With all the additional blessings
the Savior provides for our home relations: love instead of
black hatred; happiness despite poverty; joy even in sorrow, the greatest wonder of our age is this, that every hovel

and palace, kraal and igloo, every basement tenement and pent-house apartment, is not marked by the cross of Jesus Christ! Instead, as the Scriptures testify, *"men loved darkness rather than light."* I hope that you Christ-denying preachers and liberal church officials who may be listening in have finally convinced yourselves in the light of the present debacle that you must silence the twiddle and twaddle about the inborn goodness of man. If you insist on burdening your souls by denying the verdict of God's Word that *"all our righteousnesses are as filthy rags,"* then look at American homes where, with Jesus, we approach heaven as closely as we can on earth, but where without Christ men and women may come nearer to hell, I think, than any other place in this life!

We hear much of "revival" today, and prayers are uttered from coast to coast that the Spirit would mightily restore faith in Christ to the lukewarm and indifferent; to smug, contented churches where, while the souls of men are dying, the chief concern often seems to be: "What will we have now? A turkey or a sauerkraut supper? a Christmas bazaar or a New Year's card party?" What America needs is repentance, a deep, personal, unreserved sorrow over sin and a clear knowledge of what unforgiven sin means in its misery here on earth and its endless suffering hereafter. And when the text reminds us to show godliness in the home, we realize that our repentance can well begin with the sins violating our family happiness.

Young people, for example, are systematically urged to set aside the divine code of purity and to live after their own lusts. God's command for youth, *"Keep thyself pure!"* and the Church's appeal that before marriage young women remain virgins and young men unsullied is laughed to scorn. Premarriage chastity is completely set aside by a growing number of young people who pride themselves that they are living full, satisfied lives, when in reality they are actually destroying their own prospects of a happy marriage, weighting their souls with sins so treacherous that the last chapter of the Bible, summarizing a hundred similar warnings, excludes from Paradise all those who continually serve the flesh.

Young people usually follow the example of their elders; and in the adult world wedding vows are often wilfully broken by the secret affairs of unfaithful husbands and wives who, imagining that they enjoy the zest of life, instead are forging fetters of death for the soul. The curse of broken marriage pledges is not only this, that it cuts off the possibility of a family's full joy, often breaks two homes, inflicts misery on the innocent, ruins reputations, frequently spreads social disease, arouses the conscience, so that many hardly know one peaceful moment, waking or sleeping; but also, a thousand times worse, the terrifying truth — mark this, you who sneer at purity! — that there is no room in heaven for impenitent adulterers.

Other family sins call for wide, yet personal repentance, when we hear the Apostle's appeal, *"Show piety at home."* Not once but three times in the Bible's first nine chapters Almighty God lays down the divine command for all generations, *"Be fruitful and multiply!"* Yet just as though there never were a Bible, as though God never existed, unnumbered husbands and wives — and, we say it with shame, many even in Christian circles — by actions that speak infinitely louder than any words say, "We will not be fruitful and multiply!" While God's Word joyfully declares, *"Children are an heritage of the Lord,"* too many people believe that babies are a nuisance restricting ambitions and personal pleasure. So tightly does the practice of keeping the family childless clutch America today that financial journals write long articles on the astonishing profits recorded by birth-control industries, which every year help prevent hundreds of thousands of children from coming into existence. Now, not the serious physical consequences that may come from this protracted practice; not the moral collapse which follows, showing young people how the consequences of personal impurity can be avoided; not the loss which our nation sustains through families wilfully kept childless, form the most serious charge against the selfish rejection of parenthood. Sins like those of Onan still arouse the displeasure of the holy God!

Men and women nowhere sink to lower levels than in their own Christless homes. You will agree with me if you have ever seen drunken fathers or, worse, drunken mothers stagger home in an alcoholic rage. Their screaming and cursing are too terrible to describe, you will say; but the filth of drunkenness, the bruised and beaten wives, the whimpering children, the pay envelope squandered in the tavern, the loss of work, good name, and usefulness in life — even all this is only a passing annoyance in comparison with the warning of the Almighty, *"They which do such things shall not inherit the kingdom of God."*

And what shall I say of children who, far from showing *"piety at home"* by loving and obeying their parents in the Lord, have time and money for every one except the father and the mother who gave them life and supported them during their childhood years? One of the most shocking warnings in the entire Scriptures is the Biblical picture which shows us a son who despised to obey his parents, as a corpse, perhaps an executed criminal, lying unburied as the ravens eat his dead body and the eagles of the air pluck out his dead eyes. Yet that horrifying end is nothing compared with the punishment of his soul!

I speak rather plainly to you; for would you want me to use vague, uncertain language when the welfare of your home and the eternal blessedness of your soul are at stake? If we are outspoken in condemning sins against the family, we can be even more definite in showing the way to hope and happiness for this group. Where, then, you ask, can we find the power to tear out the weeds of wickedness that sometimes flourish particularly in the garden called the Christian home? Are those right who say that we must build the family with new domestic laws? Is it true that particularly the divorce statutes of the nation should be purged of their opposition to God's marriage code? But just as little as men could ever build a barricade to keep the storm-swept ocean off the length of our Pacific and Atlantic coasts, so impossible it is to stop the riptides of human passions by a protective wall of heavy law books.

Are those doctors of home troubles right whose diagnosis of our family sins reveals that we must have more enlightenment? Even worldly wisdom can help to a certain extent; but when education assumes an antichristian bias, when it deliberately degenerates into a tirade against God and His Word, it becomes an invisible T. N. T. that can blast the home's moral and spiritual walls into irreparable ruins. So much of American culture is veering toward practical atheism that thoughtful leaders in Protestant churches are aroused. Many have come to the deliberate conclusion that their groups must follow the practice long ago adopted by my Lutheran Church, the Catholic Church, and the Christian Reformed Church. This removes the child from influences indifferent or hostile to Christ and puts education under the direct control of the churches themselves. Our entire American system for higher education demands a fundamental reshaping to the end that the most essential part of American college and university life must become not head-training but heart-training, not only brain-building but character-building.

Once more, are those right who say that the hope of the American home lies in the overthrow of the family, the program advocated by radical Socialism and atheistic Communism? We hardly need answer this question after the recent tragedies and the horror that has sickened the minds of millions throughout the world, the diabolical campaign to crush Finland and destroy its Lutheranism. It was dastardly enough when the Red bombing planes rained destruction on Finnish homes, set fire to villages, raped and killed the women; but even more repulsive is the whole communistic program for the home, that would make the wife common property, the children wards of the state — a proposal born of hell itself, as it helps to produce unparalleled numbers of unmarried mothers, a neglected childhood, a riot of divorce, and a devastation by disease unequaled in modern history. As throughout the United States the organized movement dedicated to extend this vileness to our own shores grows, we must not only oppose the encroachment of this Red terror but also with redoubled prayer invoke God's power and with increased effort seek to counteract the new support this Red scourge will receive from that doubly tragic war now fought in Europe.

Because all else fails, the cry of this hour must be: Christ first for the family! We put our appeal into this definite plea: If you live as though Jesus had never died for you on the cross, stop in this moment, which may help to decide your destiny for a blessed eternity, and pray God for guidance, so that you may have Him as your Savior and the welcome Guest in your home. Let us send some helpful Christian literature or have one of my fellow-pastors call to show you positively what Christ will do for you and yours! By His own promise the eternal Christ will bring peace into your soul, help you start a new chapter in your home life, and strengthen you by His power to love good and hate evil. If you are Christ's, let me ask that at this beginning of another church-year, when our hearts are directed toward receiving the Savior, you make pointed resolutions that Christ will be the First in your families. Young folks often think the counsel of the Church and of their parents old-fashioned and unsympathetic with youth. Believe me when I tell you that youth has no greater friend than Christ, who Himself knew the problems of young manhood and *"was tempted like as we are."* Plan your future home with Him! Avoid every thought of marriage with an unbeliever, for only in exceptional cases can a home divided, for Christ and against Him, have any hope of real happiness! Avoid those mixed marriages that would unite Protestants and Catholics. We have seen too much of the sorrow they produce to keep silent and refrain from warning you! Write this down as your determination, "My partner in life must be of the same true faith; we must worship the same Christ!" Plan to build your own home on the Bible, and it will be built, as the Savior Himself promised, on the immovable Rock.

Parents who know that this is the truth, keep your home a sanctuary of the Almighty! Make the family altar the symbol of the Savior's presence! Raise your voices in prayer and hymns! *"Let the Word of Christ dwell in you richly!"* Keep all suggestive pictures from your walls, lustful volumes from your bookshelves, vile magazines from your reading-tables, programs endorsing divorce and triangle relationships off your radios! Make Christ the unseen Guest at every meal! Too many in America believe the bounties we enjoy daily as the rest of the world gazes in astonishment are automatic and can never be taken from us; but a nation even as large and wealthy as ours can be gripped by famine, and we ought to raise our hearts to God every time we are privileged to enjoy our meals.

Before Michael Faraday, electrical genius, began his dinner, he prayed with such force that another scientist who visited him recalled, "I am almost ashamed to call his prayer a 'saying of grace.' In the language of Scripture it could be described as the petition of a son into whose heart God had sent the Spirit of His Son and who with absolute trust asks a blessing from his Father." How tragic by contrast is the fact that many in our country begin their meals as the animals do, without a word or thought of gratitude to Him from whom all blessings flow!

II

CHRIST FIRST FOR THE BLESSING OF THE HOME

When Jesus cleanses the home, He also blesses it with the power to meet the requirements of the text, *"Learn first to show piety at home."* Have you ever realized how Jesus brought comfort, strength, and help to the families that received Him, how His mercy in those ancient days carries a meaningful lesson for modern homes? Are you handicapped by want? Are you one of the Ohio relief families that tomorrow will receive apples and cornmeal as the weekly ration? The Savior whose first miracle was performed in a humble dwelling in far-off Cana as He changed water into wine for a Galilean wedding couple can direct the power of His omnipotence to *"supply all your need."* Instead of turning from this Savior, let Jesus prove His love in your home! Resolve: "Christ shall be First in this family! Show your faith, and He will show you His power! Trust Him completely, and His mercy will provide for you!

Are you afraid you have closed the door on Christ because of your sins or the bad repute you or your children have brought on the family? In this very moment He stands at the entrance to your heart and home, knocking to gain welcome entrance and promising, "*If any man hear My voice and open the door, I will come in to him and will sup with him.*" In the days of His flesh His self-righteous and scornful enemies objected, "*This man receiveth sinners and eateth with them*"; in Jericho He entered the house of the notorious publican with the greeting, "*This day is salvation come unto this house.*" Believe with all your heart that the same Savior can bring peace and pardon over your threshold!

Are you clutched by religious doubts? Do you question the power of Christ to keep His word? Because some prayers have not been answered immediately and in the way specified, do you declare that Jesus has failed? Instead of protesting, "I am through with the Church!" invite Jesus to your home, as the disciples did on the Emmaus road when they pleaded, "*Abide with us, for it is toward evening, and the day is far spent,*" and as your soul in penitent and trusting faith sings, "Abide with me, Lord Jesus," your home will be brightened by a radiant faith.

Is sickness the cross imposed on you? Many of your hearts are heavy because for long years you have not known a single day entirely free from pain. Instead of harboring dark, resentful thoughts, exalt Christ as the First in your home, and you will have the assurance that the same Savior who entered His countrymen's homes to lay His healing hands on fevered brows and to remove the pains of palsy can restore your health, if it be for the welfare of your soul, and, if not, strengthen you for greater joy!

Many young women pray that, if it be God's will, they may have a loving husband and children; yet in His wisdom God has not answered; and it may seem that the chance for this happiness dwindles each year. Rather than lapse into bitterness, protesting against what you call the unfairness of life, give Christ the first place in your heart, and as He brought joy into the family circle at Bethany with its two unmarried sisters and its unmarried brother Lazarus, so the blessed Savior can grant you overflowing happiness. He may have spared you unspeakable suffering. He may have far-reaching plans for your usefulness. If it be His will, He can still grant you the blessing of your own home.

If it seems that death has inflicted a wound that can never heal; if your eyes moisten at the sight of an empty chair; if you listen in vain for a voice forever silent and find a loneliness that can hardly be removed, don't raise your voice to accuse God! Don't charge your heavenly Father with cruelty! Ask the Lord Jesus to rule in your home, and the same ever-blessed Redeemer who proved His power by giving life back to a Galilean girl, stopping a funeral procession to restore a deceased son to his widowed mother, approaching a tomb to speak words of resurrection to the moldering remains of His friend — that glorious Christ, who Himself rose from the dead, will banish brooding darkness from your family circle by His promise, *"Because I live, ye shall live also."*

Hear the Apostle's appeal once more: *"Learn first to show piety at home."* Mothers of America, if your club duties, your social obligations, employment and business, even your church-work, interfere with the proper care of your children and prevent the necessary supervision of your home, resign from your literary and musical clubs; give up your office job; reduce the time you are spending for church suppers, ladies' aid entertainments, and stay with your children, the precious souls whom God has given you for molding! Bring them to Christ and by the Spirit's help keep them with that Savior! Live for your husband and your family!

Fathers of America, whom God has appointed the

priests and guardians of the home, whom He wants to be His priests, proclaiming the love of Jesus Christ to your own beloved ones, what are you profited if you gain business success, but, without Christ, lose your own soul and see your own children similarly lost? What advantage will there be for them in eternity if you leave your sons and daughters real estate, stocks and bonds, bank accounts, but do not give them the inheritance of Christian faith? If you are too busy for Christ and His Church, too busy for prayer and the Bible, may God Almighty bring you to your knees (if necessary, by sickness, loss, reverses, collapse of hopes), so that you will realize how terrifying it is to live without Jesus, to deprive your own children of His love! Thousands of shrewd business men are sacrificing their greatest joy and blessing by keeping Christ from their family life. If you have no time for Jesus, *make* time for Him! If your bowling club, your service club, your political club, and, again, even your church club keep you away from your home and restrict your spiritual direction of your family, drop some of these activities! Remember, you must first *"learn to show piety at home."*

Children of America, help to keep Christ first in your family! Obey your parents gladly and willingly! Learn about Jesus! Recall how He provided for His mother during His last hours on the cross! Pray to Him morning and evening! Ask your parents to have family prayers! If you want to attend Sunday-school, send me a postal card, so that I can help you hear more of the blessed Jesus!

Let all of us, young and old, learned and simple, white and black, yellow and red, wherever we are and whatever our homes may be, resolve, our faces directed toward Christ's coming, that our Savior shall be First in our family, the Guest of our hearts and homes, until we are with Him in the unbroken eternity of His heavenly homeland! God grant it for His sake! Amen.

GOD, SEND OUT THY LIGHT
AND THY TRUTH!

"O send out Thy light and Thy truth; let them lead me; let them bring me unto Thy holy hill." — Psalm 43:3.

Strengthening Spirit of God:

Enter our homes with Thy cleansing power, so that during these Advent days we may give our hearts and lives to the blessed Savior! Once, in the fulness of time, He came into this world to save us. Today He comes to sustain His own through His sacred Word and ordinances. Tomorrow, in the appointed time, He will return to judge the quick and the dead. Help us receive Him as our royal Redeemer, our King of full power, mercy, and glory! To this end make us love Thy holy Word, read it, believe it, spread it, — all for the salvation of our blood-bought souls and the eternal deliverance of many who walk in darkness and error, without Christ, the Light and the Truth! Bless many hearts today by His unfailing promise! We ask it in the Savior's glorious name. Amen.

LAST week a leading Saint Louis newspaper featured a three-column full-length advertisement of fifteen books that ridicule the Bible, blaspheme Christ, and sneer at everything we Christians hold sacred. Now, we do not question a publisher's right to accept advertisements from freethinkers and atheists. If he wants to make money by promoting attacks on the Bible, we must tolerate this as part of the price we pay for the freedom of the press. Nor are we chiefly concerned with the fact that this anti-Bible, anti-Church, anti-God announcement is misleading, since it describes the books as "huge volumes," although some are only pamphlets, and hails these "huge volumes" as "a new approach," when in truth much is only the reprint of old material, some dating back to the eighteenth century. Chiefly, however, do we charge that newspapers which pride themselves on their high ethics have no right before God or man to feature printed material that wallows in sexual perversions. One of these fifteen books through which the Christian religion is to be destroyed comes from the pen of Voltaire, an utterly unprincipled libertine. A filthy product, conceived by a degenerate mind, its story deals with a social disease so vile that the Federal Radio Commission does not want its name mentioned in a broadcast.

That advertisement brought the publishers, if paid at regular rates, about $390. Think of it, for $390, not in Russia, but in the United States, a newspaper urges its readers to buy a book that is obscene from cover to cover. For $390 a newspaper calls the readers' attention to a man whose writings on sex no Christian parents would want their children to see. For $390 a newspaper is willing to assist in supplying the godless masses of the United States with ammunition for destroying Christ's Church!

Before these announcements spread throughout the land, will you, the friends of decency, not write for a copy of this broadcast message and present it to the editor of your newspaper? We hope it will not be necessary again to remind American publishers that they display misrepresentation and immorality only at the risk of alienating the support of Christian readers. But if certain journals persist in arraying themselves against uprightness, you know what to do.

Whatever the press does, the battle against the Bible will continue; for never before in American history have men of opposite extremes been as completely united in their hatred of God's Word. The Communist, who draws filthy cartoons of Scriptural characters, and the capitalist, whose millions sometimes support pulpit apostasy, the degenerate, who curses every New Testament passage, and the college president who tries to argue down Old Testament miracles and morality, atheists with their flamboyant advertisements calling for the destruction of Holy Writ, and high-society churchmen, often well-paid for their suave undermining of Biblical authority, — all these, though they oppose each other in many ways, work shoulder to shoulder in tearing the comfort of Christ and His Word from a groaning world!

If they are banded together to destroy Holy Writ, why should we who love the Lord Jesus and accept His Word not show more unity in teaching and spreading His promises? I know, of course, that God Almighty often seems to work most powerfully when His Church is small and oppressed. Sometimes a single soul with Christ can defeat formidable organizations without Christ; but those of us who find in God's Word the inerrant truth and who acclaim His Son our only Savior should — and this is our constant plea — seriously study the differences that separate us and ask the Father for a closer approach, not in the interest of size or numbers, but for true, complete spiritual agreement on every revealed doctrine — and for the wider spread of Christ's Gospel.

Today, then, as Christians throughout the land commemorate Bible Sunday, we pray God that His Book may have free and glorious course into many hearts. Contemplating the darkness of our age and its lies, we ask,

GOD, SEND OUT THY LIGHT AND THY TRUTH!

repeating David's ancient prayer (Psalm 43:3), *"O send out Thy light and Thy truth; let them lead me; let them bring me unto Thy holy hill."*

I

THE BIBLE IS GOD'S LIGHT AND TRUTH

David voiced this appeal during one of his darkest hours, probably when trouble, originating in his own family and resulting in Absolom's rebellion, drove him from the throne. There in the wilderness, so we may well reconstruct the background of this psalm, David, burdened by sorrow, disgrace, and loneliness, asks God, *"O send out Thy light and Thy truth!"*

Many in this audience grope in similar gloom. They, too, have family trouble. After the message last week almost 9,000 friends wrote, and many letters gave us an insight into modern family life that few men can have, a survey of misery, suffering, unbelief, unfaithfulness in the home, the one place where above all peace and joy should reign. Your daughters have disgraced themselves. Your parents are too proud to be concerned about their souls' salvation. You have $7.50 a month and no other help with which to provide for the family. You have deformed, subnormal children. Death has crossed your threshold. Now letters begin coming from Canadian mothers, who write that an only son was killed in active duty somewhere overseas. Outside the home these personal problems multiply. You are discouraged, lonely, misunderstood, opposed. Your health is impaired. Constant worry makes you afraid of life or, a hundred times worse, afraid of God, the conscience, and the hereafter. Some of you young folks have gone too far and, terrified, you realize that the temptations which seemed delightful have destroyed your peace and marred a happy trust in God. Some of you older folks who sowed to the flesh are seeing the Bible warning fulfilled; of the flesh you are reaping corruption.

This pall of suffering that hangs heavily over many lives is increased by the horror of war, which will end — who knows where? — perhaps not until the regiments of rebellion against God seriously threaten our own country with the destruction of our churches, family life, and government. Yet, thank God, in the darkest blackout that peace and progress may ever endure, as in the longest night of your sins and sorrows, one light never fails. It is our Bible, acclaimed by the psalmist as *"a lamp unto my feet and a light unto my path."* When men have given Scripture more than lip-service, they have found that it led them through the midnight of their anguish to the dawn of a radiant day. Augustine wasted his earlier years in the service of sin; yet when a voice called, "Take! Read!" and he took his Bible to read its warning and comfort, he saw the light. Luther was tormented by a desperate search for the forgiveness of his transgressions; but when he turned from all the failing light of human reason to the Book and in the Epistle to the Romans read, *"Therefore we conclude that a man is justified by faith, without the deeds of the Law,"* he saw God's light streaming from the cross of Christ. David Livingstone, in the jungle of sobbing Africa, was surrounded by disheartening opposition, yet he could find in his Bible heavenly light, which guided him through constant perils and later led him to say, "All that I am I owe to Jesus Christ, revealed to me in His divine book."

You, too, can have that light if only you will take the Scriptures and, as you pray David's prayer, *"O send out Thy light,"* believe that within the covers of this Volume you have heavenly illumination for any gloom. What more helpful cry can the Church raise in these darkened days than the plea: Back to the Bible, the light of God! Back to the Christ of the Bible, the light of the world! Back to the faith of the Bible, the light for our lives!? A hundred other appeals direct themselves to you as men's hopes are contradicted by their fears; but the remedy which Christ Himself prescribes for every overcast hour is, *"Search the Scriptures!"* Read the Word reverently, faithfully! Study its personal promises! Read its blessings to your family! Support its spread throughout the world!

The more you read this Word of light and life, the more penetratingly you will see God in His might, Christ in His mercy, and the Spirit in His strengthening grace. Sir Walter Scott wrote: "The most learned, acute, and intelligent student cannot in the longest lifetime obtain an entire knowledge of this one Volume. . . . New light continually comes from this one source of heavenly knowledge." George Muller, who established and supported his orphanage at Bristol, England, entirely by prayer to give the world an exhibition of God's power, stated toward the end of his life: "I have read the Bible through more than a hundred times with great delight. I have for many years read through the whole of the Old and New Testaments with prayer and meditation four times every year." Whenever he finished reading a chapter, he found that God had sent out His light to guide him along the best way. Because many people even within the churches go through life blindfolded as they neglect the Bible or walk with a faint flicker of light, since they hear or read only snatches of the Scriptures, we declare again, the universal direction of our age should be, Back to the Bible! Our continued plea must be, "O send out Thy light!"

Don't listen to arguments by freethinkers! Many of these scoffers actually do not know the book they attack. America's earliest notorious unbeliever was Tom Paine. Yet when he wrote the first part of his The Age of Reason, "he was," one of his biographers admits, "without a Bible, neither could he procure one." Daniel Webster tells how a French enemy of God who continually sought to discredit the Scriptures one day found in his library some stray leaves of an unknown volume, pages of the Bible, containing a part of the Old Testament, the prayer of Habakkuk. "Being a man of fine literary taste, he was captivated by the poetic beauty and hastened to the club-house to announce the discovery to his associates. . . . They were anxious to know the name of the gifted author, and to inquirers the elated infidel replied, 'A writer by the name of Habakkuk; of course, a Frenchman.'" He had assailed the Scriptures but with characteristic unfairness had never read them. No wonder Dr. Johnson insisted that no honest man could be an atheist! If these blasphemers would be fair enough to let God's Word prove its power, they might stop their efforts to becloud the light. It has frequently happened that those who approached the Word to scoff remained to adore Christ as their Savior. Lord Rochester, a proud infidel, seeking material for his battle against the Bible, read Isaiah's fifty-third chapter with its eleven statements of Christ's atonement for sins. He was converted and convinced of the Bible's inerrancy and our Lord's divinity. Giovanni Pappini, Italy's literary genius, was so embittered against Christianity that he was called an "anarchist, atheist, nihilist." In his eagerness to discredit the Scriptures, Pappini had to study both Testaments. Then the miracle of God was enacted in his life. He who had been the devil's advocate defended the Cross instead of trying to destroy it. Hear him acclaim Jesus "the Prince of Peace, . . . the Savior, the Anointed, . . . the Son of God and Son of man."

How often those who boasted that they were through with the Bible and cursed its God have found themselves in despair! Whenever Voltaire thought that he was dying, he sent for a priest; and those who testified of his death say that "he expired under the torments of the Furies." When earnest Quakers told Tom Paine on his death-bed that they had thrown his book into the fire, he replied: "I wish all had done as you. For if the devil has ever had any agency in any work, he has had it in writing my *Age of Reason*." In his last hours he was heard to say, "O Lord Jesus, have mercy upon me!" Ethan Allen, the Revolutionary hero, was a notorious unbeliever; his wife, however, was a God-fearing woman. When their daughter took mortally sick, she summoned her father and said: "I am about to die. Shall I believe the principles which you have taught me, or shall I believe what Mother has taught me?" When his child hovered on the edge of eternity, Ethan Allen confessed the whole bankruptcy of his unbelief, declaring, "Believe what your mother has taught you!"

Think also of the darkness with which the rejection of Christ and the Bible has enshrouded some of the blackest chapters in history! God's enemies took the Bible out of North Africa in the seventh century, and that country's glory disappeared. They banished the Holy Scriptures from France during the French Revolution, and the Paris gutters flowed with blood. They exiled Christ from Russia, and one sixth of the earth's surface under Soviet control is now afflicted with moral leprosy. The same sworn opposition to God's Word is extending its effort in this country through the most lavishly financed anti-Bible program the United States has ever seen. On the one hand we have the Communists; they claim 100,000 paid members in our land now, a group many times larger than the number which overthrew Russia, dedicated to destroy our Bible and our churches. Supported by cultural leaders who have made their classrooms hotbeds for radical hatred of Christ, Communists thrive because of unbelief in high church positions throughout the land. When a leading clergyman writes a really huge volume as a guide for the understanding of the Scriptures and calls portions of the Bible "old forms of imagination," "mythology," "folk-lore," "less humane and civilized than the Code of Ham-murabi," a pastor using the same expressions infidels like to spread; when he asserts that the Scriptures present exaggeration, survivals of pagan worship, contradictions, superstitions, primitive hatreds, magical and outworn ideas, we leave it to you who love the Lord Jesus to decide whether the time is not here for a sharp division in the churches of this country along lines which separate those who ac-cept the Bible as God's true light from those, however powerful their influence, who set themselves the task of extinguishing God's Light for our darkened age.

Again, what help and hope can all these foes of the faith suggest with their cleverness and ingenuity? What has any atheist offered for the permanent spiritual uplift of his suffering fellow-men? The Church can summon millions who will gladly testify that through Christ faith in Bible promises has brought them to joy and light; but where are the men who honestly maintain that peace, strength, happiness of soul and mind are theirs through the denial of God and the rejection of His Bible?

"O send out Thy light!" we plead with God as we think of many hearts and homes now in contact with us through the radio, many churches in which free thought instead of Christ's thought keeps the worshiper in the rest-less night of dark sins and black sorrows. *"O send out Thy light!"* we pray when we think how carelessly American Christianity has often dealt with the Bible and know that many of you in our stream-line age have time for every-thing except God's Word in your private lives and your family devotion. *"O send out Thy light!"* we cry as we survey the growing opposition to the Bible in a country where Scripture-loving men and women have given the nation its greatest moral strength.

Continuing in David's prayer, *"O send out Thy light*

AND THY TRUTH!" we realize that our Scriptures are the light because they are the truth. On the night of His betrayal Jesus prayed to His Father for His disciples, *"Sanctify them through Thy truth; Thy Word is truth!";* and Christ's verdict should stop all argument and convince us that our Bible from cover to cover is divinely inspired and therefore the pure, errorless revelation of God Himself. Yet men persist in branding the Scriptures untrue. School-teachers repeat catch phrases and laugh at "the mistakes of Moses." But that does not settle the issue. How about the fact that the most marvelous minds of the Christian ages — men to whose thought, discoveries, and scientific achievements we are indebted almost every moment we live — have been simple, trusting, reverent children of God, who loved the Bible and who, could they be assembled with us here, would endorse the verdict of that prince of scientists, Sir Isaac Newton, "No sciences are better attested than the religion of the Bible"? How about the claims of prophecy and fulfilment, that supernatural ability by which events are foretold with exactness centuries before they occurred? If only some of you who are prejudiced against the Scriptures by some fatal hatred would take time to study God's Word in the light of history, this alone ought to convince you that the Bible is what no other book can ever be, the true revelation of our Lord. Can you account for the wonderful power the Word has exercised? A New Zealand unbeliever once scoffed at the Bible before a Maori chief. The native leader pointed to a huge stone and said: "My forefathers and I were bloodthirsty cannibals. We slaughtered our human victims on that stone and then roasted and devoured them. Now all that has passed away. We are Christians. What raised us to what we are from what we were? The Bible at which you sneer." The bishop of Moosonee declared that in a gathering of Indians on the Hudson Bay shore every one of the natives present had murdered his own mother when she had become too old to work. That brutality stopped. Why? Those Indians have the Scripture and, as their missionaries assure us, study it earnestly. No error, no superstitions, could ever accomplish these and other unnumbered, stupendous changes in entire nations and individual lives. So when modern unbelievers in the growing ranks of freethinkers, in the antichristian press, in the unmistakably increasing menace of Communism, in faith-breaking theological seminaries, in modern Christ-denying pulpits, assert that the Bible is full of contradictions, we say, Let them produce these errors!

Every year since we have started this crusade for Christ, we have challenged all skeptics in this audience — and, thank God, many infidels have tuned in! — to produce a single instance in which the Bible can be proved historically or scientifically incorrect. The only answers which we have received in six years are those moth-eaten, threadbare arguments about Cain's wife, the number of quail in the desert, and similar objections, every one answered scores of times. When cynics list the charges by which they would discredit God's Word, remember that within the last century a hundred different anti-Biblical claims have been disproved by the astonishing results of excavations in Babylonia and Assyria, Egypt and Palestine. When they ask us to substitute reason for revelation, while paying unstinted tribute to true scientists, we recall the mistakes, contradictions, absurdities, right-about faces, disavowals of previous opinion that constantly mark the history of human thought.

Insistently we must pray, "*O send out Thy . . . truth!*" Ours is a lying age, with malice and vile propaganda combined to send our sons to Europe's battle-fields; a dishonest age with deceit in the home, fraud in business, deception in some courts, duplicity in politics, and even untruth in religion, where the souls of men are involved. God bless the Bible-printing and -distributing societies that are counteracting this falsehood by sending out God's truth, circulating the Scriptures in more copies and in more languages than ever before! God bless the efforts of you pastors and teachers of the truth who, without public acclaim and with small salaries, teach the Word in its purity! God bless the homes in which the parents do what the Apostle specifically requires of fathers and mothers, bring up their children *"in the nurture and admonition of the Lord"!*

II

GOD'S LIGHT AND TRUTH CAN BRING US TO HIS HOLY HILL

David had a special reason for asking God's light and truth. He says, *"Let them lead me; let them bring me unto Thy holy hill."* Exiled in the wilderness, he longed for Mount Zion, that height in Jerusalem where he had erected the Tabernacle and where God came to bless and guide him. In the midst of his suffering he looks not for vengeance nor victory but for the sacred privilege of worshiping his God at that holy place.

Today we repeat David's prayer, but we look to another holy hill. No earthly glory was attached to this elevation. It was so despised and avoided that we do not know with certainty just where near Jerusalem it was. No tabernacle crowned its height; instead, a cross of shame and agony. No hymns were sung on its slopes as pilgrims voiced their doxologies when they approached Zion; instead, the cry of a dying Sufferer pierced the rumbling thunder. No presence of God marked that hill as the Shekinah which blessed Zion; far from being present to help, God was distant from Christ, and His shriek of wounded trust demanded, *"My God, My God, why hast Thou forsaken Me?"* No sacrificial lamb was slaughtered on that summit as atoning offerings were made at David's hill; but, thank God, there on the cross, the one altar for all ages, all races, all sinners, there on Mount Calvary, earth's holiest spot, we behold *"the Lamb of God which taketh away the sin of the world," "wounded for our transgressions," "bruised for our iniquities,"* accursed so that we might be blessed, dying that we might live.

It is to this holy site that the light and truth of the Bible must lead us. We do not now ask you who may not know the Bible to appreciate its language and its forceful presentation. Nor are we primarily interested in its history, the precepts of its proverbs, the practical wisdom of its teachings. Today we push all that aside with the prayer that somehow, by His Spirit, God may lead you to Golgotha. For, my fellow-redeemed, you must stand beneath that cross if on the day of Christ's second advent you are to stand before His throne. If you come to that holy hill — and Jesus now calls you, the indifferent, the unfaithful, the disquieted, the tormented, the sin-stricken, the bereaved, the lonely, the desperate, the proud, the scoffing — to Calvary, you will be assured that, because Christ died for you, you are saved, and the only thing which can keep you from eternity's blessing is your own wilful rejection of the blood shed to cleanse you from your sins.

At the cross you who were well satisfied with yourselves until something broke your happiness and who now, without Christ, are destitute of joy and strength, can learn that this Bible *"is able to build you up."* It can take your weak faith, weighted down with doubts, questions, objections, and give you (the longer you study your Bible and hear its promises, the more clearly will you understand this) light and truth for your soul and body. That precious Book with its thousands of promises, a dozen for every dark day, a score for every problem, a hundred for every besetting sin, can transform your heart with its promise of forgiveness, revive your drooping spirit, change despair into devotion. It gives you the power to leap over everything which keeps you from Christ, your Savior, the strength to rise refreshed after each new blow with which an unsympathetic world may strike you down to the dust.

I am not theorizing, and all this is more than vague, wishful thinking. It is a truth you can experience in your own lives. Unchurched friends throughout the land, will you not come to the holy hill with us? We beseech you as though Christ Himself were appealing to you: Will you not give yourself, your family, your children, the blessing, both for earth and heaven, that this Word of grace offers you freely, without condition, simply by faith? Two weeks from tomorrow even the world pauses to observe the birthday of Christ. In all this holiday preparation that engulfs many homes, will there be time for you to read, study, and believe those 261 simple words in the Christmas-story, with their gift of salvation? If you have rebelled against God whenever you have heard the invitation of His grace, will you not in these blessed advent days give yourself as a Christmas-gift to the Savior?

This mission of the air for Christ is growing with such rapid strides, by the blessing of God, that on this earth I can hope to meet only a few of you, dear friends in Christ. But we have earnestly besought God (and I never approach this microphone without the repeated prayer that the Savior's blood may not have been shed in vain for you) that by His grace we who stand in spirit beneath the cross at Calvary, perhaps unknown to each other, will meet in the holiness of the heavenly homeland. There, when *"I shall know even as also I am known,"* with every burden removed because every sin has been forgiven, there, face to face with Jesus, we shall find that God has kept His word. We will join — O glorious blessing! — in Joshua's ancient testimony, *"Not one thing hath failed of all the good things which the Lord, your God, spake concerning you."* God grant us this faith in His Word, this triumph through the Savior's grace! Amen.

———————

"PREPARE TO MEET THY GOD!"

"Prepare to meet thy God!" — Amos 4:12

Spirit of the Coming Christ:

*T*ake possession of our hearts and minds, so that in these overbusy days of Christmas preparation we may worthily adorn our souls to receive in the Christ-child our God, our Savior, our King! Forgive us, for Jesus' sake, the indifference our lives often betray, when we complete day after day without reverent thought for our blessed Redeemer, who once came to be born, to live, suffer, and die for our atonement! By Thy miraculous power purify and strengthen us all for greater devotion to this Savior, for more unselfish service to our fellow-men, and for deeper personal concern over our own soul's salvation! Mightily use this broadcast for calling many now without Christ to meet their God! Help us all, despite losses and crosses, to find in our faith the victory over sin, sorrow, the world, our flesh, death, and hell itself! We ask this in Jesus' blessed name. Amen.

DURING the height of Israel's prosperity and luxury a strange preacher suddenly appeared on the streets of the capital city, Samaria. He was not dressed like a prophet, nor did he act like a prophet; but he had God's courage in his heart and God's Word on his lips. A herdsman from Judah, he had received the summons of the Lord, *"Go, prophesy to My people,"* and leaving his flocks, he went. With a Spirit-born zeal for justice, decency, and the true worship of God he flung his scathing denunciations at the king, the priests, the nobility, the moneyed classes, the whole smug, sin-laden nation. As few others in all history this untrained working-man pleaded passionately for a repentant return to God; yet his invitation was rejected. The perverted nation continued its sins and cruelty; yet in a dramatic episode that herdsman champion of the Lord arose to majestic heights. See him there at the market-place, confronted by a threatening crowd, his whole body aquiver with zeal for Jehovah, his eyes flashing the fire of holy anger, his words rolling out as the thunder of God. A momentary awe seizes the mob, silencing their laughter, and you can hear the prophet's momentous words ring out to be repeated through the centuries in practically every language spoken and to be engraved on the living conscience of multiplied millions. Slowly, with deadly finality, he warns, "O Israel, *prepare to meet thy God!*"

Today we need clear voices like that of this prophet— whom many of you have recognized as Amos from Tekoa— to cry out, "America, *prepare to meet thy God!*" In principle the same sins burden our age: an alarming social gulf between the arrogant rich and the destitute poor; worldliness in religion, with priests in politics and churches in business; sins of lust and greed; and, worse, the same sullen rebellion against God Almighty. We need champions of Christ not only in the clergy, but also among those who, like Amos, come from the working-classes. The last years have revealed a radical, destructive element in the ranks of American labor, which, opposing God, refuses Him all recognition. May the Holy Spirit use these words to call some of you laborers, tradesmen, workers, of America, to Christ, for the blessings of His grace! If labor could only follow the Savior, who Himself, for a part of His life at least, was a working-man! Jesus learned His trade in a carpenter's shop at Nazareth and through His death on the cross He offered the one sacred element this hate-poisoned, strife-torn world needs sorely, the love for our fellow-men and the spirit of self-giving sacrifice!

As Amos brought Israel only the Word of God, so this critical hour calls, first of all, not for the theories of economists, the studies of scientists, the charts of statisticians, but for true prophetic voices that proclaim, "*Thus*

saith the Lord." Too many preachers declare: "Thus says
Albert Einstein; thus says George Bernard Shaw; thus
says Roger Babson; thus says Neville Chamberlain"; and
they do this with such frequency that the decisive "*Thus
saith the Lord*" remains unspoken. Consequently, above
the honeyed, sugar-coated messages of the day and the
almost endless plans devised to solve our financial, social,
industrial problems, we should hear this divine proclamation,
"PREPARE TO MEET THY GOD!"

These are the words of Amos 4:12, and may we, under the
Spirit's guidance, find in them a cry of warning and a
cry of hope through Christ!

I

A CRY OF WARNING

Nothing in all our experience is more certain than this
truth that we must meet our God. A thousand other issues
are unpredictable, but the ingenuity of man, with his marvelous scientific equipment, cannot change this fact of facts.
In years to come we may be rich or ragged, strong or
sickly, brilliant or broken, influential or insignificant; but
we must meet our God. Countless statements of leaders,
pronouncements of specialists, assurances of experts, have
proved absurd guesses and mistaken prophecies; but be
clear on this: Nothing in earth or heaven itself can ever
keep you from meeting your God!

Before we go on with the unquestionable certainty of
this fact, let us see what it means to stand before the
Almighty. The Lord of life, who created us; the God of
mercy, who sustains us; the God of wisdom, who protects us; the God of perfect holiness, against whom you
and I sin daily and grievously; the God from whom men
flee and for whom they grope as a last refuge; the God

whom the wicked desecrate by profanity, perjury, and blasphemy; the God whom the ungrateful forsake despite His rich and repeated blessings; the God whom sinners deride as they deny His existence and challenge His power — that God, my friends and fellow-sinners, is the Lord whom you and I must inevitably face, no matter how self-confident and self-sufficient we may seem to be.

If only I could meet all unbelievers in this audience and with the Spirit's help burn into their souls this truth that, unseen, I can give them now only from a distance of hundreds or thousands of miles! Your God is so holy, perfect, stainless, infinitely removed from all sin and wrong, that you will be summoned before the throne of His divine justice to account for every wicked thought in your heart, every hateful word on your lips, every evil work of your hands; and you will be condemned for eternity unless those sins are removed and you can approach the sinless Lord without the brand of iniquity on your soul. If you think He is not concerned about what you call "mistakes" in life, listen to this warning from His own truth, *"The soul that sinneth, it shall die."* If you try to ease your conscience by concealing secret sins, private vices, double lives, let the Word that never made a false statement shake you out of your security as it declares, *"Be sure your sin will find you out,"* and repeats, *"We must all appear before the judgment-seat of Christ that every one may receive the things done in his body, according to that he hath done, whether it be good or bad."*

Often God begins to execute judgment during this life. The reason many of you without Christ have suffered severe money losses, sacrificed your peace, had hearts filled with fear, permitted dark, desperate thoughts to prey on your mind and suspicion constantly to lurk at your side; the reason everything seems to have turned against you, the

skeptics and unbelievers who have never found God in
Jesus Christ, is this, that God has met you, whether you
know it or not, and even now you are beginning to pay
the penalty of your unbelief. You have tried to hold back
the rushing tides of God's Word, but its breakers are
hurling you to destruction. You have sought to undermine the eternal mountain of divine truth, but you have
started an avalanche which will crush your soul forever.

We know, of course, that often the godless appear to
flourish in brazen prosperity. Like the psalmist of old,
many of you keep asking why these scoffers seem equipped
for all pleasure, while the followers of Christ are told
to take up the cross, deny themselves, endure persecution.
This perplexity is fully solved in the Scriptures, which ask
us to behold the end of these boasting individuals and to
realize that, even if God's judgment may be postponed in
this life, an inevitable reckoning comes in the next.

How men shun the thought of death! The publisher of
a mighty newspaper chain in our country, lord of a baronial
estate in California, master of castles, yachts, sky-scrapers—
everything money can buy — forbids the mention of death
in his presence. On the other side of the country, in
a 110-room Long Island mansion, a baby girl is being reared
for immortality. As she grows up, she is to abstain from
meat, alcohol, tobacco, to be kept from destructive thoughts.
Instead she is to hear good music and elevating conversation and in this way cling everlastingly to life. That newspaper tycoon and that Baby Sunshine will die; for no
matter how we shrink from this thought, ignore it, postpone
it, rebel against it, the summons comes to each one of us,
"Set thine house in order, for thou shalt die." And what
then? Does death end all? Must we sink like beasts into
eternal decay, without any hereafter? You know better
than that. Why is it that, when a torpedoed ship lurches

into the North Sea or a mine-struck tanker becomes a flaming inferno, many victims of these harrowing disasters fall on their knees in prayer even if they have never prayed before? Why is it, when self-confident men suddenly realize their end is only a matter of hours, they try to raise their hands and voices to God? Must we not concede that today, as throughout the ages, men know that there is a future beyond the grave in which they must face the holy God? Even if some deluded individuals refuse to recognize this truth, here is the verdict of the unbreakable Word: *"It is appointed unto man once to die, but after this the Judgment."*

Don't be misled by the unholy scoffers our age has produced in large numbers! Many of you recall how an American novelist, a Nobel prize winner, a man much of whose energies have been concentrated on attacking the Church and ridiculing our faith, stood before a Kansas City audience, damned the whole Christian religion, and gave God five minutes to strike him dead. When the Almighty, for reasons He knows best, refused, the free-thinker triumphantly claimed that the whole Bible was false. Yet on other occasions the wrath of God's vengeance has struck swiftly. Only a few years ago George Whale, chairman of the Rationalist Press Association, was the chief speaker at a London banquet of unbelievers. For a long time that night he ridiculed the Holy Spirit, threw his jabs of sarcasm at Christ, mocked the whole New Testament, while two hundred like-minded guests cheered until the room reechoed with their applause. When he finished his blasphemy, another atheist at the head table arose, proposing a toast to the chairman for his ruthless assault on the Bible. Cheers rang out; glasses were lifted high; but suddenly the orchestra stopped, and before the toast could be given, George Whale, challenger of the

Almighty, denier of Christ, had slumped forward, his face an ashy gray. In less than five minutes after he had concluded his assault on God, he was a corpse.

Talk to the natives around Casco Bay in Maine, and they will tell you the story of atheist Herb Beals. He lived on Pole Island in the bay, and with satanic delight he used to stand in his doorway with a mangy dog and scream his defiance of the Almighty. One day, while a religious gathering met on the opposite mainland, a heavy electrical storm broke. Witnesses recount how this enemy of God tried to shout his blasphemy across the water and above the thunder; how, while they looked on, a jagged streak of fire flattened him to the ground. Only a few years ago lightning, which, it is said, does not strike twice in the same place, again sent its jagged arm to demolish even the hut of Herb Beals, denier of Christ.

Go up to Newburgh, New York, and in well-authenticated records you can read the startling end of an atheist in that Hudson River city. One Sunday night, after the Lord's Supper had been celebrated in a local church, a clique of scoffers publicly gave mock communion to a dog, "using the words of our blessed Redeemer when He instituted the Holy Supper." On the following Sunday evening, as Dr. James Carnahan, president of the College of New Jersey, recounts, the leader in this sacrilege was found "lying on the floor of his room, convulsed with awful spasms." He "expired without being able to utter a word." *"Be not deceived; God is not mocked."*

Now, you, despite your quiet and sheltered lives may unexpectedly be called to meet your God and stand before His judgment. Every day on the average one hundred people in the United States leave their homes in the best of health, but they never return. Within a few hours they meet sudden death on the highway or in some other accident. A distracted widow in Baltimore writes us: "I married at the age of nineteen. My husband and I . . . followed the easy-going, care-free sinner's life. Money rolled in, and our every wish was fulfilled. Let me admit with shame that in our first year of married life we never once attended church, said a prayer, or thought of our spiritual needs. In fact, we boasted that souls were something that cost us a dollar and a quarter at the shoe-repair shop. One year passed. Just one week after our first wedding anniversary my husband left for work, hale and hearty. In fact, he had never been sick a day in his life. That night he was brought home to me dead." This woman, who has now found Christ through the radio, knows how quickly death may strike. Do you?

In the daily average 1,000 Americans die of heart disease. Many people rise in the morning, as a California death last week reminds us, with their usual strength; but before night falls, their hearts stop, and their souls leave them. We institute safety campaigns to reduce accidents (and God bless all these efforts to save lives!); but somehow quick death laughs at our best measures. Medical scientists and biological technicians work overtime to conquer sickness and lengthen life; but new epidemics take the place of vanquished diseases, and we have not definitely added to the life span. We ought to realize that we are constantly surrounded by death; that in the next moment we may be in eternity, face to face with God.

Don't delay in preparing to meet your Maker! Postponement has sent many souls to hell. Some years ago, when the steamship *Central America* foundered, the captain of a rescue ship came close by the doomed vessel. Because night was descending and the sea rolling high, he signaled the captain of the *Central America*, "Had you not better send your passengers on board directly?" But the captain of the derelict answered, "Stand by until tomorrow." The rescue ship objected, "We will try to stand by, but you had better send your passengers on board now." The advice was unheeded; and within a half hour the ship, trembling from bow to stern, plunged into the ocean, carrying the crew and most of its passengers to death. That destructive "Tomorrow, not now," that accursed "A little later, not just yet," can do more than drown your body; it can send your soul to hell. Why do so many of you persistently toy with eternity, delay in preparing to meet your God? You show remarkable care in guarding everything else you own. You have insurance for your life, your home, your business, all your possessions; you see your dentist twice a year, have your physician check your health; but your soul, to which Jesus attached such value that He said, *"What is a man profited if he shall gain the whole world and lose his own soul?"* that priceless eternal gift of God remains neglected. *"Now,"* the eternal Word appeals, *"is the accepted time."* Now, in this moment, get right with your God!

Our generation has another reason to prepare for meeting its Maker. More than any previous age, we today are close to the time when Jesus Himself will return in His second coming to judge the quick and the dead. If in the early Church the faithful could say, *"The Lord is nigh,"* we are at least nineteen centuries closer to His return. Examine the present-day signs of the end, fulfilled, we claim, more vividly and literally in this generation than in any other age. Sign Number One: Before the end, Jesus says, there will be *"wars and rumors of wars."* Forty million Chinese have been driven from their homes. Five to ten million are dead from disease and privation. Hundreds of their cities and towns lie in ashes, and lest we forget in smug self-righteousness, our country has supplied much of the means for this destruction. Not savage peoples, but the most advanced nations of Europe, have twice opposed each other in war in two and a half decades, so that serious minds are forced to wonder whether our modern culture is worth saving.

Sign Number Two: Jesus predicts that in the last days *"false Christs and false prophets shall rise."* Has our country ever before witnessed so many and such brazen counterfeits of the Savior's holy creed? A cult leader permits himself to be worshiped as God. Entire denominations are sold down the river of doubt by men who preach a false Christ, minimizing His deity so that they may magnify His humanity.

Sign Number Three: Christians are to be afflicted. In the last twenty years more Christians have been murdered and martyred in the bloody conquest of Communism than in the first Christian centuries. The war is causing untold damage to many mission-fields. Christians in Finland are suffering indescribable hardships and sorrows.

Sign Number Four: Saint Paul writes that, before the course of the world is run, men *"will be lovers of pleasure more than lovers of God."* Three hundred thousand people in Atlanta glorify a story in which the heroine's father wins his plantation in a poker game; the scheming heroine herself, although married, is found in compromising situations with the husband of another woman. If there is anything of beauty, honor, decency, truth in that, tell me where! America's moral foundation will be "gone with the wind" if public favor continues to blow in misleading directions.

Sign Number Five: Men will be *"without natural affection, incontinent,"* the Bible predicts. When has America seen more frequent and perverted sex crimes? Was there ever an age in which children, as God's gift, and parenthood, as His blessing, were more widely despised?

When have people been more incontinent? Compare the last generation with this! Since 1870 the number of marriages has increased four times, but the number of divorces twenty times.

Sign Number Six: The enemies of Christ in the last times shall be *"ever learning and never able to come to a knowledge of the truth"* — a forceful description of the modern antichristian, anti-Biblical culture, which stands baffled before the problems of men's souls.

Sign Number Seven: The false teachers in the end days are described as *"forbidding to marry and commanding to abstain from meats,"* in other words, destroying the liberty in Christ, and in place of offering justification by faith through His free mercy, enslaving millions by man-made restrictions.

Sign Number Eight: Many, Saint Paul assures us, shall have a *"form of godliness,"* but deny its power. That is the picture of cold, formal Christianity, the modern tendency to use the cross and the name of Christ merely as an outward mark.

Sign Number Nine: *"The love of many shall wax cold."* In numerous churches the fire and flame for mission-work have been subdued. Congregations raise money by suppers and sales, by theatricals and musical comedies, sometimes even by lottery and gambling.

Sign Number Ten: Men will be *"blasphemers,"* the Word predicts. Go back even to the rationalism and free thought of the eighteenth and nineteenth centuries to convince yourselves that, as destructive as those away-from-God movements were, they are not to be compared with the present-day opposition to the Savior's Cross.

Sign Number — but I must stop. Read the first verses of 2 Timothy 3, where in plain language it is foretold that in the last and perilous days men will also be *"lovers of their own selves, covetous, boasters, proud, . . . disobedient to parents, unthankful, unholy, . . . truce-breakers, false accusers, . . . despisers of those that are good, traitors, heady, high-minded."* Ask yourselves whether Saint Paul did not foresee our times when he penned these lines. If, then, the coming of our Lord, with His day of Judgment, is at hand, what other appeal can we direct to you than this insistent *"Prepare to meet thy God"?*

II

A CRY OF HOPE THROUGH CHRIST

How — and may this be the question that clamors for answer in your heart! — how can we prepare to meet the Lord? How can we remove all damning iniquity from our souls and stand purified before the holy God? We must have more than human power to secure this peace and pardon! Twenty years ago a League of Nations was organized, in the exact words of its covenant, "to achieve international peace and security." Millions of dollars have been spent to carry out its purpose. Experienced statesmen have lent their help; but if we realize that even these vast sums and this political intelligence have not been able to keep Europe from becoming a madhouse, then we understand that for the peace of our souls, for our reconciliation with God, we need more than men, money, and brains. We must have Jesus as our Savior!

As the Advent cry resounds, *"Behold your God!"* look to Jesus, believing with all your heart that He is your God. Understand this keystone doctrine clearly: Jesus had to be God because no man, no saint, no angel, no legion of cherubim or seraphim, could offer the ransom required for our souls' redemption. He had to be God to bring the one sacrifice by which sin, death, and hell could be defeated forever. He had to be God to pay the appalling debt that humanity with all its sins had incurred throughout the aging centuries. Praise be to the eternal mercy of Heaven, Christ, our God, with a love too high and holy for our dwarfed minds, who fulfilled the Law for us, gave Himself into death on the cross as our Substitute, removed our transgressions, and, conquering death by His own resurrection, grants us eternal life!

So prepare now to meet your God in Christ, during this busy week. If only one tenth of the time, energy, and money spent in the pre-Christmas days could be devoted to the preparation for receiving Christ, who still offers peace and pardon, how the hearts of many could be changed and the fires of hatred checked! This message may be the last God Almighty will permit you to hear. Many of you have had years in which to prepare for meeting your God, and stolidly you have let this long period of grace slip away. It may be that, if what I now tell you in Christ's name does not move your heart and bring you, penitent and contrite, to Jesus, nothing in this world will ever save you. When we stand before the Throne in eternity, I do not want you to point to me and say, "I heard you on the radio, but you did not tell me of my soul's danger." To prevent that tragedy, forget everything else as we repeat to you that without Christ you can never face God, but with Christ the portals of heaven itself will swing wide amid the hallelujahs of the angels, welcoming you when your hour comes. Don't delay! Don't postpone! Come now, in the Advent season!

You of the faith, who know Christ and can testify that every word I have spoken concerning His mercy is the eternal truth, must help prepare others to meet Jesus. God give us a radiant, Christ-centered Christmas this year! What is any earthly Christmas gift you can offer in comparison with Christ's blood-sealed redemption, which you can bring to others? Resolve that, knowing the grace of the Lord Jesus, you will gladly testify to others of the Christ-child and His blessed coming. We have millions of tracts available. Thousands of our pastors will gladly help you.

How terrifying is the thought that many who call themselves Christians never help their fellow-men (sometimes not even their own relatives) come to Christ! Charles Simeon, last-century British Gospel-preacher, was forced to hear his doomed brother accuse him, "I am dying, and you never warned me of . . . the great danger . . . of neglecting the salvation of my soul." When Charles Simeon replied, "My brother, I took every reasonable opportunity of bringing religion before you and frequently alluded to it in my letters," the dying man answered: "Yes, but you never came to me, closed the door, took me by the collar of the coat, and told me that I was unconverted and that, if I died in that state, I should be lost. Now I am dying, and but for God's grace I should have been undone forever." Too many of us, I am afraid, have never helped other people meet their God. Therefore let our prayer be a plea for forgiveness, a petition for strength, an appeal for power, as we say: "O come, Lord Jesus, bring us by Thy Spirit to a deeper, truer, nobler faith, so that, having Thee, we are prepared to meet our God and help others meet their God in Thee! O Lord Jesus, our only Savior, our merciful Redeemer, our eternal Atonement, our all-sufficient Substitute, come to us! *'Yea, Lord Jesus, come quickly!'* Amen."

HAVE YOU ROOM FOR THE CHRIST-CHILD?

> *"And she . . . laid Him in a manger because there was no room for them in the inn."* — Saint Luke 2:7.

Holy Christ-child, our only Savior:

Across this broad land hearts are now raised to Thee in joyful thanks for the unfathomable mercy by which Thou wast born of a virgin for us, so that by faith we might be born again in Thee. O precious Savior, if on this day before Thy Christmas we are too preoccupied to prepare our hearts and homes for Thy love, too crowded with pleasure or worry to welcome Thee, — by the never-ending mercy of Bethlehem's miracle forgive us and send us Thy Spirit to impart the joy, the radiance, the everlasting hope of Christmas! Be with the poor and the helpless, the sick and forsaken, the afflicted and despairing! Especially do we ask Thee, O Jesus, Prince of Peace, if it be Thy will, make an end to wars, their blood and terror! Hear us and bless us, Thou Christ-child of endless compassion! Amen.

ONE of the most famous and costly paintings of recent times — a picture that produced perhaps a greater effect than any other religious canvas of its century — is Holman Hunt's "The Light of the World," depicting Christ as He seeks to enter the human soul. In an unforgettable manner the artist portrays the Savior knocking at the door of a humble home and, as His lantern indicates, ready to bring light into the darkness of human sin and suffering. When the canvas was exhibited in England, it immediately became "the subject of discussion and wide interest from one end of the island to the other," and the artist, who only a year or two before was so discouraged that he was at the point of leaving England and starting life anew in a distant colony, became a success almost overnight.

As this message speeds across the continent, with Christmas only a few hours distant, we picture to you the Christ-child as the divine Light for every dark hour, the blessed Savior eagerly seeking entrance into your heart and home. We cannot hope that, as Hunt's "The Light of the World" became the subject of nation-wide discussion, our words will be the topic of continued coast-to-coast comment in this country; but may God in His grace give thousands of American homes a pause in their holiday preparations, so that they may prepare for the Christmas glory. We cannot promise that, as Holman Hunt found international recognition through his reverent portrayal of Jesus, so, by the Christ-child's impress on your soul, you will discover that the world honors you for your loyalty to Jesus; but in His holy, precious name, we can promise — and the Savior keeps His pledge — that, when Jesus abides in your heart, you will be a spiritual success, a distinction incomparably more blessed than all human achievement.

So that the inner joy of Christmas may not be lost for you amid the holiday eating and drinking, cleaning and cooking, giving and receiving, preparing and decorating,— or even more amid the sorrow and anguish that often seem to reach a climax at Christmas, — we should put the most vital issue of these pre-Christmas hours squarely before ourselves. Above the thousands of questions you are asking, "What dress will I wear tomorrow?" "How can I pay my Christmas debts?" "I wonder what he will give me?" "What will I do with my Christmas bonus?" "Why, of all times, do I have to be sick during these days?" "What if I can't find work next week?" "Why did God take my baby just at this time?" "Why should I be lonely while others find no end of pleasure?" — as high above all this as the heavens tower over the earth, one sacred question awaits your answer. Listen to it, fathers and mothers of America, overburdened by the festival strain! Pay careful attention, you young folks, so that this year on the Savior's birthday new faith, joy, loyalty, may be born in you! Push everything else aside and concentrate on your answer, you with burdened and blighted lives, for here is help, hope, happiness! Give me the next fifteen minutes, you to whom Christmas is just another celebration, who have ignored, denied, or opposed the Lord Jesus; and it may be that this coming quarter hour will bring you Heaven's highest gift! For as I try to depict in words the theme Holman Hunt immortalized on canvas, Jesus pleading to be welcomed into your soul and family circle, I ask for an honest, personal answer to the Christmas question,

HAVE YOU ROOM FOR THE CHRIST-CHILD?

that all-significant issue suggested by the Nativity record (Saint Luke 2:7): *"And she . . . laid Him in a manger because there was no room for them in the inn."*

I

HOW DANGEROUS TO REJECT CHRIST!

The story of the overcrowded inn is well known to both friend and foe of our Lord; but have you ever stopped to ask why no room was made for Jesus in that public resting-place? Perhaps because no one was ready to surrender his shelter to the coming Christ-child, just as today few people are willing seriously to deny themselves ease and luxury, so that the Gospel can be brought into more human hearts. We can almost hear some of the Savior's fellow-countrymen safely settled for the night in the warmth of that inn, protesting, when they were told that outside a young woman and her husband asked for lodging, "Why didn't they come earlier? We were here first, and we insist on our rights."

Ah, that is the trouble today! People everlastingly insist on their rights, rather than heed the appeal of their suffering fellow-men. Defiantly do they stand their ground instead of giving way to the need of others. See where this "we-are-right-and-we-don't-care-what-happens" obsession has brought our conceited culture today, with war-torn Europe tottering on the edge of international bankruptcy! What penalties this "I-want-my-rights" spirit has inflicted on the working-man and his employer, when, for example, in a recent Detroit automobile strike the total salaries' and sales' losses reached $117,000,000. Or, to come closer to our every-day lives, picture to yourselves the deep-grooved tragedies in the home resulting from this "I-was-here-first" spirit when men reject Jesus and the appeal of His word, *"Husbands, love your wives, even as Christ also loved the Church"*; when women forget that they are to be their husbands' helpmates and children refuse to obey their *"parents in the Lord"*; where all, leading their narrow, selfish lives, — grumbling over their grievances, sullen, silent, resentful, even hate-filled, — concede Christ no place in their hearts.

Another reason no one in that public khan at Bethlehem would make room for Christ was this, that Joseph and Mary were poor people, common folk from the laboring classes. The world now as then had little interest in men and women without money. A subtle propaganda spread throughout the land whispers into the ears of underpaid and unemployed masses, the WPA laborers, the dissatisfied workers, false charges, claiming that all churches are favorable to the rich but hostile to the poor. In dangerous days like these religious groups in the United States should avoid every semblance of preference for money and earnestly show a whole-hearted concern for the masses. If you are planning a new church, make it solid and beautiful; but do not spend a single dollar just for a large and pretentious building which, you think, will attract the high and mighty. The tragedies enacted in Russia, Spain, and Mexico may be repeated wherever the churches' size and wealth can be used by atheists as an argument against their continued existence.

Remember, too, that Mary and Joseph came from distant Nazareth, and little sympathy was shown travelers from despised Galilee. The same ugly class hatred tries to provoke its havoc in our world. "Why don't you come out against the Jews?" people ask us repeatedly. "Why do you mention the Negroes so frequently?" others inquire. The answer to all such questions is the same: When a man's heart has made room for the Christ-child, heralded by the angel's announcement of good will toward men, he cannot hate any one. He must love even his enemies and pray for those who persecute him. As soon as he believes that the Christmas-message of salvation is the *"tidings of great joy, which shall be to all people,"* he knows that every one who accepts the full atonement of the Lord Jesus is his spiritual brother, regardless of race or rank, color or clime.

Perhaps the Holy Family was excluded from the inn at Bethlehem because it was known that Mary would soon have a child and the guests were unwilling to be annoyed by these special circumstances. — Has our age altogether lost this aversion? If all the hospital beds were filled, how many hotels would knowingly give shelter to an expectant mother? The largest and the best apartment-houses often have scant room and less enthusiasm for children.

Even many homes, were the true sentiments of husband and wife known, would have this notice on their walls, "No children wanted!" Herod took the brutal way by slaughtering the innocents; but frequently a criminal hatred of children similarly expresses itself, as it did last week when a Philadelphia mother suffocated her twenty-month-old son, sawed up his body and threw some of its parts into the gutter — because, as she herself admitted, the child interfered with her parties and her work. Most of the children murdered in our country, however, are killed before they are born. Even the United States Department of Labor lists 800,000 abortions in our country every year. "No room for children!" — that is the cry of our perverted generation, to which, in effect, some members of the medical profession have lent their approval. Common sense dictates that before long appeals will come from Washington and from officialdom throughout the land demanding that American homes and families make room for children.

Bethlehem and its inn were not the only places closed to the Christ-child. Have you ever thought of this? Not more than two hours before they arrived in over-crowded Bethlehem, Mary and Joseph had doubtless walked the streets of Jerusalem, only six short miles away. The palace gates could have been thrown wide to welcome the mother and her son, the King of men's souls; yet Herod had no room for Christ. The Temple attendants could have found shelter for Him before whom seraphim chant their *"Holy, holy, holy!"* But there was no room for Christ among the priests, whose satanic jealousy later screamed, *"Crucify Him!"* Here is the divine record — after 1900 years we can hardly believe its tragic truth — *"He came unto His own, and His own received Him not!"*

Before we begin to shake our heads and think how

much better we are, we ought to ask ourselves pointedly: Where would the Christ-child find room in our twentieth-century civilization? Among the influential and mighty of the land? While we thank God that it has been our privilege to know industrial and business leaders who are humble followers of Bethlehem's Babe, we feel that for multitudes in the upper strata of American society with its all too frequent immoralities, its luxurious eating, and protracted drinking, Christmas is not far different from the heathen Saturnalia that pagan Rome used to celebrate at this time of year. Is there room for Christ in the homes of the wealthy? Thank God, there sometimes is; yet how often money proves a curse! The founder of a large concern chiefly engaged in producing Christmas-greeting cards left each of his children a huge fortune with the proviso that none should every marry a Christian. He hated the Christ whose birth had helped him make millions of dollars.

Is there room for Jesus in American business? Many tradesmen today, gleefully rubbing their hands over the holiday sales, will call this the best season since 1929; but we are shocked at the crude commercializing that sprawls advertisements like this over our newspapers, "No other gift says 'Merry Christmas!' just the way our whisky does." Another distiller suggests, "Giving a man a quart of our whisky, or two if you are really fond of him, is a grand way of saying 'Merry Christmas!'" If you could read what whisky has done in some homes that write us in the despair of broken hearts, you would know that for many people this would be a hellish way of saying "Merry Christmas!"

Is there room for Christ in all the churches of America? Read in this excerpt from a Sunday-school leaflet what Modernism has done to the beautiful story of the angels' appearance to the shepherds: "Two little boys, one of whom had come to visit his cousin in Jerusalem, were watching the strange multitude of people as they came to the city. In prowling about that night, they saw a strange light and thought that the strangers who opposed the taxing were setting fire to the city. So they went and awakened the boy's father and told him. Then together they went to investigate the light and found the baby Jesus." No room for the angels, no room for the shepherds, no room for the Virgin Birth, no room for the deity of Christ! Tomorrow thousands of buildings called churches will have room for decorations and garlands of green, time for special music and Christmas carols, plenty of interest in fashionable worshipers and prominent guests, but no room for Jesus Christ, the Son of God and Son of man, no time or interest for the Redeemer of our entire wayward, sin-laden race.

The most vital of all Christmas questions, however, is personal. It asks, Will there be room for Christ in your home and, more pointedly, in your heart? Before you answer, think of the tragic consequences of being too crowded, preoccupied, disinterested for Christ! The sorrows that throughout the centuries have swept over the nation which rejected Christ are only part of the penalty exacted by divine righteousness. The siege of Jerusalem not long after the Savior's death, when mothers, almost insane from hunger, ate their own children; when others gnawed at leather; when thousands were ripped open alive, so that the conquerors could find gold that had been swallowed — the many other indescribable aspects of that torture were only the beginning of the long-drawn anguish following the rejection of Christ. If you have no room for Jesus on earth, He will have no room for you in eternity. He warns, "*Whosoever shall deny Me before men, Him will I also deny before My Father which is in heaven."* For peace with your conscience and your God, for escape from death's terror, hell and its torture, make room for the Savior! Repeat the prayer which some of you learned in your childhood:

> Ah, dearest Jesus, holy Child,
> Make Thee a bed, soft, undefiled,
> Within my heart that it may be
> A quiet chamber kept for Thee!

Many of you, undecided about receiving Jesus, write that you are preparing to join the Church. You are almost convinced that what I say is right; you are seriously planning to be instructed in the Christian faith. But "almost" and "planning" are not enough. You may lose everything by delay. With Christmas music in the air; Christmas bells ringing from church towers; your homes filled with the Christmas gleam which should symbolize Christ as *"the Light of the world";* with the Savior knocking at the door of your heart and the portals of your home, accept Christ now! Say, " 'Come, Lord Jesus,' we have room for Thee, blessed Child of the cradle, in the sanctuary of our hearts! Come and be born in us today!"

II

HOW BLESSED TO WELCOME CHRIST!

One small spot in Bethlehem had room for the Christ-child. Reverently we read that *"because there was no room for them in the inn,"* Mary laid her new-born Son in a manger. Bible students have long debated whether the manger was in a stable or, according to tradition, in a cave; but either location, they are agreed, would be the last place in which a human being, let alone the mighty Immanuel, our God-with-us, should be born. Archeologists are likewise by no means unanimous in identifying the present Church of the Nativity in Bethlehem as the spot of the Savior's birth, but whether it is or not, what a contrast to the glitter of the overmany decorations in that Palestinian grotto the first cradle of Christ presented! Tomorrow, according to the law of averages, 6,000 children will be born in the United States, and not one of them will come into the world as destitute of human interest and help as the Christ-child came.

It was not by accident that the Savior's birthplace was in the small province of despised Judea, a vanquished, plundered country, in a village, small even according to that day's impoverished standards, and in the humblest spot of that village, a lowly manger. These details were part of a divine plan to show, first of all, the mercy which the manger cradle reveals. Christ, the great and glorious God — and only when you find in Jesus the Lord of lords and the King of kings, can you understand Christmas aright — the marvelous and mighty God, through whom this universe and its vastness came into being, loved every one of us, despite our sins, with a heavenly devotion so wide that for the ransoming of our souls from death He became man and, leaving the glorious heights of heaven, descended to the lowliest depths of this world, to be born — an outcast, rejected even by those whom He had come to save.

Besides, Christ's birth in the manger foretold that He was to be the Friend particularly of the poor and the underprivileged. Artists have painted our Lord in robes of costly fabric; sculptors have chiseled His form in marble with ornate embellishments; but the real Jesus, your Savior and mine, as He walked the pathways of Palestine, wore a workman's garb. Throughout His life He knew the price the poor have to pay in suffering; for later He was to have less shelter than even the Bethlehem manger provided. He cries out, *"The foxes have holes, and the birds of the air have nests; but the Son of Man hath not where to lay His head."* Yet in faith you, the poor in earthly goods, can be rich in Christ's Spirit; for here is the promise of God's Word, *"Though He was rich, yet for your sakes He became poor that ye through His poverty might be rich."*

A few nights ago we brought the Christmas-message to 300 homeless men at a Saint Louis municipal shelter. After the services a middle-aged man without a penny in his pocket, owning in all the world only the threadbare clothing he wore, came to me — his face gleaming with the radiance reflected from Bethlehem's manger — and said, "I cannot tell you how happy I am to hear about Jesus!" I think by contrast of some multimillionaire families which with all their money have not been able to capture even a fraction of this happiness because they are without Christ. My friends who are living on relief or who ought to have this support; you, the disillusioned who have seen the little money you once had snatched away by dishonesty and greed — when you open your hearts to Jesus, there will be strength, guidance, blessing, from Heaven itself for your darkened paths. Sometimes God blesses the impoverished in a special way. Why are more sons of the poor enshrined in New York City's Hall of Fame than sons of the wealthy? Because the Lord dearly loves those who as they suffer loss, turn humbly to Him! In multiplied instances God Almighty has lifted His children from poverty to plenty if this has been in keeping with their souls' salvation; but always, without question, the needy can look to Jesus, and their faith will hear Him say: "O my beloved, I was poor once, so poor that at My birth they had no room for Me in the inn; so destitute that at Calvary I left only My cloak and a few pieces of blood-stained clothing; so impoverished that at My death I had to be buried in a borrowed grave. I know the privations you endure; but by this poverty I promise you the riches of heaven." In the name of that merciful Christ I ask those tempted by the false promises of social revolution and communistic upheaval: Make room in the grief-embittered recesses of your heart for the Christ-child!

Again, it seems to me that Jesus was born in a manger that He might give emphasized comfort to those who feel that the whole world has no room for them. The Christmas days, more than other times, seem to heighten the burden of loneliness by contrast with the season's joy. So I ask you who today and tomorrow will be separated from your homes or hear this message in a public institution; you children orphaned by sudden death; you husbands or wives facing life without the sustaining companionship of your loved ones — look trustingly to Jesus, and you will hear Him say: "I was lonely, too, so forsaken that in Bethlehem no one save Mary, My mother, and Joseph and the lowing cattle welcomed Me. I was alone in the Garden, when even My disciples slept; alone on the cross, deserted by men, and forsaken by My heavenly Father. I know your numb, aching pain, your lonely anguish. But come to Me now, and your faith will feel Me constantly at your side." With this trust your Christmas devotion can sing, "Joy to the world!" because the joy of the Savior's companionship reechoes from your heart. Without this blessing you have no protection even against yourself. You who write me dark, morose letters, surrendering to despair, declaring that you do not know how to meet another day, must approach the manger, and in the name of the Christ who promised, *"Him that cometh to Me I will in no wise cast out,"* I assure you that, though in all the world you have no other friend, kneeling before the Christ-child, you, too, can say:

> What a Friend I have in Jesus,
> All my sins and griefs to bear!

This lowly birth at Bethlehem brings us a final message. It foreshadows the free approach every sinner can have to the sin-bearing Savior. Suppose Jesus had been born in a royal palace. How He would have been guarded that only a select few might behold Him from a distance! Credentials would have been required for admission, and many would have brought costly gifts in order to gain entrance. But no guards surround a stable. No certificates are demanded for the inspection of a public manger. Did this not reflect the full grace of the Infant Jesus, so that, as the shepherds, far down on the scale of human society in that day, were the first to hasten to the manger, today every one of us has the unconditional invitation of Jesus *"Come unto Me, all ye that labor and are heavy laden, and I will give you rest"*? We can go to Him just as we are, trusting only but wholly in the power of His blood to save us to the uttermost.

Since the Christ-child came to bring us salvation from our sins, to offer His grace particularly to the poor, the lonely, the distressed, to grant Heaven's blessings through faith, can you not see that we would be untrue to the Christmas Gospel if we were not to plead with you, "Make room for Christ!"? Jesus will never force His way into your home. When critics called Holman Hunt's attention to the fact that his picture showed no handle to the door at which the Savior knocks, the artist, an eminent disciple of the Lord Jesus, replied: "I did not paint a latch on the outside of the door because it can be opened only from within. The Lord Jesus Himself cannot open an unwilling heart. He must be invited to enter." And

He, we add, must bestow such willingness. In this spirit we invite you, our fellow-redeemed, to join us in a mighty appeal for the Savior's abiding presence. Bowing your heads in reverence and raising your hearts in assurance, pray: "O Lord Jesus, blessed Christ-child, by Thy Spirit we open our souls and our homes to receive Thee. We are not worthy that Thou shouldst come and abide with us; yet Thy love will not cast us off, and Thy mercy will be renewed for us every morning. O come, then, blessed Jesus, come to us with Thy forgiving grace, Thy radiant light, Thine ever-strengthening hope, Thy blessed promise of heaven! Come to us, abide with us, bless us, now and forever, Thou Christ of endless compassion. Amen."

BEHOLD THE GLORY OF THE CHRIST-CHILD!

"The Word was made flesh and dwelt among us (and we beheld His glory, the glory as of the Only-begotten of the Father,) full of grace and truth." — Saint John 1:14.

Blessed Babe of Bethlehem — our God, our Savior, our King:

With hearts humbled by the unfathomable mystery of the first Christmas, but with souls rejoicing in the grace and truth of Thy birth, we kneel in Spirit before Thy manger to acclaim Thee our Immanuel, our God-with-us, the long-promised Redeemer of the race. O Jesus, on this day of Thy birth we know with redoubled conviction that because of the endless mercy which brought Thee from heaven with its majesty to earth with its sorrow, Thou wilt receive us despite our sins, our disloyalty, our hatreds, if only we bow before Thee in faith, with repentance and trust. So we beseech Thee, give Thyself to us as the most glorious of all Christmas gifts, that we, reborn by Thy Spirit, may cast off the weight of our sins, the heaviness of our sorrows, the pressure of our pains, the burden of our doubts. Let Thy joy and peace reign completely in us! Thou Christ-child of all truth, give us this Christmas grace for the sake of Thy name, Wonderful, Counselor, the Mighty God, the Everlasting Father, the Prince of Peace! Amen.

HOW far from the radiant joy of the Christ-child this Christmas finds our world! *"Glory to God in the highest!"* the angels caroled on the night of our Savior's birth; but where is the glory that men should give the Almighty? Within the last twenty years the government of an entire nation numbering 170,000,000 people, occupying one sixth of the earth's surface, has officially denied God's existence and constantly blasphemed the Lord Jesus Christ. In our own country we not only have several avowed atheistic organizations, many outspoken

[122]

freethinkers, and overbearing enemies of the Bible, but on Christmas Day we also remind ourselves that at least 70,000,000 people in our God-blessed nation are not sufficiently interested in Christ to join a church for their souls' strengthening and His kingdom's existence. During the past hours even more millions have been so preoccupied with the holiday rush, so engrossed in their personal plans and problems, so completely dedicated to carousal, that they found no time whatever to show their gratitude for the Christ-child's mercy. Where, we repeat, amid all our blessings of soul and body, is the glory we should give our gracious God?

Again, the angels sang, "*On earth peace!*" But where is this soul peace? Despite our twentieth-century learning and roseate claims for progress we have been unable to establish even outward tranquillity. Forgetting God, we have forgotten the love for our fellow-men; and this Christmas Day finds more than half the world's population involved in warfare. "*Peace on earth!*" But behind the Maginot and the Siegfried lines millions of Europe's choicest youth are being trained in the science of wholesale slaughter for a struggle which, if long protracted, may shake the foundations of all civilization. "*Peace on earth!*" If the hundred millions of dollars spent to produce international harmony, the thousands of groups organized to banish war, have failed as the lust for money makes men more cruel than stalking jungle beasts, how can all human agencies combined hope to bring us the deeper peace, divine rest, and inner blessings for our souls?

"*Good will toward men!*" the first Christmas carol concluded; but we wonder where the good will is, with race pitted against race, color against color, class against class, creed against creed. How completely opposed to the spirit of the Christ-child the present steady, insistent effort to breed fanatical hatred in the American people, to hurl our country into Europe's war — for the enrichment of those who profiteer through the large-scale murder of young lives!

You can understand, then, that with conflict instead of cooperation, mass murder in place of mutual understanding, hatred crowding out happiness, the voices of radical agitators will assert boldly that the Christian faith has failed and Christmas must be discarded. Thank God, Christianity has not failed; on the contrary, the failure of our age lies in its unwillingness to apply the Savior's Gospel. Christmas cannot be discarded; instead, the true Nativity joy must be restored wherever men have lost it. At the manger side struggling, embittered souls can find the peace of pardon, the calm joy of trusting faith.

What higher privilege can we have, then, on this anniversary of the Savior's birth, the day for which generations longed, which prophets foretold throughout aging centuries, than to ask you to drop every distraction and

BEHOLD THE GLORY OF THE CHRIST-CHILD!

This personal appeal to you is based on the words of Saint John's gospel (1:14), "*The Word was made flesh and dwelt among us (and we beheld His glory, the glory as of the Only-begotten of the Father,) full of grace and truth.*"

I

HE IS THE SON OF GOD!

No uncertainty lingers in Saint John's mind about the meaning and importance of Christmas. In plain language — most of the words are of one syllable — he testifies, "*The Word was made flesh,*" that is, Jesus Christ, called "*the Word*" because He conveyed the thoughts and

the will of God, as the words you speak express your will;
that blessed Lord *"was made flesh."* I repeat, for as
incredible as it may seem people write me that they do not
know who Jesus Christ is, since they have heard His name
used chiefly in cursing and profanity: Christmas, above all
else, marks the glorious, victorious truth that the Son of
God — eternal praise to His name! — left the majesty of
His throne for the lowliness of the manger.

Note also the conviction which rings in our text. *"We
beheld His glory,"* Saint John writes. Don't overlook
that, you skeptics, who like to put a question-mark behind
the Gospel-story of the Savior's birth at Bethlehem. If you
boastingly endorse the claim of a noted educator that, if we
regard the Christmas-story as a myth, it can have more
meaning for us than if we accept it as true, take time to
study this decisive fact: Saint John says that he and others
"beheld" Christ's glory. They were witnesses. They saw
with their own eyes the most convincing evidence that the
Christ of Christmas was the Son of God, *"the Only-
begotten of the Father."* I submit to you that Saint John
knew whereof he spoke. He was with the Savior from the
beginning of His public ministry. He enjoyed, as none
other of the chosen dozen, an intimate fellowship with
our Lord; for he was the disciple whom Jesus loved with
particular devotion. John saw Christ both in His trans-
figured glory and in the deep humiliation of His atoning
love, when at Calvary the crucified Lord spoke to him
the only words directed to a disciple from the cross. When
a man thus testifies on the basis of more than three years'
personal experience that Jesus Christ is the Son of God,
that during all this time he beheld His divine glory, such
evidence should convince even the most skeptical.

John's testimony is only a small part of the proof that
this Child in the manger, whom hundreds of millions today,

willingly or unwillingly, recognize, is the Son of God made man. Long before the first Christmas, prophets and psalmists had foretold with increasing clarity that the promised Redeemer would be the Lord, almighty and eternal. As inspired Isaiah, beholding Bethlehem seven hundred years before the shepherds saw the Christ-child, declared with rapturous joy, *"Unto us a Child is born, unto us a Son is given; and the government shall be upon His shoulder; and His name shall be called Wonderful, Counselor, The Mighty God, The Everlasting Father, The Prince of Peace,"* so other messengers of God had proclaimed a Deliverer who was to be human, born of a woman, yet divine, because He would destroy the power of sin and death.

When Jesus came and these prophecies of His birth, life, and death were fulfilled, He repeatedly asserted His deity. The miracles which proved His heavenly power, the divine names and honor which men and angels accorded Him, combine to impress on our minds the glorious truth that the Babe in Mary's arms — and here we bow before the sacred mystery of the ages — is our God!

Do you object that today no one can believe this? If among the earliest to pay the Christ-child tribute were the intellectually advanced of the first century, the Wise Men from the distant East; if through all subsequent centuries geniuses, scientists, inventors, discoverers, scholars, in the varied fields of cultural activities, have likewise been humble followers of Jesus Christ; if even boisterous unbelievers who at first sought to destroy what they called "the superstition of Christian faith" later came to worship Jesus — why do you assail our Lord's deity when minds far more profound than yours have reverently acclaimed Him?

Don't tell us that, because you cannot understand the

Christmas miracle, you will not believe it. Of course, neither you nor any one else can explain how this helpless, new-born Babe is the almighty God. The Bible itself concedes that the birth at Bethlehem is a great mystery. Can you account for the thousand wonders of nature surrounding your life every day, that you unhesitatingly accept as true? The winter brings snow; you see it, you feel it; but can you solve its mysteries? Can you or any scientist tell in detail why these snowflakes, each hexagonal, yet all different in form and beauty, cover the ground? Now, if without being able to comprehend the marvelous processes of the snow that comes down from above, you nevertheless accept each snow-storm as a reality, why do you insist that before finding the Son of God in Mary's Child your puny intellect must be able to analyze what even angels cannot explain?

Or why dim the Christmas radiance by referring to the many large churches and highly publicized preachers who openly reject the claim of our text and of a hundred other passages that Jesus is God's Son? We know that unbelief has gained control in sections of certain denominations and that false teachers have long denied the Savior's deity and His atonement, without which no one can ever be saved. But are you ready to take man's word instead of God's? Are you willing to entrust your soul's destiny to preachers who constantly change their opinions even concerning worldly affairs?

Instead of closing this Christmas Day with a question-mark, examine more closely the Scriptural claims for this keystone truth — the Savior's deity. Behold the Christ-child's glory with the eyes of faith, and you will realize that He had to be God. Search your heart to discover your personal sins; survey your own wants, your failures, your weaknesses, and will you not agree that for the answer to the pleadings of your soul, for forgiveness, light, and strength, you need more than human help?

How deceptive men have shown themselves within our generation! Imposing promises of peace are signed and sealed, only to become scraps of paper in the first crisis. One nation pledges another effective military aid in the event of war; yet when hostilities break out, no help is sent. Investment houses and financial enterprises solemnly obligate themselves to repay with interest the money lent them; a crash comes, they fall into bankruptcy, and their guarantees mean nothing! Do you not realize that for help against the most insidious soul enemies, the legions of temptation and the regiments of hell; for peace with your God, your conscience, your fellow-men; for the one unfailing assurance that never proves unreliable, you need the Lord Jesus Christ, not merely as teacher or leader, example or guide (even men can be all this and more), but as your Savior and your God? When physicians stand baffled before new and devastating diseases of the body, must you not plead with your whole soul for a heavenly Physician who, applying His divine remedy, can restore you to God's grace? If chemical research is unable to find an antidote to some of the deadliest poisons or discover a cleansing fluid to eradicate certain stains, must we not, our entire being saturated with sin's venom and our souls spotted by iniquity, pray that God Himself will come to us, remove this poison, and cleanse us? Say what you will about the needs of men today; describe all the commendable steps necessary to give them a sense of stability and security; when you have finished, we will still maintain that the crying necessity for every human soul is God's forgiving presence and His purifying help.

This is the blessed glory of Christmas: when you behold in the Christ-child your God; when you join the entire

Christian Church in saying, "I believe . . . in Jesus Christ, His only Son, our Lord, who was conceived by the Holy Ghost, born of the Virgin Mary," then you have a God who can supply every want, defend you in every distress, and deliver you in every dark hour. On the other hand, if you do not sincerely believe that Jesus is your Lord and God, you do not know the true Christ. You may exalt Him over other men; you may extol Him as the greatest Figure of history, mankind's most unselfish Martyr; you may put Him in a class by Himself and agree that no man has ever done what Jesus did; yet, if on Christmas Day you say nothing more about Christ than this; if you refuse to bow before Him and declare, *"My Lord and my God!"* no matter how much you may think you know about Jesus, — and I have an acquaintance who has studied thirty-two biographies of our Lord, mostly, I fear, the wrong books, without acknowledging His deity, — you know neither the true Jesus nor the glorious Christmas blessing.

The Savior proved Himself God when His Spirit made a persecuted Paul of a sword-bearing Saul. It was a divine Christ who triumphed over the Roman Empire in the fourth century when the senate, called to decide whether the worship of Jupiter or that of Christ should be the worship of the Romans (who up till this time had murdered thousands of Christians), by a large majority formally condemned Jupiter and acclaimed Christ. As Jesus demonstrated His divinity in millions of similar transformations by which the world has been entirely changed, may He now convince you that He is not a human theorist but the almighty God! Blessed will this Christmas be if you, taking your reason captive and joining in the spiritual pilgrimage to the manger side, fall on your knees before the Christ-child to declare: "O blessed Babe, I come to Thee on this day of Thy birth, for Thou art my God. I believe it with all my heart, incomprehensible as Thy deity is, and I kneel before Thee so that I, born again in Thee, can testify to the world, I also have *"beheld His glory, the glory as of the Only-begotten of the Father."*

II

BEHOLD THE FULNESS OF HIS GRACE AND TRUTH

The Christmas appeal asks us to behold in the Christ-child not only our God but also our Savior; to understand that Jesus, the Word, *"was made flesh and dwelt among us,"* so that He could fulfil the Law we had broken, pay the debt incurred by our sins, and in our stead satisfy divine justice. That is what our text implies when it says that Jesus was *"full of grace."*

If you look up the word "grace" in a large dictionary, you will find fifteen distinct meanings; but Christ's grace means only one heavenly blessing, God's divine and unmerited love. The forgiveness of all sins, the deliverance which we ourselves could never secure by a lifetime of sacrifice, long centuries of repentance, or thousands of dollars of indulgences; the soul's pardon which we could never purchase though the accumulated billions of national treasuries were ours; the promise of salvation which no one else, not a thousand saints or ten thousand holy angels, could acquire for us, this sacred pledge is granted — oh, may your hearts leap with joy at this most magnificent grace! — by the pure, free mercy of God and the self-giving of Jesus Christ!

The evangelist describes the Christ-child as *"full of grace,"* and can we ever worthily thank Him for the overflowing measure of His mercy, its pardon for every sin and its peace for every sinner, its love so constant and complete that we never need present credentials, perform a prescribed routine of works, recite required rituals, assume any part, however small, in the completion of our salvation?   The joy of Christmas cries out, *"Only believe!* Take Christ at His word, *'full of grace'* as He, the blessed Savior, is."   If heretofore you tried personally to pay your own way to heaven or to let some one else pay for you after your death; if until the dawn of this Christmas Day you have not been satisfied to let Jesus do everything for your redemption but have tried to earn what He had already secured for you, then may God's Holy Spirit grant you personally and penetratingly the Christmas conviction that rejoices, *"By grace are ye saved, through faith."*

We hear, among other explanations for Christ's birth, that He came for social justice, the improvement of race relations, the establishment of international peace; but social justice, world brotherhood, universal peace, will never be attained in this sin-saturated world.   While Christ's Gospel does change men and in their twice-born lives gives them a helpful service program, the one purpose of Jesus' advent is to save souls, and the one objective He has in coming to you through these words and pleading that you believe in Him, is to redeem you, individually and personally, for His eternity.   There can be no doubt about that; for in repeated declarations our Lord has outlined the purpose of His incarnation and His death on the cross. He proclaims, *"The Son of Man came . . . to give His life a ransom for many," "The Son of Man is come to seek and to save that which was lost."*   He reassures us, *"I am come that they* [all who accept Him] *might have life, and that they might have it more abundantly."*   There, in Christ's plan for your blessed eternity in heaven, you have the Christmas-message and the fulness of its grace.

Combined with His overabundant mercy you can find

in the Christ-child a fulness of *"truth."* Far above the lying propaganda, the perjury, the dishonesty, the falsehoods, of our deceptive day, the Christmas verity seeks to flash its hope into every burdened life. The glory of our faith is this, that in our own lives we can experience how the Savior faithfully keeps His word. We know that this Christmas many hearts think they are too securely gripped by earth's sorrows to believe the angel's proclamation, *"Behold, I bring you good tidings of great joy."* Some of you hear these words from sick-beds, and there may be an upswelling bitterness that protests against what you miscall God's "cruelty" toward you. Others had to forego the usual Christmas Eve celebrations and are preparing only a scanty meal, because the past year has brought one financial reverse after the other. If a tabulation could be made of the homes now joined in this Christmas service from the Atlantic to the Pacific, what revelations of tragedy and sin's hideousness would appear! How many husbands or wives have been deserted and forsaken! How many young folks are suffering from broken promises! Into how many hushed chambers has death entered to bring its anguish, always agonizing, but completely crushing, it seems, when the rest of the world observes the year's happiest day. My friends among the sorrowing and afflicted, believe me when, in the name of Jesus, I promise that this Christmas has come especially for you and that the comfort of Christ, *"Your sorrow shall be turned into joy"* will ultimately be proved true, if only you will trust the Savior and realize that because He suffered more than you can ever suffer, He understands your pains; that because He loved you and gave His own holy body for your sins, He will guard your blood-bought soul, so that even your adversities, losses, bereavements, by the miracle of His guidance, will work together for your good.

During the Christmas season Columbus, distracted by Indian attacks and the rebellion in his own ranks, was on the verge of despair. In that hour of gloom it seemed that a voice in the night spoke these comforting words to him: "O man of little faith! Why art thou cast down? Fear nothing; I will provide for thee. . . . I will take care of thee." That assurance sustained him, and on the next day unexpected supplies of gold were discovered. We cannot promise you material wealth, but we can tell you that, if you trustingly say to the Christ-child, "O Jesus, thou art mine and I am Thine," then in every black midnight of sorrow the strengthening *"Fear not"* which announced His birth will be spoken by Christ Himself into your sad heart with the promise that He will provide for your needs according to the richness of His grace.

My Christmas wish for you asks: "May the Christ-child, the Word made flesh, '*the Only-begotten of the Father, full of grace and truth,*' today be born in your heart, adored and proclaimed in your life, until we all may blend our voices with the angels' chorus to sing the Savior's praise in endless glory and majesty!" O God Almighty, hear this prayer and make Thine answer a divine, radiant Christmas gift to every struggling, groping soul! Grant this for Jesus' sake! Amen.

"A MIGHTY FORTRESS
IS OUR GOD!"

*"The Lord is good, a Stronghold in the
day of trouble."* — Nahum 1:7.

Jesus Christ, the same yesterday and today and forever:

As another year draws to its close, help us to remember our sins,
our failures, our weaknesses! Make every one of us understand
that the year's end must remind us of our life's end and that we
are 365 days closer to eternity than we were twelve months ago!
Despite this inescapable flight of time and the burden of our sins,
lead us to find forgiveness and refuge in Thee, whose grace never
changes and whose blood-bought mercies are renewed every morning!
Send us Thy Spirit with special force, so that none of us will close
the old year without Thy pardon and blessing. When tomorrow
comes and with it the beginning of another period of grace,
strengthen us, Thou merciful Savior of our souls, to start anew
under Thy guidance, with both fear and pride banished by Thine
abiding presence in our hearts! We face the future undismayed
because we face it with Thee, O Christ, our Savior, our Lord,
our God. Amen.

WHEN the fighting Finns, battling for their country's
existence, went out against the overwhelming Red
forces, company after company, so the newspapers reported, marched to the front singing the hymn with which
every one of these "Bringing-Christ-to-the-nation" broadcasts starts — the most widely known and best-beloved
of all sacred songs, translated into more languages (185, to
be exact) than any other lines outside the Bible. That
strain of courageous confidence is the victory song of the
Reformation, Martin Luther's "A Mighty Fortress Is
Our God!"

In many other crises, men have sustained their courage
with this grand old hymn. On the eve of an imperial
council Luther himself repeated these words, so one his-

torian claims, to revive the drooping spirits of his fellow-laborers, and so strengthened were they by the power of God as their mighty Fortress that they testified unhesitatingly before that council, protesting against the many errors in the churches of their day.

A century later, when that Protestantism lay bleeding on the battle-fields of religious warfare and Gustavus Adolphus, intrepid young king of the Swedes, came down from his northland to help protect the cause of Christ, he at Breitenfeld led his troops in singing "A Mighty Fortress Is Our God." A year later, in the decisive battle of Luetzen, when a heavy fog prevented his forces from starting the attack, the Swedish monarch had his musicians play the same magnificent melody to which the army raised its mighty chorus. When the sun broke through the lifting fog, Gustavus Adolphus himself kneeled to pray, "Jesus, Jesus, Jesus, help me today to do battle for the glory of Thy name!" With the cry "God with us!" he led his troops forward. For several hours the outcome seemed doubtful. Shortly before noon the young king was mortally wounded; but instead of losing heart, his soldiers found new help in God, their mighty Fortress; and when that day of blood drew to its close, the victory was theirs.

In dozens of other crisis hours men have similarly found courage by singing "A Mighty Fortress Is Our God!" As this broadcast brings us to the last day of the year, we hope that you, too, reviewing the past and surveying the future, may take refuge in Heaven's unchangeable strength. Only a few more hours, and the year, which twelve months ago seemed to stretch out almost interminably, will draw to its close. We may avoid this truth and seek to escape from its warning, but here is the unalterable fact: Within less than twelve hours another year will have been removed forever from the one life that we have to live. We will be fifty-two weeks closer to the grave, 365 days nearer eternity and its judgment. Now, what assurance do we need for the sins and sorrows of yesterday, what pledge for tomorrow with its fears, if not the promise

"A MIGHTY FORTRESS IS OUR GOD!"?

We ask you to conclude the old year and start the new with this confidence not because Luther had this heroic faith but because the Scriptures themselves want you to have it and give you the pledge (Nahum 1:7), *"The Lord is good, a Stronghold in the day of trouble."*

I

GOD HAS BEEN OUR MIGHTY FORTRESS IN THE PAST YEAR

For their size the prophecies of Nahum say more about war and grim destruction than do any of the other sixty-five books of Scripture. But as the prophet portrays the fall of Nineveh, proud mistress of the world, and envisions the international tumult, long-drawn bloodshed, and wide-spread sorrow, he comforts those who put their trust in God with this sustaining hope, *"The Lord is good, a Stronghold in the day of trouble."* What a graphic, faith-strengthening picture that is! Just as a soldier, Nahum implies, outnumbered by his enemies, hard-pressed by the terror of the conflict, can find refuge, rest, protection, and power behind the walls of a fort, so God's children, who must daily battle against life's sins and sorrows, can find support and joy in knowing that through faith in Christ their heavenly Father is their mighty Fortress and Defense.

Before the old year passes into history beyond the possibility of recall, let us ask, "Are we blessed by the protection of this mighty Fortress? Or do we rely on ourselves and our fellow-men?" To see how misplaced human dependence is, survey the many futile predictions made during the closing year. Twelve months ago today Roger W. Babson, America's No. 1 financial forecaster, asserted in print that during 1939 Great Britain and France would enjoy another twelve months of peace. Last February George Bernard Shaw, British author and playwright, wrote an article entitled "Never Another War!" In April Sir Samuel Hoare, England's Home Secretary, declared that a committee consisting of Europe's dictators, America's President, England's prime minister, and France's premier could bring a golden age and "transform the whole history of the world." But in September, after these promises of peace had multiplied, the world was sickened by the contradictory realization that new destruction was at hand. The past year should have taught us that if diplomats and experts, with all their charts and studies of statecraft, cannot correctly foretell the course of the nations even a few months in advance, but instead record only a series of bad guesses, then for heart problems and our souls' welfare, which no graphs can measure and no statesmanship control, we must have an infallible source of defense and protection.

Where men failed, God and His Word have prevailed. Heaven's truth has never made a mistake, and Biblical promise has never miscarried. Examine the little book of Nahum with its score of predictions depicting Nineveh's fall long before that city's end, and remember with what startling detail history reveals how these prophecies were fulfilled. Can you, the skeptics in our audience who delight in ridiculing the Scriptures, produce any human book that foretells the future with such exactness? It has always seemed to us that the multiplied evidence of God's ability to execute His threats and His pledges should convince even the most doubtful that the Bible is a stronghold of divine, errorless truth.

How positively Nahum's assertion, *"The Lord is good, a Stronghold in the day of trouble,"* proved its truth in this country during 1939! Hundreds of millions in Europe, Asia, and Africa are directly or indirectly involved in bloodshed; yet the Lord was good to us and gave this country another year of peace. While disaster overtook one nation after the other, — and in these days we think particularly of the earthquake in Turkey, with its toll of 50,000 lives, — we should raise our hearts in sincere gratitude to God that no destruction of such proportions has been visited on our land. In China millions, threatened with famine and starvation, would be deeply thankful for the waste discarded by the average American family. The United States has had plenty for almost everybody, with generous Government and private relief for the needy. Who can thus review God's bounty without repeating Nahum's verdict, *"The Lord is good, a Stronghold in the day of trouble"*?

Inestimably more than in these physical blessings has God's goodness been revealed in His rich spiritual benedictions. During 1939 the Gospel has had its free course throughout the United States. In thousands of churches men of God have proclaimed the whole divine counsel for salvation. They have pictured God the Father as the Creator and Sustainer of our lives, the bounteous Provider and heavenly Protector; they have preached Jesus Christ as the Son of God and Savior of all men; they have shown the Holy Spirit in His cleansing and enlightening grace. Unmoved by fear or favor, they have declared what we constantly reemphasize to you, that mankind in its sins is under God's wrath, driving itself to everlasting perdition; but pointing to Christ and His cross, they have restored joy to troubled souls with the assurance, *"He is the Propitiation"* (that is, the Forgiveness) *"for our sins, and not for ours only, but for the sins of the whole world."* They have unsparingly denounced false, destructive creeds, and focusing their attention exclusively on the Savior, they have proclaimed, *"Neither is there salvation in any other; for there is none other name under heaven given among men whereby we must be saved."* There was opposition, of course, to the preaching of the Gospel; yet God continued to give us remarkable means for spreading His message, notably the radio, by which millions without the Church and multitudes beyond its reach have been assured of the full grace in Christ, with no transgression too horrifying and no transgressor too vile to be saved by the Savior's free and unconditioned mercy. Contrast conditions across the seas, with thousands of churches closed, preachers thrown into prison, witnesses to Jesus martyred, mission-work paralyzed, and you will see that, despite our unworthiness, for us *"the Lord is good, a Stronghold in the day of trouble."*

All this, however, means little unless you yourself acknowledge the good God as your mighty Fortress; and since the last day of December is one of the best possible occasions for moral and spiritual inventory and the balancing of life's book, we ask you pointedly: Did you find refuge in Christ during 1939? Did you give the Savior opportunity to prove Himself your Defense and Protection? Millions in this God-blessed nation began and closed every day without a thought of prayer for divine blessing. They sat down at their tables and rose again without voicing their gratitude to *"the Giver of every good and perfect gift."* Are you one of those who refuse to recognize God? Some of you boast that you do not need God; during the past year you made money hand over fist; your business prospered; you built a large, attractive home, increased your reserves; and you feel you can continue to get along without God. But all the while you are losing your precious soul, and Jesus says that the whole world's riches cannot compensate for this loss. You may not realize how true His words are now, but the day is coming, just as surely as year follows upon year in the steady grind of time, when your boasting will turn to chattering fear as the Almighty demands an exacting account of your entire life, with its thoughts and actions. You cannot escape God, and you cannot buy His justice.

Others in this audience started 1939 with Christ, but are concluding it without Him. They have turned away from the cross and the Savior of the outstretched arms. If only they knew the pain and defeat toward which they are hastening! In the early Church, Julian, baptized into the Christian faith, was no sooner crowned emperor than he did what some of you have done: he solemnly renounced his Redeemer. To show his disregard of Baptism and his preference for pagan rites, he bathed himself in the blood of bulls. But before he met his end on the battle-field, he had to scream that the Galilean, Christ, had defeated him, the Roman emperor.

While the last falling sands in the midnight hour-glass show that 1939 is slipping away forever, look over the 365 pages in this current volume of your life. As you find the daily entries blotted by sin, crowded with the evidences of your indebtedness to God, spattered by tears that you made others weep or that dropped from your eyes, may you realize that, while you have no resources to pay these obligations, God, our Strength and Protection, *"is good,"* so good that Christ came to meet our staggering debts, remove these spots, and through faith give us heavenly power for every burdened pathway of life. It is not too late to appropriate His atonement; with only a few hours of the declining year left, do not try to hide your transgressions. On the contrary, *"be sure that your sins will find you out."* A few days ago a murderess was traced by the impression her pencil had left on a newspaper below a motion-picture-contest coupon which she had signed. Don't think lightly of your rising up against God; for the very pleasures that keep you in sin now will certainly haunt you. Listen to the French author Lavredan, a confessed atheist, who after the agony of the first World War made this startling confession: "I laughed at faith and thought myself wise. Finally this laughter became hollow and vain, for I saw France bleeding and mourning. . . . How difficult it is to remain an atheist in a national cemetery! I cannot, I cannot, I have deceived myself and you who have read my book. It was a delusion, a giddiness, an evil dream. I see death and call for life. . . . France, turn back to faith; to forsake God means to be lost! I do not know whether I shall live tomorrow, but I must tell my friends, Lavredan is afraid to die an atheist. . . . Rejoice, my soul, that you have been permitted to experience the hour when on my knees I can say, I believe." In the name of Jesus Christ you, too, can take your sins and come, just as you are; lay all your iniquities and your fears at the foot of the cross and hear Jesus say, *"Thy sins be forgiven thee."* Then in the joy of your life you will know that God *"is good."* You will find Him a mighty Fortress to protect you against the onslaughts of your personal sins and private vices, a Stronghold for the building of your character; with Luther you will confess and exult:

> With might of ours can naught be done;
> Soon were our loss effected.
> But for us fights the Valiant One,
> Whom God Himself elected.
> Ask ye, Who is this?
> Jesus Christ it is,

We hear individuals objecting: "Well, I cannot say that God has been good to me during 1939." "Think of my money losses!" "I spent months in bed and am not cured yet." "My husband left me and ran away with another woman!" "My home was taken away because we could not meet the mortgage payments." "The doctor doesn't want to tell me, but I know I have a cancer." "My wife died this fall." "I buried my only child during Christmas week." — Many of you hear the promise of our text, *"The Lord is good, a Stronghold in the day of trouble,"* and you demand: "How can God be good when He deliberately tore away that which is most precious to me? How can God be a Stronghold when again and again during the past months He let me face the world alone and suffer defeat without His strength and protection?"

We can understand that sometimes the pressure of sorrow's burdens seems beyond the carrying; but, thank God, even this weight can be removed before the year closes. Remember, in the first place, that this promise of God's guidance and protection in our text is extended only to *"those who trust in Him."* If you turned your back on Christ and cursed His holy name; if Jesus has repeatedly pleaded with you, *"Come unto Me!"* and you have pushed His outstretched arms aside, then don't accuse God of cruelty when you suffer the consequences of your unforgiven sins. Blame yourself and your own stubborn, foolhardy resistance to the Savior's grace. But if you are Christ's; if that disconsolate "Why must I suffer?" comes from the same lips that hail the power and love of Jesus' name; if the same eyes that now brim with tears look trustfully to the Savior's cross, then let these last hours of the declining year be blessed as I repeat, thinking only of *your* afflictions, *your* sorrows and problems, *"The Lord is good."* To you, as to every humble believer in Christ, God was good when you were born and He will be good when you die. God is good when He extends His blessings and when He permits agony to overtake you. He is good when He grants health and when sickness brings you low. The Lord is good if He gives you a home-life of happiness or misery. He is good if you marry or remain single, if He gives you many children or no children, if your children live or if they die. He is good if your husband is a loving helpmate or a drunken sot, your wife a faithful mother or an unprincipled woman. He is good to you whether you live to be a hundred years old or die an early death of tuberculosis or heart disease. God is good through Jesus Christ — praise be to His eternal mercy! — to every believer in every way, time, and place!

Some of you have been shaking your heads in protest; but we do not want the old year to leave you in any uncertainty regarding this blessed conviction: Whenever a sinner has been justified by faith, purified through Jesus, reborn into a new, blessed existence through Baptism and the Holy Spirit, his life is *"hid with Christ."* There may be a great deal of mystery to us in God's unsearchable ways and the divine judgments that are past finding out; but when our Savior says, *"What I do, thou knowest not now, but thou shalt know hereafter,"* believe that the day will come when in far clearer, in heavenly vision we can behold the marvelous direction of God's providence and see how He turns sorrows into joy. We will learn that as Christ's redeemed we lose in order to gain, that by the marvels of divine forethought the sicknesses of our body have been promoted for the health of our souls. There, face to face with Jesus, we will understand how all things, even the apparent defeats, stinging failures, heart-crushing disappointments, work together for our ultimate good, because we love God in Christ. We will know that the money we lost through the dishonesty of others or through our own fault was taken away so that we would not spend

ourselves into hell; that the six-year old son whose body
was crushed to sudden death by a truck was called home
that he might be blessed the longer with the glories of
heaven and that his parents might be led to prepare themselves for reunion in eternity. Friends and sufferers in
Christ, we cannot ask you to rime God's providential love
with your reason, but we plead that you trust the promise
and power of the Lord Jesus and believe that the Savior
has hallowed the adversities in your life, that they may
help strengthen your faith, tear your heart from earthly
distractions, deepen your trust in God, and bring you ever
closer to Him.

As this year with its sins and sadness closes, will you
not turn to the empty space on the last page of your current
life volume and write: "O Father, I thank Thee with all
my heart for another year of grace. I do not know from
how many unseen dangers Thou hast protected me and
how often I have found safety within the fortress of Thy
love; but I do know, O Lord, that Thou art good and
that by the blood of Jesus Christ, my Savior, every sin
recorded in these pages has been washed away. I know,
too — thanks to Christ, — that the trials and temptations
which crowded this busy year have resulted in my blessing
and promoted my welfare. As I inscribe these last lines
that could have ended with disaster and eternal loss had
it not been for Jesus, I bow before Thee, O Lord, to say:
Praise, glory, and everlasting thanks be to Thee, God my
Father, God my Savior, God my Sanctifier!"?

II

GOD IS OUR PROTECTION FOR THE COMING YEAR

But what of 1940? Let no one enter this year without a full realization that it may be the most disastrous
period our age has ever witnessed. We shall face not only

a new year, but also a new period of problems, greater, we believe, in 1940 than in 1930. We still see more than 9,000,000 unemployed. Our national debts are too great to be expressed so that people can really understand their staggering amount. Trade journals are optimistic, of course, but war profits are unhealthy and cannot bring permanent gain. In our religious life the very foundations have been attacked. The denial of God's existence has become almost a commonplace. Intellectual and radical circles sarcastically belittle every Scriptural promise, and church leaders are often among the foremost to express their rejection of the Bible. Even a notable magazine like *Fortune* feels called upon to start its New Year issue with an editorial charging that the churches of this country have compromised instead of maintaining the absolute truth, that they are not offering the guidance required for these critical days. Adding to the confusion, our Government now deserts a traditional American policy by entering our religious life. Millions of Protestants and many others are disturbed by the occurrences of last week, when the President of the United States saw fit to appoint a personal representative to Vatican City. This arrangement, as cautiously as it is advanced, unmistakably endangers the principle by which Church and State are to be completely separated. Our republic should have no political contacts with any religious denomination. Besides, this inauguration of diplomatic relations is an unmistakable preference for one church. The White House does not suggest sending an envoy to the Lutherans of the world, numerically the largest Protestant group, nor do we want one. The President does not have a personal representative among the 240,000,000 Mohammedans, nor does he recognize any other denomination. We are distrustful of this arrangement because it may be the beginning of further discriminations and a potential start for additional encroachments. We demand that the Government follow the constitutional principle of keeping its hands off our religious life.

Many of you, of course, are untouched by these larger national and world-moving issues; but you have personal problems in the smaller circles of life. Tomorrow many a father in this audience, and particularly among those who have reached the age limit, which heartless industrial competition is continually lowering, will wonder how he is going to see his family through another year, with the stack of unpaid bills confronting him. Now, we cannot promise steadier work and higher wages, but by the grace of the Lord Jesus Christ we can say that if you come to the Father in His name, beseeching His help, the God of all power and might, if it but be His will, can banish want from your family and give you the most prosperous year you have ever enjoyed; and if this would not be helpful to spiritual growth and God wants to purify and strengthen you further, His love will still support you, even through miracles. Say to your heavenly Father now, "O God, through Christ Thou art good, my Stronghold in my day of trouble"; and in response He will say, *"I will never leave thee nor forsake thee."*

In the same way the Lord will provide all your needs according to the riches of His grace. If you mothers are worried about the possibility that your sons will be drafted and sent across the ocean, pray and work for peace, and then escape fear by taking refuge in the mighty Fortress, knowing that whatever God ordains is good. If you young folks who for several years have been planning to establish a home feel thwarted again as the new year seems to preclude all possibility of marriage, do not give in to the easier, yet sinful way; but go to the Arsenal of faith for weapons that can repulse the assaults of lust. If you want a deeper knowledge of Jesus, a more personal, intimate faith in His forgiving love, a more constant victory over besetting sins, power to resist temptations and to lead clean, courageous and godly lives; if you want the joy of Christian faith to displace encircling gloom, don't trust yourselves. Go directly to the mighty Fortress, and *"the victory which overcometh the world, even our faith,"* will be yours.

The new year may be the last for thousands in this audience. It may bring twelve months of upheaval such as we have never witnessed; but one comfort we do have: through all the change and decay our eternal Rock of Ages, *"Jesus Christ, the same yesterday, and today, and forever,"* will remain unmoved amid the raging storms of mass-hatred and the turbulent tides of adversity. Cling to that Savior from the first days of the new year, you, the disciples of Christ! Come back to Him, you, the unfaithful, for whom His blessed mercy has plenteous grace! As Peter was strengthened after his denial, so you, too, may be recalled to a courageous discipleship. Come to this good God, the Fortress of faith, you, the indifferent, on whom the doom of God may even now be descending, but who have a period of grace in which to escape! Come and learn with what blessed hope and promise you can start the new year once you have Christ! Throughout this country thousands of pastors associated with us in this mission of the air are eager to help bring you and your home to the Savior. May we not have the privilege of sending one of these messengers of God to you, so that, with Christ in your family circle, your children baptized in the Christian faith, your household blessed by His presence, you may find in 1940 the joy and gladness in life you may never before have thought possible?

We ask no formal New Year's resolution of you, for we can well understand this personal confession by Samuel Johnson: "I have now spent fifty-five years in resolving, having, from the earliest time almost that I can remember, been forming schemes of a better life. I have done nothing. The need of doing, therefore, is pressing, since the time of doing is short. O God, grant me to resolve aright and to keep my resolutions, for Jesus Christ's sake!" Yet, my fellow-redeemed, we do ask you now, throughout the land, to give the next minute entirely to God, to stand or kneel before Christ as though He, the blessed Savior, were visibly in every room into which the marvels of the radio bring this message of His grace; and with hearts removed from all else but the endless, limitless love that brought Him to the cross for us, let us say: "O Lord Jesus, by Thy birth at Bethlehem, Thy death at Calvary, Thy resurrection at the open grave, we know that Thou art our good Lord, a Stronghold for us in every day of trouble. In Thy name, strengthening and sustaining above every name, we will begin and — if it be Thy will — end the new year. Help us by Thy Spirit every day to live this resolution in firmer faith and a life constantly guided by Thee! Amen, our God and gracious Savior, our mighty Fortress! Amen."

"O COME, LET US ADORE HIM!"

> *"And when they were come into the house, they saw the young Child with Mary, His mother, and fell down and worshiped Him: and when they had opened their treasures, they presented unto Him gifts: gold and frankincense and myrrh. And being warned of God in a dream that they should not return to Herod, they departed into their own country another way."* — Saint Matthew 2:11, 12.

Our God of Grace and Truth:

As once a gleaming star led distant seekers to the Christ-child, so may Thy Word and promise now lead us to worship Thy Son, the Savior of our souls! Enlighten us to know and believe, by the illuminating power of Thy Spirit, that Jesus was born to save us all, to remove sin, share our burden, lift each sorrow, and heal every wound! Teach us to trust the Savior with our whole hearts, as He offers every one of us, Jew and Gentile, rich and ragged, white and black, men and women of all colors, conditions, and classes, the full atonement in His blood, the free redemption by faith, and the final deliverance through His promised grace! Withhold from us whatever else Thy wisdom and love may decree, but, O Father of all mercy, give us persevering faith in Jesus! We ask it in His name and by His pledge! Amen.

DEEPLY thankful to God Almighty, we begin this afternoon with a report on the remarkable growth of this radio mission for Jesus. Six years ago we resumed our work of "Bringing Christ to the Nation" by using only two outlets (and, I confess, not without marked misgivings). In the succeeding five years station after station was added, until today, by the grace of God, about 140 cities throughout the United States broadcast our message.

But the best is yet to come. You will rejoice with

us when we announce that within the next weeks our Gospel radio system will be extended into foreign lands. Messages such as you hear Sunday after Sunday will be broadcast by Station HCJB, "The Voice of the Andes," in Ecuador, which will bring the hope of salvation in the crucified Savior to vast areas in South America as well as to islands in the South Pacific. At the same time our appeal will also be spread abroad through the Orient's largest station, KZRM in Manila, Philippine Islands, which will touch the interior of Southern China, Formosa, Japan, the Malay Peninsula, Cambodia, Cochin-China, Australia, New Zealand, Borneo, Sumatra, and many other hitherto inaccessible countries. I firmly believe that this is only the start. These weekly appeals for repentance and faith are now being translated into Spanish, and we hope under the continuance of God's guidance to link many places from Central America to Argentina in an international Gospel system.

For continued growth we urgently ask your prayers, your interest, your zeal, your financial help; for, unlike some religious broadcasts, which receive the facilities of other networks free of charge, we must pay for our chain programs at full station rates; and it costs immense sums to maintain and increase our mission of the air. The radio may be God's final gift for the proclamation of the eternal redemption in Christ. Who knows whether in these last, perilous days God Himself will give us a more powerful agency than the radio to tell men of every color, clime, and condition that Christ was born for them, lived for them, died on the cross for them, and rose again for their eternal salvation?

The glorious invitation that would bring all, regardless of national, racial, social differences, to Christ, is the theme on this Epiphany Sunday, with its mighty missionary challenge. For Epiphany, marking the visit of the Wise Men from the distant East and their homage to the Christ-child, asks us all:

"O COME, LET US ADORE HIM!"

And may God's Spirit so take possession of your hearts that you will follow these Magi, of whom we read in our text (Saint Matthew 2:11, 12): *"And when they were come into the house, they saw the young Child with Mary, His mother, and fell down and worshiped Him; and when they had opened their treasures, they presented unto Him gifts: gold and frankincense and myrrh. And being warned of God in a dream that they should not return to Herod, they departed into their own country another way."*

I

WORSHIP CHRIST DESPITE DIFFERENCES IN RACE AND NATIONALITY!

No one knows exactly who those Wise Men were, how many of them followed the gleam of Bethlehem's star, or from what Eastern land they came. One fact, however, is decisive. These travelers seeking the Christ-child were not Jews, born into the chosen race; they were Gentiles. It was widely expected even in heathen circles at this time that a mighty world-conquering ruler would arise in Judea, and it may be that the Magi had studied some of these startling auguries. More probably they had become acquainted with Old Testament predictions. Whether they did or not, God's plan of salvation provided that Christ, His Son, would be the Savior of all mankind, irrespective of language and ancestry; and this promise, foretold in dozens of prophetic foregleams, was fulfilled when these Oriental worshipers laid the tributes of their love at the Redeemer's feet.

What unbounded comfort for every one of us lies in the fact that Christ is the atonement for every sinner; that in His sight, as far as the human soul is concerned, there are no Negroes or white men, no native-born or foreign-born, no pure-blooded or mixed-blooded, no Aryans or Semites; but that all, whoever they are in the hundreds of racial groups, wherever they may live in this world's far-flung stretches, whatever language of the thousand different tongues and dialects they may speak, are on the same common level, the fallen children of God, whom Christ loved with such divine devotion that He was born as every man's Savior, lived and died as every man's Substitute, rose again to become every man's Resurrection and Life!

Read the Koran, and you find yourself in the Arabian Desert. Page through the Vedas, India's sacred books, more than a hundred in number, and you put yourself on the banks of the Ganges. Study the writings of Lao-tse, and you are restricted by Chinese horizons. Examine some of our modern cults, and you will discover that the United States marks the limit of their extent. Take the Bible, translated into more than a thousand languages; the Christian Church, with adherents on each of the five continents and the islands of the seven seas; the Christian creed with its glorious Gospel, *"God so loved the* WORLD *that He gave His only-begotten Son, that* WHOSOEVER *believeth in Him should not perish, but have everlasting life"*; read these blessed *"whosoever"* passages: *"Whosoever shall call upon the name of the Lord shall be saved"; "Whosoever believeth in Him"* [Jesus Christ] *"shall receive remission of sins"; "Whosoever believeth that Jesus is the Christ is born of God,"* and you have a creed, invitation, and appeal that attract the Eskimo and the Zulu, the head-hunter and the bushman, the English as well as the German — and have you noticed that the Bible is still the best seller in Germany, far outdistancing even *Mein Kampf?* How seldom we read that a normal American or European becomes a Mohammedan, a Confucianist, or a Hindu? Yet millions of the followers of Mohammed and Confucius and Buddha have turned to the Redeemer. For when any man believes that Jesus is the Savior of the world; that soon after His birth He was visited by the Magi, the representatives of the Gentiles; that on the cross, with its superscription in three languages, Jesus shed His blood for sinners and, since *"all have sinned and come short of the glory of God,"* for all humanity, — that man, saved by grace, knows that Christ, far from recognizing racial, national, or social barriers, offers the mercy bought by His blood without restriction to every man, woman, and child.

We hear much today of international understanding; but the League of Nations has failed, and have we any reason to suppose that the United States of Europe, which, some hope, will emerge from the war, will succeed? From Moscow Communism sends out its agitators to the workers of the world, asking for international uprising against the present order for the establishment of Soviet brotherhood; and masses in this country, as among the unemployed, poorer classes in other nations, listen with cupped ears to their lies and shameless falsehoods. Where has Communism ever raised sums comparable to the hundreds of millions of dollars Christians give to help benighted races, to heal the sick in body and in mind, to provide for the suffering poor at home and abroad? Workers of America, close your ears to the chants of Communism! Turn to Christ, who has proved Himself the divine Savior of all men, whose Spirit has helped ten thousands of missionaries sacrifice almost everything men regard as precious in their effort to bring eternal help and hope into the night of heathendom!

How tragic that the universal appeal of Christ's love is so frequently rejected! If only it were possible to stand in Europe's No-man's Land between the two lines of concrete, steel fortresses and proclaim, "Soldiers of France, Germany, Britain, why do you hate one another? Why do you lust for blood? Here is Jesus, the Lord of love, His divine soul filled to overflowing with compassion for all men; the Savior who gave Himself into the soul-crushing death of the cross for all the English, the Germans, the French, so that you, loving Him, might love one another! Come to Him! Fight for peace instead of war, for the salvation of souls instead of the slaughter of bodies!" The one effective method of taking millions of Europe's soldiers out of the trenches would be to fill the hearts of Europe's statesmen and their nations with the love of Christ. Never before have the churches of America been called on to preach the eternal mercies of Jesus as the Redeemer of the race with the emphasis this hour requires. In our own country diabolical forces attack Christianity as a creed reserved for a selected few. We must have more soul-saving activity among the foreign-language groups of the land; more missions for our colored citizens; more humble churches in the less attractive parts of the city; more contacts with the unemployed, the disheartened, the destitute; for our faith teaches, and the needs of this hour demand, a Christ who is the Savior of all mankind.

Before the radiance of Christmas recedes too far into the background of our lives, let me point you to the Magi on their knees before the Christ-child and tell every one that Jesus Christ is *your* Savior; that His blood was poured out for *your* ransom; that He rose again from the dead to give *you*, through faith, that righteousness which alone can justify the sinner before God; that the Savior, now glorified at the right hand of God, His Father, is making intercession for all men but particularly for *you*. If you can begin to fathom what an eternity of terrors means, kneel before the Christ-child, God incarnate, and adore Him as your Redeemer!

Crush every objection which says that your sins are too great; for His holy blood can cleanse the vilest iniquity, remove the most bestial crime. If you are almost too ashamed even to have your letters unburden the agony of your transgressions, believe that Jesus has atoned a thousandfold for you. Don't say that your sins are too small, that you need no Savior, since you "live right and act right," and when you die, God will pat you on the shoulder and offer heaven as a reward. If you are honest, you will not dare to lift up your eyes to God's holiness, but, overcome by the evil in your heart, on your lips, on your hands, you will bow your head before the Almighty, strike your breast, and gasp, "Father, be merciful to me, a sinner." And if the self-worshiping in this audience need to be humbled so that they can behold themselves as they really are, lost in sins, not as they think they are, models of perfection, then I pray that, as Saul was hurled down on the Damascus road they, too, may be sent prostrate on the path of life and learn that they must get right with God through Jesus Christ.

If you feel that Christ will not enter your house because yours is a humble home in the wrong part of the community, you do not know the Lord Jesus; for He is richest when you are poorest, strongest when you are weakest. And if you, the surfeited, self-satisfied rich, tell me that you do not need Him, that you have money, education, power, and an unshakable sense of security,

I ask, Have you the real security which will sustain you if in the next few days you are suddenly brought face to face with Almighty God? Have you peace and happiness with your money? Recently this letter came from a sixty-five-year-old widow in Philadelphia: "I have just finished my Christmas dinner of warmed-over spinach, made three days ago, some crumbs from old bread, some celery and onions mixed with the spinach. But how I thank God for that, and how appetizing the Lord made it taste! I was invited to a sumptuous Christmas dinner with dear friends, but I refused because I knew, that if I accepted, I could not hear your broadcast and not feel the presence of the Savior. How full of joy I am after hearing again that the Savior was born for me!" As you listen to this remarkable letter, think of thousands of wealthy American families which, despite their holiday wining and dining did not feel one small part of the happiness without Christ that this poor woman enjoyed with her Lord. Much more than the ragged, the rich sometimes need the Gospel of grace, since family trouble, self-trust, disregard of divine support, often crowd their lives. To them especially the Epiphany scene, with those Oriental men of means kneeling before the Christ-child and bestowing their royal gifts, *"gold and frankincense and myrrh,"* calls out, "O come, let us adore Him!"

II

WORSHIP CHRIST DESPITE THE CONTRADICTIONS OF LEARNING!

These Magi were scholars, scientists, among the highest intellects of that day. Since then mighty minds have shown similar reverence for Jesus. Today some scientists are atheists, pantheists, skeptics, who openly attack Christ and His saving Gospel. Last week the American Association for the Advancement of Science met in Columbus, Ohio, and if the invitation for this day, "O come, let us adore Him!" could have been extended to that gathering, many of those present would have refused to worship Christ. We may be equally certain, however, that many devout Christians in the numerous sections of these assemblies would have followed the Magi in bending their knees before Christ, their Savior and King. We are told that no modern mind can believe the Bible; but too often these objections are voiced by men who themselves do not know God and His Word. Out in Girard, Kansas, an infidel publisher, who blasphemously calls Jesus "crazy," recently showed again how he attacked the Scriptures without understanding what the Bible really says. In a deceptively advertised pamphlet he glorifies Huxley, particularly because of that skeptical scientist's motto, *"Prove all things; hold fast that which is good."* He implied that this maxim is out of harmony with our acceptance of Scripture. But he does not know enough of Holy Writ to recognize that the words *"Prove all things; hold fast that which is good"* are taken from the Bible itself.* High-school students, college men and women, who daily meet opposition to your creed, don't surrender your Christian faith! Teachers far greater than your instructors have had the mind of the Magi. Do you mention the name of a heavily headlined Chicago lawyer who scoffed at everything sacred? Then recall also that peer of American attorneys, Daniel Webster, who declared: "I believe Jesus Christ to be the Son of God! The miracles which He wrought establish, in my mind, His personal authority and render it proper for me to believe whatever He asserts. . . . And I believe there is no other way of salvation than through the merits of His atonement." If you know some scoffing doctor who likes to

---

* 1 Thess. 5:21.

say that man is only a high-grade animal and that death ends everything, think of physicians who never begin an operation unless they pray, many of them on their knees. If high-school teachers tell you that the Bible must be discarded, remind them of Sir Isaac Newton, universally conceded to be one of the world's most profound thinkers, who confessed: "We account the Scriptures of God to be the most sublime philosophy. I find more sure marks of authenticity in the Bible than in any profane history whatever." Or read this statement by the learned John Selden: "I have taken much pains to know everything that is esteemed worth knowing among men; but with all my reading, nothing now remains to comfort me at the close of this life but the passage of Saint Paul: *'This is a faithful saying and worthy of all acceptation that Christ Jesus came into the world to save sinners.'* To this I cleave, and herein do I find rest."

If some say that science and the Bible conflict, challenge them to explain why we should accept a theory that may be here now and gone tomorrow in preference to God's eternal and immovable truth. Demand that they show us which scientific opinion we must substitute for the Bible, the attitude of an American expert or of his European opponent! Ask them if science has ever made mistakes and if authorities have ever been wrong, and then ask yourself whether you want to entrust your soul, your own blood-bought soul, to a system that can be wrong!

Teachers of America, don't ever raise your voices to destroy the Christian faith in the hearts of your pupils! Read what the Scriptures say about the millstone and drowning in the deep sea. Above all, you who have the privilege of shaping the plastic minds of the rising generation in our public schools, don't bring antireligious remarks or suggestions into the lives of our boys and girls! For here not only the ordinances of God but even the law of the land prohibits you from attacking Christian faith. Oh, that with much of tomorrow's destiny, humanly speaking, in your hands, you would follow the long procession started by the Magi, since maintained by the highest minds and directed to bring you, the teachers, scientists, scholars of America, to the feet of Jesus!

III
WORSHIP CHRIST DESPITE ALL OPPOSITION!

Now these Magi came to worship Christ despite Herod's murderous intentions, and *"being warned of God in a dream,"* they refused to tell the envious monarch where the new-born King could be found. Obeying *"God rather than men,"* they took a different road back to their homeland.

We may well pause to study the policy of this Herod, miscalled "the Great." The man who murdered his own wife and children, slew his enemies in vast numbers, massacred the innocents at Bethlehem, herded his enemies into the arena at Jericho with the instruction that they be put to death the moment he breathed his last; Herod, who was soon to die of a horrifying, loathsome disease, whose body was to rot away as his soul went to hell — that fiend was the first ruler to interfere with the Christian Church and ruthlessly to cross the line separating the domains of Christ and Caesar. But he was not the last. Soon came the Roman rulers who condemned children and aged, helpless men and defenseless women, to torture and death because they were Christians! Hear the groans of 10,000 in France on Saint Bartholomew's night and through the ensuing massacres, as Charles IX continued his meddling in religion! Read the hideous catalog of those murdered in the Spanish Inquisition, more than 18,000 unfortunates burned alive during only the first chapter of this state tyranny! Try to visualize all the gallows on which official hangmen swung the victims of religious intolerance; the blocks on which state executioners cut off martyrs' heads; the stakes where public servants lighted the fires that were to consume faithful disciples; the religious wars in which hundreds of thousands were cut down in cold blood by royal regiments! Because all these deep and indescribable tragedies can be traced to the fact that the government wilfully denied its subjects the freedom of conscience, you will see why today we must whole-heartedly resist every intrusion of the state into our spiritual lives.

In the United States we should be ready to repel every State encroachment on our God-given liberties. There has been an unmistakable increase of governmental interference in our religious life. Not long ago a Secretary of Commerce overstepped his role to outline a church program. Among other things he stated that the churches should cooperate with law-enforcement agencies; develop the musical talents of young people, provide recreational facilities. The Church's one duty, however, is to preach the full Gospel of Jesus Christ, and no cabinet official can change that supreme commission. But more: He told the religious groups that they should forget their differences, get together, and establish national headquarters where leaders can be trained. Those who refuse to join in such a combination — and many of us want loyalty to the full Gospel rather than a new merger that agrees to disagree — those who cling with adamant allegiance to Christ, were denounced by the Secretary of Commerce as "causing men and women everywhere to despair . . . and in some cases to take their own lives." We submit to you that, when a high Government official makes suggestions to the pastors and openly attacks those religious bodies which do not agree with him, it may be, particularly in some hour of emergency, only a short step to Government direction and totalitarian control.

The time to resist these encroachments is in their beginning, and I appeal to all who love our Christian heritage and American liberties not to think lightly of this vital issue. That is why last Sunday I voiced the opinion of millions of my fellow-citizens and fellow-Christians in protesting against the establishment of diplomatic connection in any form whatever with a religious body. According to the Bible and American tradition, Church and State are to be rigidly separated. We hear much of Jeffersonian democracy today, but we ought to hear more of this Jeffersonian conviction, "I consider the Government of the United States as interdicted by the Constitution from intermeddling with religious institutions." Every statesman in this country should be guided by the absolute verdict of Christ Himself, *"Render to Cæsar the things that are Cæsar's and to God the things that are God's."* Blessing and prosperity have always followed the policy of keeping the secular and the spiritual completely separate. Why should we now forsake the old American and the Christian pathway? We all want the end of Europe's war, of course, but the same approach to peace can be made, as in the past, without allying our Government with any religious body.

This is a distasteful matter, and we would rather pass over a public issue of such scope in silence, were it not for the pivotal principles involved. We have been bitterly attacked in the daily and religious press for uttering what hundreds of thousands of you know to be an eminent American truth. May our heavenly Father give you who love Christ and His faith the interest, earnestness, and zeal to repulse, if necessary in an organized way, every assault, no matter how insignificant it may seem, on the complete separation of Church and State!

We have worked together shoulder to shoulder as citizens, Catholics and Protestants, with no Church officially preferred above another. Why must this change? Why must the stories of old hatred and bloodshed be revived? May every one of us today in our American homes think of Herod, the first ruler to interfere with the Gospel! As we hear the Epiphany appeal, "O come, let us adore Him!" may we, with the mind and the faith of these Far Eastern Wise Men, pray God that the American and the Christian heritage of free worship be safeguarded for us and our children!

Under the evangelical summons of Epiphany we lift up our eyes to behold hundreds of millions in the world about us perishing because they do not know the Lord Jesus. Rising to our feet from the adoration of our blessed Christ, the Son of God and Son of Man, let us go out not only with the mind of the Magi, but, having found Jesus, our King, approach those without Him, at home or abroad, through our personal testimony and the mighty power of the radio, asking, "O come, let us adore Him!" Continuing to bring Christ to this nation from coast to coast, we also resolve in His name, for the glory of His kingdom, the salvation of preciously bought souls, to bring Him to the world, from continent to continent! May He bless our zeal throughout eternity! Amen.

FIRST OF ALL —
CHRISTIAN EDUCATION!

*"The fear of the Lord is the beginning
of wisdom." — Psalm 111:10.*

Almighty and all-merciful God, our Father in Christ:

*Our prayers are raised to Thee, together with Thy Son and Thy
Holy Spirit, in behalf of this nation's youth. Guard the rising
generation during these perilous days, and if it be according to Thy
will and for our best, O God, keep our sons off the battle-fields of
Europe! Enlist them in Christ's service and for His holy warfare
against sin! Bless our homes with the Savior's presence and the
strengthening power of family worship! For His sake forgive us
all our sins, especially those committed against our youth, our failure
to give them Christian example, Christian training, and Christian
power! Bless all who hear these words with the sincere resolution
to acquire that wisdom which starts with the reverence of Thy
name and the love of the Savior! Come to us with Thy Spirit
and help us to build better homes, more consecrated churches, a more
godly nation! We ask it by our Redeemer's precious promise!
Amen.*

CRIME keeps marching on, and too often American colleges are the leaders in its procession. During the past
one week, for example, — and these were seven average
days, — campus criminals and academic lawbreakers, as
usual, made heavy head-lines. A University of Pittsburgh
senior held up a telegraph office and deliberately shot a
guard to death. A Harvard graduate, prominent athlete,
socialite, and industrialist, first fired a bullet into the head
of his dog and then blew his own brains out. A Dartmouth
College professor, an internationally known poet, closed the
doors of his garage, started his automobile, and took his life
by carbon monoxide. A University of Missouri junior died
under circumstances which made the coroner suggest sui-

cide, and a University of Michigan department head similarly plunged four stories to his death. A graduate of Fordham Law School was charged with embezzling large sums of money from a mentally incapable woman. A Yale graduate, head of a gigantic public utilities concern, paid an annual $60,000 salary, was threatened with Federal investigation on the charge of illegal political influence and tax evasion. Pictures were reprinted showing the former president of Louisiana University not in his academic robes but in a convict's striped garb, — a condemned fraud and thief. A University of Wisconsin graduate wrote a magazine article and, describing his own college experiences, brazenly declared: "Many of us got dead drunk about twice a week. . . . Free love on the campus was a familiar practice." — All this and much more in a single typical week!

American education has often failed in building character. Too frequently our schools have produced brain power but not moral power. They have specialized in graduating nimble-minded but not noble-minded students. Too often they have given information but no inspiration, cleverness but not cleanness.

Now, why this frequent failure? Why do some of our penitentiaries list enough college graduates to supply a teaching force for a moderate-sized college? Not because we have neglected education and refused to provide adequate funds for our schools. No other age and no other land has received as many hundreds of millions of dollars every year for public education. Nor are the modern teaching methods responsible for the crime wave. Too often, of course, the schools fail to equip youth for the opportunities and responsibilities of life, since frills and fads and fancies push solid learning aside; but the reason modern education has helped produce lists of criminals lies deeper. This appalling condition can be explained only by the fact that many American children and young people receive a daily schooling which is either unreligious, irreligious, antireligious, or even atheistic. We are training the mind, appealing to the senses but are too often perverting the spirit, heart, and soul.

Because no single issue is of more vital importance for this nation, its churches, and the world of tomorrow, we protest against the dangerous tendencies in our modern Christless culture and urge:

FIRST OF ALL — CHRISTIAN EDUCATION!

And for this appeal we find Scriptural endorsement in the words of Psalm 111, verse 10: *"The fear of the Lord is the beginning of wisdom."*

I

WHY WE NEED CHRISTIAN EDUCATION

This *"fear of the Lord"* which the psalmist mentions as *"the beginning of wisdom"* is no cringing terror. When we realize how deeply God loved us despite our unholiness and His complete holiness; when we know in positive assurance that God grants us forgiveness, free salvation, eternal life, not through a mere decree, but by accepting as the atonement for our sins the holy, precious blood of the Lord Jesus Christ; when our faith tells us that the almighty God swings the gate of heaven wide to welcome us, not if we come with any human admission price or the credentials of our own faulty righteousness, but if we approach trusting in the Savior's mercies; when we summarize these divine riches of grace in Christ, we cannot fear God with an animal, slavish terror. Indeed, it is the glory of our faith that *"perfect love casteth out fear."*

So when the text speaks of *"the fear of the Lord"* as *"the beginning of wisdom,"* this means the reverence of

God, the humble worship of the Almighty, the unreserved honor of a contrite heart confidently offered to the Lord Jesus. On such reverent fear of the Almighty as *"the beginning of wisdom"* we are to build the training of our children and young people in their search for wisdom. We are to bow down before the Lord in Jesus' name and say: "O God, mighty and magnificent beyond all measure and understanding, Thou art the Potter, and we are the clay. The truth is in Thee, but we behold error all around us, and therefore we will believe, accept, and teach nothing that contradicts Thy Word. Because we know that before Thee the stars and the planets and the gigantic bodies of the heavens are but as glittering dust strewn across the firmament; that the oceans, unfathomed and overwhelming to us, are to Thee but drops in an immeasurably vast universe; and that all the strength of men in Thy sight is but as the weakness of the worm to us, we bow submissively before Thy Word, knowing that 'heaven and earth shall pass away' before Thy Gospel passes away. If men's scientific claims ridicule Thy truth; if their evidence seems to contradict it, we know no wisdom except that which begins with the reverential awe of Thy majesty. And though we cannot always understand Thy ways nor explain the unnumbered mysteries that surround us, we repeat: We will believe, accept, and teach for ourselves and for our children, in the churches and the schools, nothing contrary to Thy Word and eternal revelation."

This fundamental principle of our faith that education must not be atheistic, skeptical, antichristian, but that real culture starts with Biblical truth, has been endorsed by great leaders whose names have made scientific history. The desire for Christian education has led to the establishment of our greatest universities, for example, Harvard, with its motto: "For Christ and the Church!"; Yale, with its seal recalling the high priest of the Old Testament; Princeton, with its love for Jesus that made John Witherspoon, its first president, formally declare: "Cursed be all learning that is contrary to the Cross of Christ! Cursed be all learning that is not coincident with the Cross of Christ! Cursed be all learning that is not subservient to the Cross of Christ!"; Wellesley, founded by a successful attorney, who, as a lay preacher of the Gospel of the Savior, devoted his fortune to establish a college for the Christian training of young women.

Each of these schools, however, as well as scores of other American colleges and universities, which were originally built by Christian founders, now employs teachers who deliberately reject the Bible, question or even deny the very existence of God. Indeed, the entire system of public education, to a greater or lesser degree, is similarly marked by indifference or hostility to the claims of Christ. Take the average American child and survey his educational career, — your own boys and girls, as they leave your homes every morning. They start at the kindergarten, but with all its commendable features, the public kindergarten cannot give your children Christian instruction, because a wise law prohibits crossing the line of demarcation between Church and State. So Hallowe'en comes, and the little tots cut out witches, ghosts, and skeletons; Thanksgiving comes, and they paste synthetic turkeys together; Christmas comes, and the teacher pictures on the blackboard a jolly Santa Claus squeezing through a brick chimney; Easter comes, and the children bring home papers pasted with pussy-willows and decorated with rabbits. But where, fathers and mothers of America, is the knowledge of the Savior, who declares: *"Suffer the little children to come unto Me and forbid them not, for of such is the kingdom of heaven"?*

In the grammar school these tots become lads and lassies; and not only does the Christless education continue, as it must, since we cannot use public funds for religious purposes, but as the child advances, he often faces a rejection of Biblical truth. That was my own experience. At home in Boston my father read the Bible to us night after night, and then on week-day mornings I went to a public school that bore the name of a great Puritan divine— to hear parts of the Bible truth rejected, to have the teacher say, for example, that millions of years ago this globe of ours was a fiery ball, which through successive ages cooled down, assumed the shape it now has, and accidentally produced life. The home teaching the Bible, the public school rejecting it! Do you know what that can do to plastic, suggestible young minds? Many of your children are subjected to the same conflict. Some of the text-books, purchased by public officials with public funds for public schools, openly picture the world as an accident instead of the masterpiece of divine creation and man as the product of evolution from the lower animals instead of the handiwork of God Almighty. These children come home from school in the afternoon and turn on the radio to hear an unbelievable array of juvenile broadcasts with criminals and gangsters. The few moments left before supper are devoted to the comic strips, which again show the details of lawbreaking and may leave an indelible imprint on their young lives. After supper, in how many homes is there not insistent begging for the price of a movie ticket? Even worse, how often is this wish not granted by parents who do not even know what the picture will be, yet who ought to know that sections of the motion-picture industry are rotten! And when that crowded, emotion-filled day is over and the youngster tumbles into bed, sometimes too tired to say his prayers, if he knows any, how has Jesus Christ found opportunity to purify that young heart, to strengthen that young mind, to build that young life with spiritual power and glory?

Then follow the high school years of adolescence, when questions of sex begin to assume absorbing interest, the practical every-day dangers of Christless or antichristian culture become evident. I certainly do not want to be a pessimist or indulge in that easy but often unwarranted comparison with "the good old days"; but I have received altogether too many letters from distracted parents, and this nation has been rocked by too many high-school scandals for the Church to maintain silence. Now don't concentrate the blame on these young people. Our age has made it easy and safe for them to reject entirely the Scriptural command *"Keep thyself pure!"* by encouraging the birth-control industry and its clutching grasp for profit. We have put the worst books and magazines within easy reach of these young people. A false example of their elders has often made them think lightly of profanity and regard gin, highballs, cocktails, as fashionable. Yet how little is done to bring the renewing, strengthening power of Jesus Christ into their lives! We have more than forty different periods broadcasting dance music on an average night here in Saint Louis, and if it were not for the station from which I speak to you now, our Gospel Voice, there might not be a single religious broadcast here and particularly no young people's message.

When the college years come, — and more than a million and a quarter of our young people are college students, — the antichristian influences reach their climax. Some teachers serve notice right at the outset of their courses that the students must "park" their religion outside the classroom. If they do not insist that there is no God, many are unwilling to go farther than to concede that there may be one. They teach that man is just another animal. He has no immortal soul. His religion is superstition. His language, the "bow-wow," "pooh-pooh," "ding-dong" theories are said to prove, is evolved from animal sounds and grunts. Everything in life is ruled by chance. No hereafter awaits man, for he dies like the beast that he is. What all this means for daily life may be seen in a recent article entitled "Bohemia on the Campus," the confession of a Madison, Wisconsin, student. That ought to make every Christian parent examine the moral conditions at any college to which he entrusts his children. The tragedy of American higher learning is this, that with millions of dollars devoted to athletic programs for the body, hundreds of millions endowed for the advancement of the mind, our present-day culture has not only left the soul untouched but has often alined itself against the cause of Christianity.

Who can measure the startling results? Voices outside the Church are constantly raised charging that the schools have given room to un-American, radical Red movements and are become hotbeds of immorality. Now, I am not here to discuss issues of Americanism and chastity, but I am before this microphone to say with all the power God gives me that antichristian education will help send many souls to hell unless there is a reawakening to the truth of our text that *"the fear of the Lord is the beginning of wisdom."* As a consequence of this soul ignorance, which now extends its handicap to the third generation in the United States, almost 75 per cent of the country's population do not attend church on an average Sunday. Since at least three of every four children are growing up without adequate religious instruction (although some churches devote more time to the religious instruction in their foreign mission fields than to American youth), we ought to realize now that for the salvation of the souls of America's youth, for the continued blessing upon our land, and for the upbuilding of the truly Christian churches we must have — and, O God, grant this to us! — Christian training and Christian schools, Christ-exalting education, and Christ-centered colleges. We must realize personally that *"the fear of the Lord"* — the reverence for God the Father as our Creator, the love of God the Son as our Redeemer, the praise of the Holy Spirit as our Sanctifier, the acceptance of the divine Word, the trust in the divine truth — *"is the beginning of wisdom"* and also its glorious end.

II

HOW WE MAINTAIN CHRISTIAN EDUCATION

How, you may ask, can we help to promote this training that starts with the fear and the love of God? We can do very little unless we ourselves revere our heavenly Father and love the Savior. It is therefore doubly important that you fathers and mothers come to Christ; for remember, your unbelief not only helps keep you from the greatest blessing God Himself can give you, but your bad example may be a fatal stumbling-block to your own children. Even if heaven or hell were not involved for *you,* I would still plead: Accept Christ so that He can help you strengthen your children through Christian faith and saving knowledge.

When Christ is yours, you must become an advocate of Christian education. I have already explained that we do not ask for religious instruction in the public schools. On the other hand, as Christian citizens we should help build our public schools. Especially must we insist, however, that no institution supported by public tax money tolerate an antichristian teaching. If your children come home with books that contain pictorial and printed attacks on the Bible, go first of all to the teacher, then to the principal, the school board, and, if still necessary, to higher authorities and demand that such un-American activities be discontinued immediately.

The churches, particularly, must lay new emphasis on Christian culture. With all due respect to the Sunday-schools and with my thanks to those of you in this audience who are Sunday-school teachers, let me say that to strengthen the immortal souls of our youth we need more than the brief Sunday-school hour. Every year we call attention to the Christian day-schools, thousands of them from coast to coast, maintained by my Church. Let me summarize for you a typical day in one of these schools. First of all, the children start the morning with reverent hymns, prayers, and the confession of their faith. Next their teachers, about 85 per cent of them men and 15 per cent women, who have been trained at Christian normal schools, employ the first and best hour of the day to instruct them thoroughly and systematically in the Word of God, in Bible History, in the Christian doctrine according to Luther's Small Catechism, in the Bible itself. Gems from Holy Scripture, Christian hymnology, and other materials are committed to memory as a lasting treasure. Then follows the instruction in the common school branches, reading, arithmetic, history, and the rest; and a thorough instruction it is, equal in efficiency to that of any other school, often superior because of the children's character. It never places a question-mark behind the Word of God but always stresses the joy and truth in our Christian faith and the application of the Christian and Biblical viewpoint to secular affairs. When the classes are over, hymns and prayers close a school-day in which instruction was supported by a consistent Christian school discipline. This Church-controlled education is receiving wide recognition and unexpected support in many Protestant circles. We believe it to be the hope of America. Don't you, too, honestly think that the child thus trained, with the love of Christ in his heart and the reverence of God in his mind, is best prepared for the struggle of life? Even if you are not ready to answer, it can be demonstrated statistically that children with this training do not frequent the courts of juvenile delinquency.

We extend a personal invitation to you: These schools, more than 1,300 of them, are open to your children, in practically all cases free of charge. They may not in every instance have large and pretentious buildings, but they are splendid schools when measured by their educational achievement and particularly by the spiritual power they radiate. Give your children the greatest blessing of life! *"Come thou with us, and we will do thee good!"*

Likewise open to your sons and daughters are Christian colleges, founded for the specific purpose of affording to our young people a cultural training free from all attacks on their faith. A college of this kind, which I mention particularly since I am intimately acquainted with its work, is Valparaiso University in Indiana. Fully accredited, it offers a thorough academic training; but it offers more: the environment of Christian young people, classroom instruction that never questions God's Word, instructors who bow submissively before the eternal truth. Again, this school and many other Christian colleges may not have the legislative endowments that State universities enjoy, but the heart of a real, character-building university is the Christian faith of its leaders, the Christian work of its instructors, the Christian spirit of its students.

Remember, however, that the Church with its schools and colleges cannot fight the battle alone. This education that starts with *"the fear of the Lord"* — and now pay close attention — must come also from the home. In the family life that has promise for the future and that, in turn, will receive divine guidance, father and mother should both be devoted followers of Christ. So we have prayed God repeatedly that He would bless this broadcast for many homes by crystallizing in your hearts the resolution now to give yourselves to Jesus for time and eternity. Nothing else that you can ever do, all the money you bequeath to your children, can ever mean as much to them as the realization that you lived and died in the Lord. In the truly blessed home husband and wife will be of one faith, and the true faith. No house divided against itself, no tragedy of a husband worshiping in one church and his wife in another, until indifference creeps in, and when children come, they often attend no church at all! I wish that every broadcasting chain in our country would give us a half hour each week to show the spiritual danger, not to mention the unhappiness, that often follows these mixed marriages. Few other appeals can be as definitely in keeping with this objective of all broadcasting, "the public interest, convenience, and necessity." In the home that will build the Church and the nation the father must have time and love and interest to teach his own children the truths of our faith. Men like to push these responsibilities on the mothers' shoulders, but God holds you husbands primarily responsible. And if you are Christ's, you ought to be the spiritual heads of the home. How terrifying this must seem to some of you men in this audience when, instead of bringing your children to Christ, you realize that your repeated sins are helping to keep your own flesh and blood away from the Savior! What a terrible thought it must be for you to know that on the day of Judgment God Himself will charge the souls of your children to your account! I must speak plainly because some of you may never hear me again; and if deep in your heart a voice pleads: "Oh, get right with God now!"; if you want forgiveness and pardon for the distress and sorrow of every sin; if you really love your children and want to stand with them on that Great Day face to face with Jesus to say: *"Behold, I and the children which God hath given me!"* then come before God now in Jesus' name! Let us send a pastor to help direct and guide you! Let us send you Christian literature, anything you may need to help make your home what it should be, a church of the living God, a school for the spiritual instruction of your children!

You mothers, to whom God has given more power for the establishment of a better tomorrow than He has to many legislators, what a blessed privilege you have in promoting Christian education! We know that the endless workaday duties in many of your homes hardly leave some of you exhausted mothers the time and thought required to watch over the souls of your children. But let Christ help you! Let prayers sustain you! Let faith fortify you! When a busy mother who has been remarkably successful in bringing up her children was asked for the secret of her success, she answered: "While my children were infants upon my lap, as I washed them, I raised my heart to God that He would wash them in the blood that cleanses from all sin. As I clothed them in the morning, I asked my heavenly Father to clothe them with the robe of Christ's righteousness. As I provided them food, I prayed that God would feed their souls with the bread from heaven and give them to drink of the Water of Life. When I prepared them for the house of God, I pleaded that their bodies might be fit temples for the Holy Ghost. When they left me for week-day school, I followed their infant foot-steps with the prayer that their path through life might be like that of the just, which shineth more and more unto the perfect day. And as I committed them to rest for the night, the silent breathing of my soul has been that the heavenly Father would take them to His embrace." Mothers of America, push everything else aside that keeps you from devoting your time, your prayers, your love, to the eternal welfare of your own children! *"Learn first to show piety at home,"* Saint Paul told certain women of his day; and in that spirit we repeat: If anything takes your attention away from your children; if it be pleasure or recreation, business or social obligations, women's clubs or political meetings, charity collections or relief drives, even certain forms of church work itself, drop it all and with God's help give your children the wisdom that starts with *"the fear of the Lord"* and leads to His everlasting adoration in heaven!

Sometimes we hear parents complain about the cost of rearing their children. You say: "My son cost me $200 in doctor's bills last year." "My daughter cost me more than $1,000 during her first year at college." But you forget what your sons and daughters, even as you and I, cost the Lord Jesus: that never-to-be-fathomed suffering, that seeming eternity of anguish, that God-forsakenness on the cross. Now, if Christ so loved your child, will you not help your child to come to the Savior?

God grant that all of you may have Christ in your homes, Christ in the lives of fathers and mothers, Christ in the obedience and love of the children, Christ as the eternal, never-failing, all-glorious Savior for the entire family — and with Him heavenly wisdom, power, and blessing! Amen!

THE ONE WAY TO HEAVEN

*"I am the Way, the Truth, and the
Life; no man cometh unto the Father
but by Me."* — Saint John 14:6.

Cleansing, strengthening Spirit of God:

We *are weak and sinful, but Thou art holy and almighty. Give
us, then, a trusting faith in the Lord Jesus, our sin-atoning Savior,
and help us through daily contrition and sincere faith to come ever
closer to Christ, the Way, the Truth, and the Life, without whom
we cannot approach the Father! Strengthen us to show the spirit
of the Savior's mercy in our love toward all suffering fellow-men!
Make us humble and Christlike in word and action, outspoken in
our testimony to the Cross, courageous — through Jesus — even
in the darkened hours of affliction! Use these broadcasts toward
convicting many of their sins, bringing them to Christ, and keeping
them — with us — in the faith forever! We ask it in Jesus' name.
Amen.*

DO you know what it would mean to lose your way
in a desolate country during the bitter cold that for
days has swept our nation? "How terrifying," you declare,
"to stagger blindly against the icy gale and face death in
forsaken horror!" Yet that tragedy has been repeatedly
enacted within the last weeks. Soviet troops marching
against screaming blizzards frequently lose their road,
wander in circles for a few hours in that fifty-four-degree-
below-zero cold and then collapse in fatal drowsiness.
Frozen death grips them so rigidly that their fingers fall
off when enemy scouts take the rifles from their icy grasp.

Yet many of you in the warmth and comfort of your
homes can lose the way and meet disaster incalculably
greater than the anguish of exposure. You have a soul
that will live after the body dies. There is a hereafter

in which you will be eternally blessed or eternally rejected. You must face a judgment in which you will be either acquitted or condemned. With no intermediary stage known to the Bible and no second chance after death, since the Scriptures clearly warn, *"It is appointed unto man once to die, but after this the Judgment,"* every one of us — and who you are or what you think you are makes no difference — is even now on the road to heaven or — may God forbid! — to hell. And terrifying beyond all measure it is to lose the way to a blessed eternity.

Too often men think lightly of heaven. A recent political gathering in Washington rocked with laughter when one of the speakers, a high authority in this nation, told a joke which had a celestial scene as its background. The public is so accustomed to this procedure on the stage, the screen, the radio, and in the press, that there was no protest whatever. Personally we feel that with all the crooked practices which mark American political life today, it comes with doubly ill grace when the sacred truths of our Christian faith are used to produce derisive laughter at $100-a-plate party dinners. Heaven is no joke. Neither is hell!

People like to postpone thoughts of the hereafter; but how suddenly they often face their Maker! Last Monday the veteran member of the United States Senate went to his physician for an examination. "You're as sound as a dollar," the specialist declared; but within less than twenty-four hours that widely respected statesman slipped, struck his head, and sank into a coma from which he never awoke. With the same swiftness eternity can approach you. What guarantee have you and I that tomorrow we may still be numbered among the living?

If you have not heard a Christian broadcast before,

listen to this message now; for in your whole life you have never been addressed on any subject more important to you individually than that which I now direct to you in the name of Christ Himself. Think of these words not as being broadcast over a huge system of 145 different stations, with uncounted multitudes tuned in, but as an appeal especially to you, because your salvation is of such tremendous importance that God Almighty is concentrating His pleading love on your soul. Here is the truth for which many of you, I hope, will thank God in eternity,

THE ONE WAY TO HEAVEN

as outlined by the Savior Himself in the deathless words of Saint John 14:6, *"I am the Way, the Truth, and the Life; no man cometh unto the Father but by Me."*

I

JESUS TEACHES THAT THERE IS A HEAVEN

When Christ on the last night of His earthly life here speaks of going *"unto the Father"* and, only a few hours before His death, promises *"life,"* He, the holy, perfect Son of God, teaches that existence does not stop with the grave; that as He, after the blackest of deaths on Calvary, rose again and returned to His Father, so we, too, rising from the grave, can follow Jesus to heaven.

Unbelief has ridiculed this promise as it has attacked every pledge of Christ's mercy. They tell us that a man dies just as a dog, a horse, a cow, or any other animal dies; that his flesh and bones, rotting away, finally become dust and nothing more. Heaven? A blessed hereafter? A glorious eternity? "Why," they answer with undisguised scorn, "tell it to the children. The only heaven men will ever get is the one they make for themselves on earth."

"We want our pie now," the Communist sneers, "not by and by up in the sky." Yet have you ever noticed how quickly this bubble is pricked? Volney was one of Europe's loudest scoffers. But once on a journey his ship was overtaken by a heavy storm, and he ran about shrieking, "O my God, O my God, what shall I do?" When the tempest subsided, he was so ashamed of himself that for the rest of the voyage he hid from the passengers who had heard his braggart blasphemies. His fellow-countryman Mirabeau boasted that there would be nothing craven about his death; he even wrote these instructions for his last moments: "Crown me with flowers; intoxicate me with perfume; let me die to the sound of delicious music." Yet when he actually faced death, he gasped, "I have within me a hundred years of life, but not a moment's courage!" Cringing coward that he was, he demanded, not flowers, perfume, music, but a dose of opium, and under the stupor of that narcotic he died. Last week a gruesome book was published — the life story of a man employed by Sing Sing to pull the electric-chair switch. Again and again, he reveals, when condemned criminals leave the death cell and face the chair, they are terrorized into silence by the presence of death, no matter how unconcerned and godless they may have been before.

If you, rejecting Jesus' promise of *"life"* and a return *"unto the Father,"* have not been impressed by the fact that unbelief fails in the greatest emergency of human experience, the hour of death, then remember that denial exposes its weakness under every burden. What comfort can the afflicted and sorrow-weighted have in a world that offers no compensation for the future? Some of you have been helplessly sick during twenty, thirty, and even more years. How desperate you would be if all we could say through this microphone would be: "Well, you won't have to suffer much longer. When death comes, everything ends"! One out of six of you, on the average, lives by federal aid grants; and you would find little sustaining power in the thought that because life is unfair, fate blind, destiny cruel, death with its annihilation will stop your troubles since it destroys you forever. You, felled by the body-blows of adversity, staggering under the impact of new sorrows, do not want death to end it all. You ask for a new life that can compensate for earth's sorrows and offset your sufferings. The promise that makes life with its unfairness and cruelties bearable for multitudes who exist only through Government support — and last week we were officially told that their number is now more than 20,000,000 — the assurance which prevents this world from becoming a complete madhouse, is the teaching of Jesus that there is a future existence, a blessed eternity, with the Father. Tear that out of human hearts — and we have too many among our modern writers, scientists, and teachers who would do just this — and you have kicked the crutches from the arms of a crippled race. If you want this world to show evidence of international dementia in comparison with which the present bloodshed and hatred are only trivial annoyances; if you wish to witness the collapse of all that still makes life worth living and have every man live ruthlessly, frantically pursue forbidden lusts, and selfishly gratify bestial desires; if you are eager to see the collapse of civilization and a reign of black terror such as not even the most degenerate ages of modern history have known, then spread the damnable delusion that there is no hereafter, no heaven or hell, no eternal judgment seat before which you must appear!

I hope that none of you questions this future blessed existence when Jesus Himself strongly testifies to its truth. Is our God who created us when our life started not powerful enough to recreate us when life ends? At a Rockefeller Institute laboratory in New York City you can see in a test tube the segment of a chicken's heart which Dr. Alexis Carrel has kept alive for twenty-seven years and which he hopes to maintain indefinitely. Now, if a scientist can extend the existence of chicken tissue to three times its normal length, cannot God Almighty, whose laboratory is the universe and whose test-tubes the mighty oceans, stretch the span of our existence far beyond everything we know? We see much of God's omnipotence; yet even more is concealed from our knowledge. We look to the heavens and see Sirius, one of the nearest fixed stars, and it seems very bright; but when Sir William Herschel beheld it with his great telescope, he reported that it appeared as a gigantic mass much larger than the Sun, and lit up the whole surrounding heavens with a splendor so brilliant that Herschel had to protect his eyes with a colored glass. Now, do you not think that the Creator, who spoke one word and all these overpowering heavenly bodies came into instantaneous existence, has the power to give us life after death? Even if you do not agree, here is Christ's promise of *"life"* and a return *"unto the Father"*! Here is Christ's power to keep His promise, His miraculous resurrecting of the widow's son at Nain, the young maid at Capernaum, and Lazarus, His friend, at Bethany. Here is Jesus' own Easter Day example, His breaking the seal on the guarded rock-hewn grave.

Instead of arguing about heaven, let us try to picture its magnificence! But in this effort human thought fails and men's words lose their power. The glory Christ has won for us is beyond description, beyond comparison, beyond imagination. Its splendor cannot be measured or even estimated. We can only peer through the heavenly gates left slightly ajar by the writers of Sacred Scripture and exclaim, "What unspeakable radiance!" When Dr. Kane, polar explorer, was close to the north pole, he wrote: "The intense beauty of the Arctic firmament can hardly be imagined, . . . with its stars magnified in glory. I am afraid to speak of some of the night scenes." If God made such glory on earth, what must the splendor of heaven be? If He gives the brilliance of beauty here below, even to His enemies, what magnificence awaits His redeemed above in the hereafter? May this be a source of unfailing comfort to you, our friends who, but for your faith in Christ, have little of loveliness and beauty in life, as day after day you see sordid, ugly sins!

Think of the peace in that Paradise, with all the differences removed which array men against one another, send armies into the trenches, and fill human hearts with black hatred! On earth we have no lasting peace. But in heaven ours shall be a never-broken, never-weakened, never-ending peace with all, regardless of race or religion, who have worshiped the Lord Jesus Christ as their only Savior, joined in complete harmony! What an anchor of hope for those who continually face hatred, even in their family circles!

What can I say of the enraptured joy? Take the supreme happiness that can come into any Christian life; multiply it as much as you will or can, and you are still far from the eternal pleasure at God's right hand. No grief or graves, no hearses or cemeteries, no blistering heat, or freezing cold, no hunger or thirst, no falling sick or growing old, no terror for the past or fears of the future! Only perfect joy and full bliss Christ offers in the prepared mansions.

Heaven will also marvelously strengthen our knowledge! "*Now*," we say with the apostle, "*we see through a glass, darkly, but then face to face; now I know in part, but then I shall know even as also I am known."* In that brighter light much before which our limited reason balks will be explained and understood. We will know how fully God has kept His promises and how truly all things have worked together for good to us who love God. There in that superior knowledge, life's afflictions will appear in their true nature, as evidences of divine grace. Take comfort in that, you of God's children who stand before unsolved mysteries and wonder why God's ways often seem to take you down to the deepest depths. Some day through Christ you will understand and praise God's all-knowing mercy.

Particularly blissful will be the associations of heaven. The poet Southey liked to say that he anticipated eternity because he there hoped to converse with Dante, Chaucer, Shakespeare, and other great men of letters. While most of us look forward to the presence of the saints and the mighty Christian heroes, we think especially of the reunion with our loved ones who have preceded us in the faith. What rejoicing there when orphans are brought together with their parents, widows united with their husbands! Let this be the balm of healing for the deep wounds of bereavement!

Above all, however, heaven offers one supreme privilege — the unutterable glory of beholding Jesus face to face. To worship the everlasting God in His majesty; to bow before the redeeming Christ as His lips speak wondrous words of truth and power; to acclaim the Holy Spirit our God and direct our praise to His enlightening love — that adoration which even now forms the highest occupation of God's holy angels will be the supreme radiance of the New Jerusalem, the ever sacred truth that has made the Church of the ages joyfully confess, "I believe in the resurrection of the body and the life everlasting."

II

JESUS TEACHES THAT HE IS THE TRUE AND ONLY WAY TO HEAVEN

God's mercy is not exhausted by the marvelous promise that there is a heaven; Jesus plainly shows the way to glory. From the very earliest days of the race, men have sought the pathway to a blessed eternity. One of the world's first great poems, recorded on Mesopotamian clay, tells of a legendary hero who tied immense stones to his feet, descended far into the ocean's depths, and there in a submarine garden found the magical plant that reputedly could bestow everlasting life. But when he brought the plant to shore and knelt beside a spring to drink, a snake slithered out of the grass and devoured the plant before his eyes. Since those early days, men have similarly gone to depths and heights to find assurance for the hereafter; but as in the case of the Babylonian seeker, it has always escaped their grasp. Towering eternally over these failures is the divine promise of Jesus Himself in our text, *"I am the Way";* in four one-syllable words He tells His disciples, simple working-men from the laboring classes, what mighty minds have often sought in vain: To escape eternal death and find the path to Paradise, men must trust not in themselves and their own ability to discover the road to redemption; they must rely not on their fellow-men, not even the most godly, learned, and powerful; they must come to Christ, hear Him say, *"I am the Way,"* and trust Him with all their heart.

To understand how Jesus can be the Road from earth to heaven, the Bridge from death to life, we must believe that He broke the power of sin which separated us from God; the evil in our hearts and lives that pays its wages in death; the transgressions responsible for every casket, funeral, and cemetery; the wrong inherent in us from our birth and increased in us during our lives; the iniquity that sends every one of us, with a sweep that knows no exception, down to the decay of the grave. That sin — and once again we stand before the glorious climax of our Christian faith — Jesus took from us. It was ours in its complete hideousness and destruction, but it became His when on the cross He, as the Lamb of God, took away the world's sin, removed our guilt forever, washed and purified us in His blood, so that in God's sight we have no sin. With our iniquities canceled, our pardon sealed, the broken Law fulfilled for us, Christ's atonement accepted for our transgressions, we can have life — eternal, blessed life through Him!

What immeasurable love God has shown us in making Christ the Way! Do you know what it cost the Lord to have His Son, Jesus, substitute for a world of sinners? Out in Kansas a father unknowingly ran over and killed his own son, who had been coasting; but there was nothing accidental about God's love for us in Christ. It had been decreed before the foundations of the world. Across the water millions of parents are forced to send their sons to the battle-fields, where thousands are destined to die for their country; but our heavenly Father was not forced to give Christ into death. It was pure, unconstrained love that sent Jesus to the cross. God loved us, every one of us, with such devotion, and so intensely desired that we should be with Him in glory, that He sent His Only-begotten to blood-marked Calvary in our stead.

Now, if Christ, as our Road, would direct us to His homeland along the hardest paths man has ever trod, we would still sing His praise. If His highway to heaven meant fighting snows higher than the Himalayas or dragging ourselves across the heat and blister of deserts far wider than the Sahara, cutting our paths step by step through swamps and jungles a thousand times more impenetrable than the Upper Amazon Valley, we would still thank him eternally. But — praise be to His ever-blessed name! — He made the road for us, filled up the deadly ravines, tore down the impassable heights, and gave us the smooth-flowing highway of faith to His Father's arms. You, the disquieted of spirit, who continually ask yourselves, "How can I earn my way to heaven?" believe that Jesus is the entire Way. Your salvation is not partly His mercy and partly your work; every inch of the trail from time to eternity has been made and blazed by the Savior Himself, your all-sufficient Redeemer, your complete Atonement.

Christ's pathway to heaven is never uncertain; you have a guide-book to explain the road — the sacred, error-less Scriptures. When John Jay, first Chief Justice of our Supreme Court, was brought down on his death-bed, he was urged to tell his children from what source he drew his remarkable consolation for the last hours. His reply was brief, "They have the Book!" You, too, have the Book; but how often do you read it? Many of you are experienced travelers and know the shortest and best auto highways from one part of the country to the other; but before God I ask you, "Do you know the most important road of all, the way to heaven?" Thousands of you fathers and mothers do not find time to study Christ's road in your own homes and with your own children. The church historian Eusebius records that one of the early Christians whose eyes had been burned out during the persecutions by Diocletian repeated the Holy Scriptures from memory before a large assembly. Bereft of his sight, he could see more than many of you can with open eyes. Read the Bible; believe it; make it yours in mind and soul, and that Book will bless you forever!

This appeal becomes the more necessary when we realize that today wilful men are building byways that lead away from this royal highway. See how even churches, sometimes unconsciously, sometimes wilfully, are coaxing people off the road to redemption on to the side lanes. We have a current copy of a Christian young people's magazine in which much is said about vocational guidance, race relations, international peace, labor conditions, and a dozen other timely questions, but in which there is not a single clear pronouncement in answer to the query, "Where is the road to heaven?" The first question for the modern pulpit to answer is, "What must I do to be saved?" not, "What must I do to save democracy?" Too many of our churches have side-tracked the ministry to the soul and the search for heaven in favor of social discussions. Preachers have always failed when they turned politicians, and the churches have always sacrificed their vital influence when they substituted popular catch phrases for the eternal promises of Christ's Gospel. At a time when spiritual ignorance prevails among the masses, including particularly our children, as the President of the United States recently emphasized, when even church-members cannot give a clear, straightforward definition of the Christian faith, our activities must concentrate on helping to save men's souls. The fundamental question which ultimately confronts every person is, "What happens to me when I die?" The church which fails to offer the positive hope given by Christ in the Scriptures will eventually destroy itself. In directing men to Jesus Christ as *"the Resurrection and the Life,"* we have the pledge of continued blessing.

As if in protest to the modern attacks on Christianity, Jesus pointedly says, *"I am the Way, the Truth, and the Life; no man cometh unto the Father but by Me."* Rebuk-

ing those who claim that the Christian, the Jew, the Ethical
Culturist, the Mohammedan, the Brahman, the Confucianist, are all bound for heaven and that these various
creeds are merely taking different roads to the same goal,
Jesus says, "There is only one way, and *'I am the Way!'*"
Christianity is not just another religion; it is *the* religion;
not one of many creeds, but the one true creed.   Since the
Bible specifically warns, *"Other foundation can no man
lay than that is laid, which is Jesus Christ";* since the
Scriptures declare, *"There is none other name under heaven
given among men whereby we must be saved"* but the name
of Jesus Christ, and our text emphatically says, *"No man
cometh unto the Father but by Me,"* neither you nor I nor
any one else should say that there are many ways to
heaven.

If we had two-way radio communications now, many
of you would raise charges of bigotry and of a narrow
creed.   But can the truth ever be bigoted and narrow?
When a competent physician says there is one way to cure
a disease, do you object and say: "O Doctor, why be so
narrow?   There must be a dozen ways!"?   If a specialist
for malaria says that medical science knows one cure for
that disease, quinine and its derivatives; when an expert
on rabies pointblank maintains that the medical world
knows no other help for infection from a mad dog than
the antirabies vaccine, do you not accept this, as most
people do?   Why, then, listen to religious quacks when
Jesus Christ, the Good Physician, has given the one
remedy that can heal us from our iniquities?   If you
were steering a ship through the North Sea and the charted
route showed a single path free from enemy mines, would
you say, "Oh, let's take a chance; let's try another
course"?   Why, then, are you ready to risk your eternal
destiny by neglecting and forsaking Christ's truths?   Sup-

pose you were a general and your troops were surrounded by the enemy; if your maps showed one and only one way of escape, would you sacrifice the lives of your men by going in an opposite direction? Why, then, in the battle of life do you run contrary to Christ?

Instead of charging the Christian creed with bigotry, thank God that for your soul's salvation you do not have to worry which road is the right road. Christ shows you the way today, and His assertion that He is *"the Truth"* has been proved in the hearts and lives of so many millions that we plead with you in His stead to take the Christ road to glory. You can always tell His way by the cross. When Von Humboldt traveled through tropical America, journeying by night to avoid the day's heat, his guides directed their course by the stars in the well-known Southern Cross. Frequently, he records, when wearied during a long night of travel, they would look up to that starry cross and cry, "Courage, comrades! The cross begins to bend." They thought that the constellation was beckoning to them. In the dark and hard-fought journeys of your life, your eyes of faith can behold Him who died on the cross as He seeks to bend more closely to you and say: "Take courage, My child, for this pathway of the cross is the right road, the true road, the only road."

Fellow-sinners, take that road today! Start now! Tomorrow may be too late! God help you for Jesus' sake! Amen.

GOD WILL PROVIDE!

*"My God shall supply all your needs
according to His riches in glory by
Christ Jesus."* — Philippians 4:19.

Christ, Thou Lord of Life and Death:

*Help us through constant repentance and purer faith to trust Thee
with the firm reliance that casts our cares on Thy mercy! Strengthen
us, especially in the dark hour of every affliction, with the assurance
that, if we ask the Father in Thy holy, redeeming name, He will
supply all our needs! By Thy Spirit put this faith into burdened
hearts and sorrow-swept lives! Prove Thyself the Helper of those
who suffer by war, the heavenly Physician for the victims of
scourges and diseases, the Provider for the destitute masses in our
country, the Friend of all the friendless! Hear us and bless us,
Savior of our souls, as Thou hast promised! Amen.*

DURING the World War I was asked to hold services
for enemy sailors in the Massachusetts War Prison
Camp. When I arrived at the prisoners' quarters, an unmistakable hostility could be felt immediately. None of
the men in the entire stockade appeared at the appointed
hour of worship. Instead, they shouted that they would
have no contact whatever with American churches. Had
they not been under guard, I might have been thrown out
bodily, so deep-rooted was their antagonism. Later, when
the Lord granted calmer moments, the sailors explained
their angry resentment by producing a scrap-book of clip-
pings, many of them hymns of hatred written by American
ministers. One of these inflammatory clerical utterances
I shall never forget. It ran something like this: "After
God had made the snakes, the toads, the worms, and the
slimy creatures, a little oozy mud was left; and out of that
He made the German people."

Can you not see how that preacher helped to keep these

men from Christ? Can you not also understand that
every time pulpit propaganda side-steps the Cross of Christ
and fans the flames of war, the churches must lose? So
when a few days ago thirty-two Protestant ministers and
laymen, including three university presidents, issued a
formal statement declaring that American churches cannot
remain neutral but in effect must support the ideals of
England and France, these ecclesiastics — many of them
Modernists — took dangerous paths by involving the
churches in war issues. The Christian clergy of our land
has one first-line duty, to preach the Gospel of forgiveness
through the blood of Jesus Christ and His atoning death
on the cross; and when Christ is all in all to us, we as a
Church will remember His admonition, *"Put up thy
sword!"* and not fail to teach the Biblical instruction, *"Seek
the peace of the city!"*

But, these thirty-two church-leaders maintain, tremendous questions of right and wrong are at stake in the
European conflict. Think of the debate they provoke!
The reply is hurled at them, "Have any of the nations
embroiled in this conflict preserved unimpeachable standards
of righteousness? Have any of the European belligerents
clean hands?" We do not condone some of the things that
have occurred in Germany; but have not its enemies built
up their empires by conquest? Thousands of Boer women
and children died in Lord Kitchener's concentration camps.
In the "Opium War" the British controlled the sale of this
destructive narcotic and, refusing the Chinese plea for
a high duty, kept the price of opium cheap to increase
sales and profits. One of the most pathetic statements in
missionary history can be found in the word of the Chinese
prince, a pagan, to the British minister, a Christian, "Take
away your opium, and . . . your missionaries will be
welcome."

Pointedly critics ask in this debate, has our own United States a clean record with our racial prejudices, our conquests by force, and the corruption in our political life? The Nazi treatment of the Jew is repulsive, but how did we treat the American Indians? We fed them whisky, cheated them, took their lands away, and locked them on reservations! What have we done to the American Negro? Try to have a colored boy enrolled in some of our upper schools, and you will find part of the answer. We despise conquest and invasion, but how did we get Texas and California? If we are honest, we shall see that guilt is international and knows few geographical bounds.

Suppose, however, that as church-leaders continue to appeal for war, the power of propaganda succeeds, where can we find strength and guidance? If we are thrown into the conflict and, as a result, the menace of atheism, the threat of radical upheaval, and the uprising against God continue, — and we believe that history will show these to be the consequences of another protracted World War,— where are we to find assurance and safety?

How I thank God that we have an answer of joy and strength for all of you! In the name of Christ we can promise that in every need of body and soul

GOD WILL PROVIDE!

For this is the glorious pledge of Philippians 4:19, *"My God shall supply all your need according to His riches in glory by Christ Jesus."*

I

HE PROVIDES *"BY CHRIST JESUS"*

Only heroic faith could express this conviction, since the Apostle, when he wrote these words, was a prisoner, paying the hard penalty for his loyalty to Jesus. It was a terrifying hatred, this persecution that started with the beginning of Saint Paul's ministry and that was to end outside the walls of Rome when his head was severed from his body. Some one has estimated that through the centuries a total of 50,000,000 Protestants have been cut down in cold blood because of their faith. Add to this the appalling number of martyrs in the first Christian centuries and those within the last years who have been murdered by atheistic terror, and you have a picture of the price paid for unswerving devotion to Christ.

Where has the world seen stronger courage than the faith of these Christian martyrs? Here is Saint Paul, despised, persecuted, imprisoned, suffering unspeakable cruelty for Christ; and in the face of certain death he not only says of himself in the verse preceding our text, "*I have all and abound,*" but he writes to his congregation in Philippi, "*My God shall supply all your need according to His riches.*"

What gave the Apostle this firm confidence that God would provide for all His children as He had provided for him? It was not Paul's training and education. Voltaire found no assurance in his literary genius when he exclaimed, "I wish I had never been born!" David Hume was one of Europe's best-read men; yet when he reviewed his own mistakes, his fears and frailties, he burst out: "I seem affrighted and confounded with the solitude in which I am placed by my philosophy. When I turn my eye inward, I find nothing but doubt and ignorance. Where am I? Or what am I? From what cause do I derive my existence? To what condition shall I return? I am confounded with questions. I begin to fancy myself in a very deplorable condition, environed with darkness on every side."

Neither was the Apostle a care-free, happy-go-lucky

spirit, who could take whatever each day might offer and make the best of it. On the contrary, life to him was real, earnest, problem-weighted, question-marked. Nor was it simply religion that gave Saint Paul his confident outlook. He had had plenty of theology before he met Christ on the Damascus road, but all his pharisaical zeal could not quiet his soul. He found contentment, and we, too, can discover the reassuring faith required to declare, "God will provide," only *"by Christ Jesus."*

It is of life-and-death importance that you realize today what these three words, *"by Christ Jesus,"* mean for you and your future. You may never know anything about the mighty figures of history, science, and art; you may silently pass the claims of your fellow-men and ignore, if you must, their accomplishments; but if you want courageous faith and assured salvation, you must know who the Lord Jesus Christ is and what He has done for humanity, particularly for you. You must believe with your whole heart that He was more than man, infinitely higher than the greatest of men; that He was, by His own declaration, by the proof of His divine power, and the public acknowledgment of His heavenly Father, the Son of the living God, made man with us and for us. His career on earth was dedicated not to a single race, a limited age, or a restricted area. His influence and blessing have been for all men, for eternal ages, for the ends of the world. His task was not simply to change human affairs, to bring better working conditions and improved family relations, to spread progress and culture; but He, the great God, became one of us, so that He might save our souls, restore us to God, and bring us, every one of us, to heaven. He died on the cross, not merely as a pattern of heroic self-sacrifice or as a victim of prejudices, but as the sin-bearing, sin-removing Lamb of God, our Savior and Substitute, our Redeemer and Ransom. He rose again from the dead on the third day, not merely in the thoughts and wishes of His disciples nor in the sagas and legends of the early Church, but in the positive truth of actual history, to give to those who believe in Him — and may you be numbered among His followers! — eternal life, with Him, the Father, and the Spirit, in the glory of heaven. To that heaven He Himself ascended, where He now rules, not as a distant King who forgets His lowly subjects, but as the loving Sovereign of our souls, who regulates the lives of His redeemed with mercy, wisdom, might, and as the heavenly Intercessor who still pleads our cause and assures us that, *"if any man sin, we have an Advocate with the Father, Jesus Christ the Righteous."*

If you come to Christ through this humble, penitent faith and say: "O my Savior, Thou art everything, and I am nothing. I was lost, but Thy grace found and restored me. I was full of shame, but Thy blood has cleansed me. I was at war with God, but being justified by faith in Thee, I have peace with my Father; I was dead in trespasses and sins, but by Thy resurrection I have life, now and forever!" — if you live in this faith, by constant contrition, and continued, Christ-exalting trust in your Lord, you, too, can calmly face the most terrifying ordeals that a mercifully veiled future may have in store for you. You can meet the threat of want and suffering with the assurance that *"by Christ Jesus"* God will provide for you.

With Jesus you spurn the very thought of taking recourse to fortune-tellers, astrologers, spiritist mediums and frauds, whose activities would be completely outlawed by every civilized government if the deep-grooved tragedy they produce were fully realized. Under the Savior's blessing you know that whatever tomorrow may bring, it comes to you as a child of God from your heavenly Father

and must therefore serve your best interests. With Jesus
you understand that life is never a gamble; that your course
is not decided by the dice of destiny or the cards of chance
but that your career was planned by the Savior's love before
you were born. When we come to Jesus as God's elect,
our names are written in the Book of Life, and from that
moment we have eternal life. This means that as Christ's
nothing happens to us by accident; luck, good or bad,
plays no part in our experience. God's angels constantly
guard us, God's wisdom daily directs us, God's love con-
tinuously strengthens us, God's power always provides for us.
For if our gracious Maker loved us with such a depth of
devotion that He did not stop short of that marvelously
merciful sacrifice, do you think that His grace can leave
those who come to Jesus the helpless victims of cruel
afflictions? As the Apostle exults, *"He that spared not
His own Son but delivered Him up for us all, how shall
He not with Him also freely give us all things"* — everything we require for our soul and body?

II

GOD PROVIDES FOR *"EVERY NEED"*

So when Saint Paul promises, *"My God shall supply
ALL your need,"* he means just what he says. *"All"* you
really need to carry out God's good purpose in your life
will be granted through Christ. Be clear on this, however,
God provides, not everything you think you need, not everything others say you need, but everything you actually
require to complete His holy design.

What are our actual needs? A generation ago the
average American had some seventy-two wants, of which
sixteen were classified as needs. Today the level of our life
has become so much higher and more complicated that we
have 484 wants, with some 94 necessities. If many of

you were asked to list your own needs, your catalog would contain items like these: fur coats, new autos, jewelry, stylish clothing, automatic heaters, trips to Florida or California, new furniture, large homes and, in general, bigger bank accounts, larger financial reserves. But these and a hundred other luxuries, as desirable as they may be otherwise, are not necessities; and in the stress of many crises money has often proved a hindrance rather than a help. During Cortez's conquest of Mexico the Spaniards, confronted by disaster, had to choose defeat with their glittering gold and sparkling jewels or safety without that heavy booty. Wisely most of the troops spurned the gold; the few who insisted on loading themselves with its weight were either killed or soon threw the treasure away. Only by the grace of God have some of you remained poor and unburdened by wealth; for if the Lord gave us all the money we wanted, many of us would selfishly spend our way to hell. America is living far beyond its means, not only as a nation but in millions of individual lives. Multitudes in this country must be prepared for a simpler life and a lower standard of living. This week the Secretary of the Treasury informed us that Congress will be asked to raise the legal debt limit of the United States from $45,000,000,000 to $50,000,000,000. You do not have to be a financial expert to foretell that even this increase will not meet the new demands, and that there are no other avenues of escape besides inflation with its suffering, repudiation with its bankruptcies, or a long up-hill pull throughout this entire generation. The many millions in Europe repeatedly limited by food cards, the swarming multitudes of China, where a recent famine took 5,000,000 lives, have accustomed themselves to a simpler mode of existence; but I wonder what will happen in this country when the adjustment comes, as it must come. Shall we be able to stand the real restrictions and the rigors of emergencies that the future may bring?

To know life's true values and to understand our basic needs, we must have the Savior's guidance; and here, as always, Jesus gives us definite directions. Surveying human ambitions, He says, *"Thy faith hath saved thee,"* the unshaken confidence that we are redeemed through Jesus Christ for eternity. When the Apostle promises, *"My God shall supply all your need,"* he declares that everything we may require for salvation is freely supplied by God. The text speaks of His *"riches,"* and you cannot exhaust the store of His mercy. Generation after generation, century after century, turns to it for pardon and peace; yet the reservoir of His atoning love is no more drained than the ocean would be if a single drop of its salty water were removed. Here in the treasury of divine love you can always find more than enough to pay the indebtedness to God incurred by your repeated sins. At the cross your faith can discover the power to remove doubt and to conquer fear. In the blood of Christ you have unfailing, purifying soul health. Human blood is often transfused to sustain physical existence; yet some rare types can hardly be matched, and often the donors lose their blood in vain; but the *"blood of Jesus Christ,"* God's *"Son,"* always *"cleanseth us"* — every one of us — *"from all sin"* and gives us the spiritual transfusion necessary for the Christian life.

Accept this magnificent mercy! Trust Christ fully! If you ask, "I wonder if I can be saved," His Word assures you, *"By grace* ARE *ye saved!"* Christ has redeemed the whole world, and it is only unbelief and the rejection of His mercy that keep the sinner from the Savior. If you hardly dare lift up your eyes to ask, "Are my sins too red, too lurid?" Christ answers, *"Though your sins be as scarlet, they shall be white as snow."* If some one tells you,

"Jesus will not accept you, you have fallen too often, transgressed too repeatedly," listen to the blessed Savior's assurance, *"Him that cometh to Me I will in no wise cast out."* Don't let anything or any one come between you and your Christ but take every burden of your soul, bring it to Him, and say: "O blessed Jesus, Thou canst supply my every need. Help me now!" and the merciful Savior, who never left a plea for His grace unheard, will always strengthen you.

I hope that you realize in a practical, every-day faith how gloriously this promise of supplying our soul's wants can enrich each passing moment. All of us need a closer walk with Jesus, a more godly life, cleaner thoughts, purer emotions, and the victory over unholy desires. You young folks, constantly assailed by the lure of the flesh; you husbands and wives, only too frequently thrown into situations that may lead to unfaithfulness and its destructive vices, take your plea for firmer trust, stronger resistance, directly to Christ, and the longer you stay with Him, the more frequently you meet Him in prayer, the more valiant your spiritual courage will become as He creates a clean heart and renews a right spirit within you!

But how about bodily needs? Can Christ grant us health and happiness, money and material prosperity, food and fuel — the advantages that engross the human mind? The Communist answers, "No; God cannot provide for the needs of the masses. Abolish private ownership! Make everything common property! Then we shall have enough to go around." The Fascist explains, "Give the state control, and then every one will have plenty." The capitalist cries, "If business and the banks assume leadership, the happy day of abundance will arrive!" The politician urges, "Follow my platform, and your worries will be over." The economist promises, "Accept this proposal, and your financial hardships will be solved." But is it not significant, for example, that multitudes have starved to death in a land where Communism has found its greatest support; that in our own country during the last ten years, a decade devoted to social questions with an intensity previously unknown, the number of people dependent on Government aid has increased six times and now totals more than 20,000,000?

Of course, the Lord wants us to employ the resources of human reason in solving the problems of food and clothing, health and shelter; but sometimes, when individuals and nations forget to praise the God from whom all blessings flow, place themselves in the Almighty's place, and think they can manage their affairs without His benediction, they meet difficulties too staggering for the best human minds. At such times especially the Christian holds trustingly to his Savior's assurance that He can provide us richly and daily with all that we need for this body and life. For, while it is true that God in His unmeasured goodness *"maketh His sun to rise on the evil and on the good and sendeth rain on the just and on the unjust,"* there is indisputable evidence that the riches of His grace have rested particularly on those parts of the globe where men revere Jesus Christ and believe His Gospel of salvation.

Our plea to many in this audience thus urges: If you are worried about your rent, your unpaid bills, your decreased income, your money losses, your work; if the coal bin is almost empty and the cupboard supply is scant; if your children are not dressed warmly enough for this biting cold, don't clench your fist against God! Don't give up in despair! Don't stoop to sin! Approach your heavenly Father in Christ! Ask Him, "Provide for me! Help me! Give me what I must have!" And if you pray for real necessities, the promise of our text will be ful-

filled: *"God shall supply all your need."* Trust Him with
your whole heart, work with all your might, and He will
provide!

The Savior, who miraculously fed the multitudes, can
similarly draft His omnipotence to provide for His redeemed. During the Reformation John Brenz, faithful
Gospel witness, pursued by men who sought to kill him,
found refuge in a barn hay-loft. For ten days he remained
safely concealed there, although inspecting soldiers thrust
their swords within a few inches of his body. On each
of those ten days a hen laid an egg within his easy grasp
and thus helped to sustain him. — Many in this audience
can likewise testify that, when all seemed lost, support came
from God through entirely unexpected sources.

For every problem that embitters your life pray to your
heavenly Father in Jesus' name, that is, in firm reliance on
His atoning mercy! Pray humbly, without dictating the
time, place, or manner of His answer! Pray trustingly,
never doubting that the Lord is able to keep His Word
to the very letter! Pray insistently! If it seems that God
does not hear, redouble your petitions! Force your way
through to the Throne of Mercy! Pray without malice
toward your fellow-men, remembering that you cannot
pray, *"Forgive us our trespasses,"* unless you yourself are
ready to forgive and forget! Pray that the Father's will be
done, not yours, since His gracious will is always the best!

Prayer like that must be answered! Melanchthon, the
gifted coworker of Martin Luther in the stupendous task
of the Reformation, once fell deadly sick, and by the
time Luther arrived, the symptoms of the end appeared
unmistakable. Nevertheless the Great Reformer knelt
more than an hour, beseeching God for the recovery of
his assistant. As if by a miracle Melanchthon was spared
for many years of additional service in Christ's kingdom.
When Thomas Charles, who in the last century started the

mighty British and Foreign Bible Society, was at death's door, his friends met to intercede for his life. One aged man in the group earnestly pleaded that, if it were the divine will, their leader might be spared, at least for fifteen years more, so that the mission of spreading the printed Word might succeed. Hardly had these words been spoken when Thomas Charles began to regain his health, and he was given an extension of life which, as remarkable as it seems, lasted the fifteen years the believers had requested of God.

Can you not see, also, that for the needs of our nation we must have Christian prayer from coast to coast? People often write to ask us why we do not urge this audience to send telegrams to Washington on this question or that. The answer simply is this, that ours is not a political broadcast but a Christian message of trust in the Lord Jesus Christ. Let the legislators give us good and wise laws if they can; and if they cannot, as citizens you have the ballot and should know what to do. But as followers of the Savior we can invoke mighty, miraculous blessings from God on our country. Give us prayer in the heart of every American who is Christ's; prayer in every home dedicated to Christ; prayer in every true Christian church from shore to shore; earnest prayer, penitent, pleading, persistent prayer, all in the name of Jesus, and we shall have God's help for our multiplied perplexities, war difficulties, labor troubles, financial problems, moral issues, and every danger before us!

Fathers and mothers of the land, for the fulfilment of this promise we beseech you: Don't let your children grow up without knowing Christ, without being able to speak to Him in confident prayer! Don't destroy their trust in God by the example of your own prayerless life and home! These boys and girls may have to face adversities that make our present troubles seem petty annoyances. For the salvation of their souls, for their peace of mind, and for the assurance that their needs, whatever they may be, will be supplied, bring them to Christ! Teach them the power of triumphant pleading to God! Pray, America, pray, and all necessary help will be granted!

III
HE PROVIDES FOR US "IN GLORY"

Do not overlook the truth of the text that our heavenly Father promises to supply all our needs "IN GLORY *by Christ Jesus.*" Bible students have debated the exact meaning of these words, but does it not seem that the Lord here offers to grant us every requirement in a glorious manner? What comfort and sustaining power we all can find in this thought! God's glorious providing helps solve the mystery of sorrow in the Christian's suffering and answers the "*why*" that surges within our hearts when we seek an explanation for our afflictions.

A few months ago one of our most experienced missionaries, a man in the prime of life, returned to his field in China. Before his furlough he had repeatedly preached in cities bombed by the Japanese invaders. He had witnessed the multiplied horrors of that conquest in personal experience; yet, because the love of Christ constrained him and the thought of China's perishing millions haunted him, he could not remain longer in this country, but leaving his wife and children here, he returned to face the perils of the field alone, yet with Christ. Last week a cable brought the sad news that Missionary Zschiegner died while on an inland missionary trip. How can we say that God granted his needs when He permitted His own missionary servant to be cut off in the strength of his life? How can we say that God provided for his widow and the fatherless children when he took away the one on whom, humanly speaking, they depended most?

It takes faith to know and believe the answer, and we pray God that this trust may be given particularly to all those burdened by the humanly unexplainable sorrows and life's apparently cruel reverses. Above and below this heart-crushing anguish we must still discern God's unfathomable love. Sometimes there may be a clash between what we think we need and what God knows we need, and when our Father prevails, we should say not only, *"How unsearchable are His judgments and His ways past finding out!"* but, though in tears of sorrow, we must also declare, *"Oh, the depth of the riches both of the wisdom and knowledge of God!"*

Because that missionary in China and his family are Christ's, even this shattering sorrow must become a blessing. Somehow and in an unseen way his home-going is an answer to some spiritual need, and by God's providence, fragments of happiness in the bereaved family that seem disjointed and contradictory to us will be realined and put together in a glorious, heavenly design. We do not know why that witness to Christ had to die a sudden, lonely death in far-off pagan China, but God knows, and therefore all will be well. Try to believe Jesus and to realize that for those who are His, the deeper the sorrow, the greater the blessing, the hotter the fires of affliction, the purer the refining; the more bitter the grief, the more glorious the divine purpose! If our loving Father lets you suffer, look to Jesus, and as the resurrection came after the cross of shame, so, by the sorrows of your life, you are having an unknown need provided, an unseen protection bestowed.

God grant that today many of you will come to Jesus, so that the multitudes of this vast audience, all sins removed, all needs supplied, may be saved for eternity, there to behold Him face to face and to exult, "O my Christ, my Savior and my God, Thou hast truly supplied all my needs, according to Thy riches here in glory!" Amen.

VICTORY FOR THE SONS OF GOD!

*"Whatsoever is born of God overcometh the world;
and this is the victory that overcometh the world,
even our faith."* — 1 John 5:4.

O Holy Spirit, our transforming, soul-cleansing Lord:

*May we be filled with power to behold ourselves defeated by our
sins without Christ, but with Christ — O glorious grace! — redeemed through faith in His atonement, reborn by the new birth in
Thee, restored to the Father's waiting arms! Give us all, particularly those who disconsolately seek pardon for their transgressions and help for their sorrows, the pledge of eternal triumph that
can be ours, through humble, sincere trust in the Savior! Grant
us all this world-conquering, self-vanquishing, sin-destroying, death-
defying faith as our greatest necessity and Thy most blessed gift;
through Jesus Christ, our Lord! Amen.*

TODAY'S broadcast is of particular interest since these
words now spoken are being recorded on durable
disks for the far-distant year 8113. Oglethorpe University in Georgia has established a Crypt of Civilization,
in which the evidences of our present age's culture and
achievement are to be locked and scientifically protected
against decay for 187 generations. By special invitation
of the university an electrical transcription of this broadcast is to be deposited in a huge vault, where, together with
other samples of our twentieth-century activities, it will
remain untouched until its sealed doors are opened in
8113. It is recognized, of course, that Oglethorpe University and even the United States may be destroyed long
before that remote day; so metal plates are being sent to
China, India, Tibet, and many other foreign countries to
keep future generations informed concerning the crypt.

Personally I do not believe this sin-burdened world will

exist for sixty-two additional centuries. That international suicide, the bloodshed across the seas, with Europe's most advanced nations bent on killing each other, seems to indicate a sort of final failure. Besides, we cannot read the Biblical statements concerning the last times without realizing that these days are upon us. Wars and rumors of wars, false Christs and antichrists, seducing spirits and the doctrines of devils, forbidding to marry and commanding to abstain from meats, lying and hypocrisy, deceiving and being deceived, self-love and covetousness, boasting and pride, blasphemies and disobedience, ingratitude and unholiness, sex perversions and family trouble, truce-breaking and false accusations, incontinence and fierceness, despising of God and betrayal, love of pleasure more than the love of truth — these Scriptural signs of the end are so strikingly fulfilled before our eyes that we should believe in the Lord Jesus Christ's imminent and personal return to judge the quick and the dead. Yet, if God's patient love permits the world to stand until 8113 and some distant generation discovers the disks on which this message is recorded, one glorious truth will prevail although in the eighty-second century the United States and every other modern nation may have ceased to exist; the eternal Gospel will have proved itself what we know it to be in our twentieth century: God's triumphant power unto salvation. So we exult across this nation as this transcription record may proclaim to a future age in the Crypt of Civilization:

VICTORY FOR THE SONS OF GOD!

For the pledge of this triumph hear Saint John's words, First Epistle, 5:4, "*Whatsoever is born of God overcometh the world; and this is the victory that overcometh the world, even our faith.*"

I

VICTORY IN THE CHURCH

Saint John here tells the first Christians that their conquest consists in overcoming *"the world"* — all hostile forces that seek to retard and destroy the Gospel's progress. That *"world"* still is, and always will remain, the Church's greatest enemy. In different lands and ages its opposition assumes various forms. Today, in our country, *"the world"* has mobilized seven formidable foes. The first is the sinister agitation that seeks to involve this nation in Europe's battles. We leave it to others to describe the horror, the sacrifice of human lives, the loss of money, and the bankruptcies that would follow through our entanglement; for we are particularly concerned about war as an enemy of the Church and a destructive force that retards the Gospel's free course. Although the present conflict is only a few months old, it has already produced serious losses in foreign mission fields where natives ask, "If white Christians cannot maintain peace among themselves, why do they send us missionaries?" Multiplied millions of dollars that should be contributed for the extension of the Savior's kingdom are consumed, instead, by war's cost and its taxes. Besides, every hostility produces a let-down in morals, a spirit of religious indifference, an age of materialism, and an organized opposition to Christ.

The second foe of the faith is the twin menace of Fascism, with its state control of religion, and the immeasurably more destructive atheistic Communism. Within the last seven years the number of officially enrolled Reds in the United States has increased and is now estimated at 100,000. — Need we wonder that radical influences have crept into the Government itself, that experts claim to have listed almost 3,000 known Communists in Federal positions? Despite their frequent smiles and declarations of innocence, thousands of American Reds have diabolically pledged themselves to close our churches and banish loyal ministers of Jesus Christ.

The third enemy of the Christian Church is atheistic education, the growing danger in our public schools, by which the minds of our children, the attitudes of our high-school youth, and the ideals of our college students are poisoned against Christ by godless teachers, who betray their trust.

The Church's fourth foe is the rampant immorality that threatens to overflow our land. Immeasurable dishonesty in business and financial circles; graft and connivance in our city, State and Federal governments; perjury and corruption in the courts; illegitimate births, abortions, adulteries; broken marriage vows, disrupted homes, and divorces; printed filth and applauded impurity; arson and robbery, murder and suicide — these reach new records as crime rides on its high crest.

Now we come to the most dangerous opposition, the assaults on the Christian cause that arise from within the churches. The fifth enemy, one of these internal dangers, is the menace of Modernism, the smooth, perfidious denial of Jesus Christ as the world's Savior, the rejection of the Bible as God's inspired, errorless Word, the unbelief that has captured many American pulpits and found lavish supporters especially in certain millionaires. Within the memory of thousands in this audience entire denominations, once loyal to Scriptural truth and Christ's atonement, have disavowed these two pillar doctrines.

The sixth menace to modern Christianity is doctrinal indifference, the delusion that the churches can compromise their sacred truth, follow a policy of pretty diplomacy, and agree to disagree even in the vital teachings of Christ. Far too many clergymen today preach the easy and convenient delusion that it does not matter what you believe as long as you sincerely follow some creed, though Jesus Himself says, *"If ye believe not that I am He, ye shall die in your sins."* It is this indifference — and indifference ultimately means denial — that permits Jewish Rabbis, Hindu philosophers, and atheistic lawyers to speak from Christian pulpits.

The last of the seven foes is worldliness in the churches, the constant erasing of the sharp line which separates the Church of Christ from the world of sin. I mean specifically the tactics that bring reproach on the Savior's name, vulgar, sometimes indecent theatricals, sensational stunts, games of chance.

Now, if the churches are to defeat these formidable enemies and emerge from our problem-weighted years stronger, purer, healthier, what do they require for that victory? What does American Christianity need if it is to be preserved as long as this world stands, even until the Crypt of Civilization be opened, should Christ tarry that long in His coming? We may think in first instance of external needs. The churches must discard political ambitions. They must not tolerate any governmental policies in Washington that would tell our congregations what they must do or suggest to the ministers what they should preach. American Christians must not permit the usurpation of power by any Church which claims that its sovereign should control public affairs and direct legislative programs. Church discipline should be revived and the congregations ban from membership those — no matter how wealthy and imposing they may be — whose lives are a public disgrace to the Savior's creed. Followers of Christ must take a firm stand against the gambling, raffling, and money-raising schemes outlawed by divine regulations and civil laws. We must remove the theater, the modern dance, the commercial amusements, from the churches and make these sanctuaries what they should be, temples of the living God, houses of prayer for all people. Christianity must not become a religion exclusively for the middle and upper classes. History demonstrates that spiritual power declines when churchmen are allied with the wealthy to the neglect of the everlasting poor. The victorious Church of tomorrow will not be built of deadening formalism, the pomp and ceremony of exaggerated ritualism, that leaves men's hearts untouched. The churches which will prevail should give to their youth a penetrating program of spiritual training, not limited to a weekly hour of haphazard Sunday-school instruction. But before and beyond this, American Christianity needs an inner reformation, the deeper conviction indicated in the text, *"This is the victory that overcometh the world, even our faith."*

What is this world-conquering trust? Many would answer that the churches must have confidence in joint endeavors, State and Federal councils, amalgamations, interdenominational programs, since strength lies in united effort. Because Christ says, *"Without Me ye can do nothing,"* we can predict that any future age in which this message now being recorded may be heard will have witnessed the complete defeat of many merely human plans for strengthening the Church. Since 1900 ambitious, expensive programs have been undertaken to promote religious work; but every one that gave room and support to Modernism failed completely. Nor is the trust the Church needs a reliance on modern methods, organizations, office machinery, twentieth-century equipment, new styles of architecture, new orders of service, new Bible translations, or anything new. Above every advantage God permits us to use in spreading His kingdom we must have — and now I sound the battle-cry of the true Christian

Church — faith in Jesus Christ, the Son of God and the Savior of the world; reliance on His Gospel as the message of full, free, and final salvation for every sinner; confidence in the merciful assurance that we are saved by grace; the trust that takes each promise of Christ at its face value and refuses to doubt or detract from it; the faith, in short, which asks us despite our sins to approach the cross, believing in the eternal mercies Jesus showed there when His suffering secured our forgiveness, His bleeding our cleansing, His dying our living eternally. Men may have a dozen different definitions for faith, but to every Christian faith means particularly this sincere, personal, trusting declaration which we shall be happy to send you so that you can memorize it and repeat it every day, Luther's glorious explanation of the Second Article of our Christian Creed: "I believe that Jesus Christ, true God, begotten of the Father from eternity, and also true man, born of the Virgin Mary, is my Lord, who has redeemed me, a lost and condemned creature, purchased and won me from all sins, from death, and from the power of the devil, not with gold or silver, but with His holy, precious blood and with His innocent suffering and death, that I may be His own and live under Him in His kingdom and serve Him in everlasting righteousness, innocence, and blessedness, even as He is risen from the dead, lives and reigns to all eternity. This is most certainly true."

This faith gave the first Church its power. Had it been foretold that twelve men, practically all workers from the lower classes, would defeat the wisdom of pagan philosophers, remove the gods and temples of the heathen kingdoms, defy the rulers of Rome, and finally destroy their vast empire, this prediction would have been laughed to scorn; yet these and much greater victories were recorded by the early Christians, who had few outstanding men, little money, no buildings in the beginning, no helpful machinery or appliances — practically nothing of the equipment and assets that many people today regard as absolutely necessary for success. But they had faith in Jesus Christ, unwavering, uncompromising, unconditional trust, and there was not enough ingenuity in the fiendishness of Nero, the brutality of his bloodthirsty successors, plus their armies and their imperial treasuries, to withhold the victory. Those first-century Christians were often tried beyond endurance. It is recorded that 6,600 Christian soldiers of Emperor Maximinus were ordered to sacrifice to heathen gods and then persecute their own fellow-Christians in Gaul. They refused both commands, preferring to obey God rather than men. Three times the enraged emperor selected every tenth soldier in that legion and sent him to a horrible death. When even this failed to move the remainder of the Christian legion to deny the Savior and attack their brothers in faith, Maximinus, the tyrant, sent his army against these loyal believers. Instead of fighting, they threw away their arms, and within a few hours the entire legion had been cut down by the sword, bored through by arrows, trampled by horses, until not one of the 6,600 was left alive. Yet despite royal fiends, executioners' blocks, flaming fires, and man-eating beasts, despite torture and dungeon, faith proved itself God's victorious power.

Today, too, when men write books to show that Christianity is in its last stages; when scurrilous attacks charge that our creed is hysteria and superstition, the same triumph is pledged those who maintain their loyalty to Christ. This triumph is not always evident to the human eye, and it may be that for its purifying and strengthening God permits His Church to suffer reverses and affliction. Some of you write that because of denominational politics and modernist boards you have lost your congregational property and must worship, as the early Christians did, in your own homes. But spiritually the Church is often strongest when it is poorest, more loyal in the darkness of oppression than in the spotlight of public approval. The sorrows that God sends the followers of Christ are for their own upbuilding. In the reign of Bloody Mary, Bernard Gilpin, loyal witness to Christ, would constantly repeat his favorite maxim, "All things are for the best." During the persecution he was charged with heresy and ordered to stand trial in London. On the way he broke his leg, and a scornful companion demanded, "Is all for the best now?" Yet Gilpin's faith was not misplaced, for before he could resume his journey, Queen Mary died, and instead of proceeding to his death at London, he went home in triumph. — Give us Christian pastors in the pulpit who, with Saint Paul, will *"count all things but loss for the excellency of the knowledge of Christ Jesus"* — ministers who strive and pray to help save the world for our Lord, and the invincible power of God Himself will work through them! Give us men and women in the pews whose souls have been enriched by a holy earnestness for Jesus, who will protest against every attack on the truth; put this faith into the family, with the home entirely dedicated to Christ; inject this trust into the congregational activities, let it produce greater personal testimony, deeper prayer-life, sincerer love for the Sacraments, nobler missionary zeal, and, under God, the Church will continue to make its way from victory to victory!

It may happen that the worship of Christ will be banned from certain countries, as events in our own day show. We may lose Christianity here in the United States if unbelief and uprising against God become too blatant and blasphemous. But at some place on this earth of sin God will have kept His Church in every age, *"and the gates of hell shall not prevail against it."* If, against our firm expectation, the world still stands in 8113, those who find this record and are able to decipher its message will say, "These words spoken in the ancient days of 1940 are the truth! The Christian religion has not been destroyed! Christian faith has victoriously maintained its power!"

II

THE VICTORY IN OUR INDIVIDUAL LIVES

Most of you, however, are more interested in the twentieth than in the eighty-second century, more concerned about your own problems than in issues confronting the Church. You have personal opposition to meet now, and you want to know where you can find victory. From Pennsylvania, for example, a distracted woman writes: "I am a Catholic. By birth my parents were good people, but I am a terrible sinner. . . . I have had trials and tribulations more than I can stand. Twice I have tried to kill myself, and once I almost committed a murder. After that my husband drove me out, and now I am living with a man for the past five years who has caused me much heartache and misery. Now he is tired of me and wants to cast me out also. I have pleaded with God not to let me destroy myself and send my soul to hell. I have repented and repented of my sins. I have cried bitter tears, pleading with God to forgive me my sins and show me the path to another way of living. My nerves are so bad I'm afraid something may snap in my mind at any moment. Oh, why did I have to turn out to be a bad woman? I've helped the poor, and I've never turned any one away from my door, and still I have to fall into this destruction. Please help me to save my soul and keep me from suicide."

That woman is listening in this afternoon; and I want to discuss this problem both for her and for all who see in her appeal the burden of their afflicted soul. First of all, I fail to find in this letter a single reference to the Lord Jesus. To have forgiveness of your sins, assurance both for this life and the next, you must know Christ in a personal, trusting faith. He must be everything to you. Then, this plea for help states that the burdened woman is a church-member, protests that she has always treated the poor well, and never sent any one empty-handed from her door. But you need much more than outward church-membership and acts of charity to be blessed by our Lord Jesus' promise and the guiding strength of His love. You must be a child of God, for our text reminds us, *"Whatsoever is born of God overcometh the world."* As the Savior Himself plainly stated, *"Ye must be born again!"*

For the assurance of His victory it is not enough that your name is written in the church register; that you attend services regularly; that you subscribe for a religious paper and pay your congregational dues. For the victorious life it is not sufficient that you belong to a young people's society, a ladies' aid, or a men's club. You cannot say, "I am a Christian" simply because you attend church suppers and entertainments. You need far more than the mere fact that you are an officer in the congregation, a teacher in the Sunday-school, or a soloist in the choir. The assurance of triumph over your sins and sorrows cannot be purchased with contribution envelopes, three- and four-figure checks, tithes and generous donations to missions and charities. You cannot rely solely on the fact that you have been baptized, confirmed, and accepted as a member in a Christian church. God is pleased with all this only when it is found with a regenerated soul, a new heart, and a twice-born life. The question your heavenly

Father first asks is not, "What church do you attend?" "Of what congregation are you a member?" "What are your annual contributions for mission purposes?" but, "Are you My child through Christ?" A mere mechanical faith cannot meet God's demands. Don't be satisfied with emotional religion, a holding up of hands or a singing of hallelujahs that has no foundation in true knowledge and that therefore can be swayed by every wind of adversity! Don't drug yourself into a false security and say, "Once a Christian, always a Christian!" Look at the examples of the high and mighty who have fallen from faith and ended in unbelief. The plain ultimatum of Jesus remains, "*Ye must be born again!*"

To the distracted woman in Pennsylvania and her co-sufferers we say that their chief concern must be: "Am I a child of God?" "Have I really been born again?" For unless these questions can be answered with a clear, ringing "Yes"; unless you have been reborn a new creature in Christ, all talk of strength and confidence in religion is only wishful thinking. And now to answer the question that has been lingering on your lips, "How can I become a child of God?" You are not the first to put that question; near the beginning of the Savior's ministry a teacher in Israel, Nicodemus, directed the same inquiry to Jesus, and even if you do not understand it, if men contradict it, if unbelief ridicules it, Christ's reply is the holy, unbreakable truth: We are born again, we become God's children with the promise of victory, our Lord says, through "*water and the Spirit.*" This means that, when God's Spirit brings us as sinners to the Savior, through this faith our whole inner life is changed; we become new creatures; for the old things of sin are passed away, and the new glory of grace has dawned upon us.

As a special gift, God's enlightening, renewing Spirit

comes to us through water, that is, through Baptism. For when we take Christ at His word, *"He that believeth and is baptized shall be saved; but he that believeth not shall be damned"*; and again, *"Baptism doth also now save us,"* we understand that by no mere mechanical pouring of water but by the living, trusting faith which unconditionally accepts God's promise, we have been washed of our sins and made heirs to heaven. Since this glorious blessing is given in Baptism, we can understand that the Savior in His last commission to His disciples declared, *"Go ye therefore and teach all nations, baptizing them in the name of the Father and of the Son and of the Holy Ghost!"* No wonder the apostles immediately followed His instruction, so that throughout the Book of Acts we read how entire households, old and young, were brought to Christ through Baptism and how sorrow and despair were turned to joy and assurance! But great wonder that despite these baptismal blessings 40,000,000, 50,000,000, 60,000,000 and more people in the United States have never received this *"washing of regeneration"*!

If only God will now lend divine power to my words, so that many unbaptized will be moved to accept the pledge of this grace! People are glued to their radios on certain nights when broadcasts offer large sums to those selected by the spin of a wheel. Today I promise you in Christ's name the victory over your sins and afflictions — a wealth of soul glory incomparably more magnificent both for time and eternity than the glitter of earthly gold, a heavenly blessing won not by lottery, but by the age-old plan of salvation that ended at Calvary, when the holy Son of God died for the unholy children of sin.

Chance plays no part when Christ addresses Himself to you. Half an hour ago you would have thought few things farther removed from your life than this, that an invitation to be baptized would come directly to you. Yet here it is. Across hundreds and, in some cases, thousands of miles a person whom you have never seen is pleading in Christ's name that you, convicted by sin's guilt and weight, yet assured by God's mercy, resolve now to receive the Sacrament of Baptism, with the instruction you require. Thousands of pastors throughout the breadth of this country, in Canada, and many foreign countries are eager to be God's agents in bringing you and your family this blessing. Will you not give us the opportunity of helping you, of explaining the rebirth through *"water and the Spirit,"* by which you become children of God? That promise grants you mastery over sin, hell, and death itself; the conquest of your fears and weaknesses; the defeat of men's hatred and opposition; the relief from anguish that crushes your soul; the complete, eternal, unchanging triumph for every soul in 1940 and, if this record in the Crypt of Civilization is deciphered, the victory for every future generation.

Heavenly Father, above everything else that we in this country and others in later generations may ask of Thee, give us — even though it may mean earthly loss and opposition — Christ! With faith in that precious Redeemer, grant us all the rebirth by which we become Thy children for eternity! Amen.

TO CHRIST FOR HEALING LOVE!

"He touched his ear and healed him." — Saint Luke 22:51

Blessed Jesus:

We come before Thee, our souls wounded by sin, to secure Thy healing benediction and Thy cleansing power. O Jesus, where can we find the cure for the selfishness and the sorrow that burden our lives, if not in Thee, our loving Savior, through a trusting approach to Thy cross? Let all else in life recede; but may the picture of the crucifixion which these Lenten weeks draw before our inner eye be irremovably etched on our hearts, so that we may always look to Thee for help! Send Thy healing mercy to our bruised spirits and broken lives! Show them, as Thou hast shown us, what an all-gracious Redeemer, ever faithful Friend of sinners Thou art to them that love Thee, our Christ and our God! Amen.

FOR millions in the United States eventually it must be either Christ and His redemption or chaos and its despair. More than a thousand people write us every day; and if you want to survey the reaches of sorrow, examine the towering files of our mail. Here are snatches from last week's letters, sent by heart-broken, peace-robbed listeners. A theological student in Georgia, a young man who is to give others spiritual comfort, writes: "I have lost all hope and have been at the point of taking my own life." An eighty-one-year-old mother in Virginia confides: "I am writing to tell you how fearful I am that I may drop into hell because of my wickedness. I can see no hope of salvation. God does not answer me." A distracted wife in New Jersey fairly screams: "It is awful to live without hope. I have been tempted very often to take my own life."

What can we tell these stricken souls? What assurance can we give those battered and broken by a thousand crushing sorrows? What comfort, indeed, if not the hope offered in this Lenten appeal:

[220]

To Christ for Healing Love!

May God's Spirit richly bless this plea, based on Saint Luke's inspired record (22:51), *"He* [Jesus] *touched his ear and healed him"*!

I

MALCHUS EXPERIENCED THAT HEALING LOVE

These words take us to the Garden of Gethsemane. Only a few days before this solemn Thursday, Jesus was welcomed to Jerusalem with enthusiastic acclaim; now a mob, armed with swords and staves, has come to kill Him! Only a few hours earlier the Savior held His final meeting with the disciples in the upper room and at that last supper instituted Holy Communion, with the blessed gift of His own body and blood. Now the time has arrived when that body, scourged and wounded, will be given into death for our sins and that blood will flow from His beaten back, His nail-pierced hands and feet. Only a few moments before, in the deepest loneliness history knows, Jesus threw Himself to the ground, pleading in never-to-be-measured anguish that, if it were His Father's will, the cup of suffering might be lifted from His lips; so terrifying was the ordeal confronting Him, the Son of God, about to bear the world's sins in His own sinless body. Now the silence in the garden of prayer is suddenly broken. From all sides, it seems, an armed mob thirsting for blood swarms into Gethsemane.

In this crisis it is a different Christ whom we behold in the revealing light of the full moon; no longer weak from that agonized wrestling; no longer terrorized into a blood-like sweat. With the courage imparted by the strengthening angel He steps before that mob of murderers to ask, *"Whom seek ye?"* When they answer, *"Jesus of Nazareth,"* the Savior unhesitatingly identifies Himself with the words, "*I am He.*" That declaration and the glance with which He pierced their hearts were so powerful that the whole throng was instantly hurled to the ground. The love of Christ was even stronger than His omnipotence. Though He could have avoided His arrest and the sequel of torture, uncomplaining Lamb of God that He is, He wanted to suffer for us!

He released the men who in a moment would take Him captive. After they had risen to their feet, their ranks seemed to part, and a sinister figure advanced toward Jesus. We recognize the form and features of that man whom all generations will despise because of His loathsome treachery — Judas, the disciple entrusted with the meager funds of the Twelve — Judas, the informer, the money-blinded wretch who, though repeatedly warned by Christ, sold His Savior and his own soul for thirty pieces of suicidal silver. His smirking kiss, it seems, fully aroused the disciples to their Lord's danger, and the hand of one of them nervously gripped the hilt of a sword hidden beneath his garment. Neither Matthew nor Mark nor Luke mentions the sword-bearing disciple's name; only John identifies him as Peter. What impressive example of Christian charity and forbearance in the silence of the first three evangelists! When their gospels were written, Peter was still alive, and with loving consideration they avoided mentioning his name, to spare him and the early Christian congregation much sorrow. But John wrote toward the close of the first century, long after Peter had died, and, both for our warning and comfort, he could well record the name of this impetuous disciple.

How sorely we need that spirit of Christian charity today in helping to protect the good name of friend and foe! Newspapers employ, and the public applauds, peep-hole columnists, who delight in publicizing private sins.

We ourselves easily put the worst construction on the actions of others. Even nations can be goaded into warfare by propaganda later proved malicious falsehood. How the ministry suffers not only from front-page space devoted to its mistakes and from the motion-picture caricatures of the Protestant clergy as snooping hypocrites, but also through the unjustified attacks of scandal-mongers and tongue-waggers in some churches! We ask this audience to reject all unfounded attacks on the ministry. Instead, let us defend the clergy and by prayer and friendly help support these spiritual leaders, who, the most easily maligned of all men, have the hardest task the ministry ever faced in the United States.

In the heat of the excitement Peter, turning to Christ, asks, *"Lord, shall we smite with the sword?"* Without waiting for an answer, he unsheathes his saber and with that single weapon tries to start a holy war. An ill-aimed blow strikes his nearest enemy — it happens to be the servant of the high priest — and cuts off his ear.

That was the beginning of bloodshed in the mistaken defense of Jesus Christ, but it was not the end. Recall the ill-fated attempt to tear Palestine from the Turks, as though some special holiness attached to the country that rejected Jesus! Think of the persecutions of the Waldensians and the Albigensians, recorded in blood-dripping chapters! Some one has estimated that 50,000,000 Protestants were massacred in persecutions and religious wars. This figure may be too high, but if the exact number were known, the total still would be appalling. We have had the sword-bearing, inquisitorial type of Christianity on this continent, too. In this age of many monuments we should recognize the first religious martyrs within the boundaries of what is now the United States and place a towering shaft at the mouth of Saint John's River in Florida. Sixty years before the Pilgrims landed at Plymouth Rock a French Protestant colony was established there. But King Philip of Spain sent merciless Menendez to Florida to kill all the "Lutherans," as the French Protestants were known. Here and in near-by places during ensuing massacres at least five hundred men, women, and children, including the aged, the sick, the helpless, were cut down in cold blood, as the record specifically states, not because they were Frenchmen but because they were "Lutherans." The bloody horror was hardly over, when those killers held religious services, "a cross was raised, and a site for a church selected on ground still smoking from the blood of a peaceful colony."

Why revive ancient history? some of you may object. Why erect a monument in Florida to commemorate a carnage that every one admits was a mistake? We answer: Because that obsession of spreading Christianity with the sword, far from being labeled an error, is often applauded. Last week a United States Federal Court indicted seventeen men on the charge of conspiring to overthrow the Government of the United States. In their headquarters investigating agents found weapons, ammunition, and material for making bombs. Who were these men, organized, it is claimed, to overthrow our existing order by force of arms? Anarchists, radical agitators, atheistic Communists, agents of foreign nations? They called themselves the "Christian Front," employing Christ's holy name to justify a campaign of bloodshed. More significantly, they received encouragement from a publicized churchman. Instead of condemning their sword-bearing crusade, he declared, according to press reports: "I shall take my stand beside the Christian Fronters. I reaffirm every word I have ever said in support of their position."

What does Jesus say about such sword-bearing? Hardly had fire-breathing Peter severed that ear, when the Savior raised His voice in warning, *"Put up again thy sword into his place; for all they that take the sword shall perish with the sword."* That stern rebuke forever takes the sword out of any church's hand. It tells all Christian denominations to forget military power, political agitation, and lobbying for their special interests. It foretells that those who thus kill will themselves perish by violence. If only today this spirit of a militarized Christianity, this delusion of arms-bearing forces regimented to cut a bloody path for Christianity, were stopped in its tracks! How much more could be won by the love and the power of faith!

Jesus was not satisfied with rebuking His erring disciple. Even in the momentous hour of His own arrest and persecution He had a remedy for the wounded man and a lesson for Peter. There is plenty of negative preaching today with the repeated prohibitions: "Don't do this!" "Stop doing that!" Pulpit harangues and moralizing orations thunder accusations right and left. But Christ is the constructive Savior. He leaves no problem unsolved, no essential question unanswered. Here, too — and in less than twelve hours He will be nailed to the cross — He helpfully performs a miracle, the last in His earthly life. He stretches out the hand that never grasped the sword, touches the wounded ear, and His life-giving contact brings immediate healing.

The New Testament accounts tell us little about the man who had the distinction of being blessed by the Savior's last miracle. Three of the gospels do not even mention his name; the fourth simply calls him Malchus. What marvelous grace, however, that, though he was among Christ's enemies and a servant to those who lusted for our Lord's blood, the all-merciful Savior loved not only His friends, but also those who opposed Him! How bitterly we, like Peter, hate! How quickly we fan our prejudices into consuming anger and resentment! Love our enemies? Some people cannot even love their own husband or wife or their own flesh and blood. Even if our soul's salvation were not involved in accepting Christ, we should follow Him, if only to learn how to love those who despise us and to do good to those who persecute us.

Malchus was a servant, a slave, of the high priest. When an acclaimed leader of men falls sick, every resource of healing is quickly drafted. Take the instance of Lord Tweedsmuir's critical illness. Outstanding specialists were rushed to his bedside; carpenters quickly erected a special platform and approach at the depot; a private train was chartered to convey him to the best-equipped hospital in Canada; extraordinary traffic precautions were exercised throughout the trip. Everything humanly possible was done to help him, for Lord Tweedsmuir was a mighty man, the King of England's representative to the Canadian Dominion. But here, in our text, is a slave, a social outcast, one whose body and life are not even his own; and as though the Lord would tell all men, no matter how despised they may be, that He is their Savior, Jesus closes the long list of His pre-Calvary miracles by restoring the ear of a bondman. Is not He, the condescending, all-loving Lord, the Redeemer whom you want? Is not His spirit the power we need to stifle the passionate hatreds that make people sneer at their fellow-men if their skin is of another hue, their families of another race, their worship of another creed?

Peter did not forget that rebuke and that miracle. Never again did he take recourse to the sword. After Pentecost and its outpouring of the Holy Spirit, the sword-wielding disciple became an apostle of patience. In his last days, when his enemies confronted him, as on that Maundy Thursday night they surrounded his Savior in the Garden, Peter did not start a second miniature holy war. Early records state that, when he was crucified for his loyalty, he asked that he be nailed to the cross head downward, since he did not regard himself worthy to die as his Lord had died. This is only tradition, but there can be no doubt that this humility agrees with Peter's spirit. Read his letters! He commits the punishment of evil-doers to the government, not to the Church. He says it is a thankworthy thing *"if a man for conscience toward God endure grief, suffering wrongfully."* He holds up the example of the persecuted Christ, who, *"when He was reviled, reviled not again; when He suffered, He threatened not."* *"Rejoice inasmuch as ye are partakers of Christ's suffering!"* he exults. Strengthened by the Spirit, fortified by faith's victories, he had learned to apply Christ's healing love.

II

WE, TOO, CAN FIND HEALING IN CHRIST

When we, too, know the healing power of Christ, we know the Savior aright. It was prophesied centuries before Gethsemane that the coming Deliverer of the race would be the Savior by *"whose stripes we are healed."* The divine cure Jesus offers us today penetrates far deeper than physical pains and means much more than the healing of a lacerated ear or a wounded body. Christ, first of all, cures our souls of sin — that fatal illness for which men have no human help whatever, the inherited disease bequeathed to each of us at birth, and the contagion we contract during life. Only one cure can banish that soul-sickness — faith in the cleansing, life-transfusing blood of Jesus Christ. Only one contact can break the power of that soul- and body-destroying terror — the touch of Jesus Christ, our God and Savior. Only one prescription can present a permanent antidote for every form of this poison — the direction of the Master Physician's apostle, *"Believe on the Lord Jesus Christ, and thou shalt be saved."* Only one hospital can offer a sure cure — the arms of Christ Himself and the restoring offered by the true Church here on earth.

As we enter this Lenten season with its clinic for our inner life, let none of you spurn Christ's healing and claim self-confidently that you are of such spiritual health and moral perfection that you need no physician! Take inventory of your thoughts and impulses, your lusts and desires! Catalog the words that proceed from your lips — often hateful, malicious, dishonest, slanderous, untruthful! Recall each act that takes you away from God and perhaps brings injury or disgrace on yourself and others! See yourself as does God, whose eyes can penetrate your heart more completely than any X-rays, diagnosing your moral illness better than any corps of experts! And in honesty you must acknowledge yourself sick and sore, mortally afflicted by a poison inestimably more dangerous than the deadliest virus known to medical science.

Under the conviction of your sin listen to Christ as He repeats for you the first recorded sermon He ever preached, *"Repent ye and believe the Gospel."* Stand before the Crucified in true contrition; that is far more than mere sorrow over your sins, much deeper than good intentions to stop drinking, swearing, cheating, lying, slandering, coveting, serving fleshly lusts. Find real repentance which moves your soul with deep-rooted grief, unreserved confession of all your sins, known or unknown, and the realization that the breaking of God's Law is far more than a disobedience soon to be forgotten. As little as a cerebral hemorrhage can be stopped with a headache tablet, just so impossibly can the cure for sin be found without recognizing this divine decree, *"The soul that sinneth, it shall die."*

Thank God, *"where sin abounded, grace did much more*

abound." In the darkness of any sin-blackened night you can see the rays of the cross pierce the gloom as, in fulfilment of the Old Testament promise, the *"Sun of Righteousness"* arises *"with healing in His wings,"* that is, with the reviving powers radiated from Christ and His cross. When you train your eyes to behold Jesus nailed to that accursed timber, all else in life recedes; when your heart, crushed by sin and sorrow, acclaims the crucified Son of God your Savior, a greater power than that which healed Malchus's ear will cure your sin-sick soul forever. A score of diseases may baffle modern science, but Christ is stronger than any sin. Believe that, my young theological friend in Georgia distracted by the specter of suicide! Hundreds of thousands may die annually because they started treatment only when it was too late; but it is never too late for a penitent soul to come to Christ. Think of the promise of Paradise given to the malefactor on the cross, my eighty-one-year-old friend in Virginia! Vast multitudes in the United States are beyond the reach of proper medical care; but no one who believes the words I now proclaim across the country by the marvels of the radio, *"The blood of Jesus Christ, His Son, cleanseth us from all sin,"* has reason to cry out, *"Oh, that I knew where I might find Him!"* for that sin-destroying Savior now stands in spirit before you to heal and help. Remember that, you in New Jersey who are continually tortured by the thoughts of self-destruction and attempted murder. Pay close attention, every one of you, particularly those whom God in His gracious guidance may have led especially to this broadcast for a holy purpose: Here is hope for your sin-sick souls! Here is help and strength from heaven itself, in this resolution of faith, "To Jesus Christ for healing love!"

Can Jesus also heal the sickness of the mind and the weaknesses of the body? Banish every doubt from your heart; the unlimited power of the blessed Savior, whose outstretched hand restored Malchus's ear in Gethsemane, can do today what He did in thousands of instances during His lifetime, when He drove out fevers, cured the palsy, healed the lepers, made the lame walk, restored sight to the blind, hearing to the deaf, and gave life to corpses. As definite proof of the healing power in Christian faith we have specific instances, unnumbered in this audience alone, in which, after medical science had exhausted its resources; after specialists had admitted, "As far as we can see, there is no hope"; after even the unmistakable signs of death had begun to show themselves, God suddenly exerted His quickening power. One of the leading surgeons here in Saint Louis, a physician who himself has performed thousands of major operations, expressly answered my question with this credo: "I believe that God Almighty can cure men and women today. I have repeatedly seen instances in which, after all human help had been tried without avail, the patient continued to live despite the prediction that he could not rally."

We will defend with all our energy this truth that Jesus can cure today as He did on that memorable night in the garden. But the decisive question is not, "*Can* Jesus heal?" but, "*Will* Jesus heal?" And here we must think in harmony with the revealed truth of the Scriptures. In the first-century Church, we know, the apostles and others enjoyed a special gift of healing. They could lay their hands on diseased bodies, and health would flow from that contact. Such cures were extraordinary endowments to the early Church by which its power could be clearly manifested in those epochal days. But where in all the Scriptures is there a statement saying that today we must not bother about doctors? To the contrary, the Bible recognizes the necessity of physicians and of medicine, stating, *"They that be whole need not a physician, but they that are sick."*

So much fraud and deceit have been attached to the delusion that certain people, once they touch a disease-ridden body, can always bring miraculous healing, and so much sorrow has come from the similar error of trying to think ourselves out of our sicknesses that we must say a word in protest. From our files we take this account of an Altoona, Pennsylvania, "healing." In that city, on a recent May 13, a man who had been a bedfast invalid for seven months was carried to the platform of a "healer," anointed, and there, before the eyes of all, walked four or five steps. The tabernacle was in an uproar. The case was pronounced an outstanding cure. Twelve days later the man died from overexertion. His physician, a reputable doctor, declared, "It is my professional opinion that his trips to the tabernacle, the exertion, and the excitement . . . hastened his death." Here is the case of a twenty-eight-year-old Kansas City young man who, seriously injured, refused medical aid and preferred the help of a so-called "miracle woman." Because he was badly crushed, his strength kept ebbing away as he sat upright in his chair, praying for hours. After resisting twenty-four hours longer, he died. The family doctor, a registered physician, wrote, "Had that man received medical attention immediately, he would have had a good chance to get better." Thus have money-grabbing, falsehood, and despair often followed this misplaced trust.

Believe, however, that, if you pray to God for health or for the lifting of any other burden — the unpaid bills after the funeral of your deceased husband; the increasing mortgage charges of 1939, 1938, 1937 and longer, for which you see no source of payment; the sorrow in your family that seems beyond remedy — God *can* help you provided you are Christ's; and He *will* help you if this healing be according to His will. If our Lord prayed in that garden of agony, *"Not My will, but Thine, be done!"* should we not go to dark Gethsemane and learn of Jesus to pray submissively for earthly blessings? God grants requests for the restoration of health, money, and happiness, for the removal of family friction and the lightening of all earthly burdens only when those petitions are in harmony with His good and gracious will, which — whether we understand it or not — always directs a Christian's life to a blessed end.

If you, my peace-robbed friends, tell me that though you are Christ's the Savior has not healed you, let me ask in reply whether you have that trusting, victorious faith which says, *"Speak the word only, and my servant shall be healed!"* Pray on your knees and with all your soul for a deeper, stronger, truer faith! Turn to the basic textbook on the curing of wounded hearts, the Bible! Daily, constantly, reverently, study the Word! Read it aloud! Have it explained to you! With this confident faith, all else may pass away; but the promise of God's healing grace positively must, through Christ, be fulfilled in your life. Perhaps, too, you have been dictatorial in asking for this healing love. You forget that sometimes God's will and wisdom must purify, refine, and strengthen your faith by repeated contact with the fires of adversity. Perhaps you have been too sure of yourself in the past, and therefore God sends no immediate help so that you may become truly humble, fully penitent, and completely reliant on Him. It may be that God has already helped you and you do not realize it because He has adopted a new and unexpected healing process.

Particularly do we ask you, our fellow-redeemed, who have not found help for your sins and cure for your affliction in Jesus, to approach the cross and there to find your Savior and Substitute, your Ransom and Atonement. Keep His cross before your mind during the day and at night, when your eyes close or when they open in sleeplessness; cling to the Crucified! Then you will have not only a cure for every sin, a healing for every sorrow, but, day by day walking more closely with the crucified, now victoriously risen Savior, you can also look to the heavenly homeland with the confidence, "Earth hath no sorrow that Heaven cannot heal!"

O Christ, grant every one of us Thy healing love! Amen.

JESUS CHRIST — CROSS-EXAMINED!

"The high priest arose and said unto Him, Answerest Thou nothing? What is it which these witness against Thee? But Jesus held His peace. And the high priest answered and said unto Him, I adjure Thee by the living God that Thou tell us whether Thou be the Christ, the Son of God. Jesus saith unto him, Thou hast said." — Saint Matthew 26:62-64.

Blessed Lord Jesus, who on the cross didst suffer agony and endure shame for us and our sins:

Help us by Thy Spirit not only to behold in Thy suffering and crucifixion the sorrow of Thine anguish, the hatred of mankind, Thy faithfulness unto that bitter end; give us also penitent, trusting hearts to find at Calvary the endless love that redeems us from sin, the limitless face that atones for our iniquities. By the contemplation of this cross may we daily draw nearer to Thee, to heaven and its eternal life. Amid the swirling floods of our afflictions give us the courageous faith that builds its strength and stability on Thee, our everlasting Rock of Ages, the hope that clings the more resolutely to Thy grace the higher the waters of agony rise upon us! O Christ, hear us now and mightily prove Thy power for Thy mercy's sake! Amen.

FRIENDS of a New Jersey detective who recently died in the penitentiary are urging the President of the United States to overrule the court verdict of "guilty" and restore the dead man's good name. During his long career, they point out, he faithfully served the interests of law and order; and the misstep near the end of his life, his attempt to solve a kidnap case by kidnaping a suspect, should not forever brand him a criminal.

In reading of this proposal during these Lenten days, many Christians doubtless have recalled a real miscarriage of justice — the most shocking mistake in legal history, the sentence that sent Jesus Christ, the innocent Savior of all men, to the cross. One can understand why certain prominent Jews have suggested that their coreligionists throughout the world choose official representatives to declare the trial of Christ before the great Jewish Council completely illegal.

No doubt should linger in any modern mind that the account of this hearing before the churchmen of Jerusalem is faithfully described in our four gospels. Dr. Simon Greenleaf, former professor of law at Harvard University and the greatest authority on evidence the legal profession of any country or age has ever produced, has shown in a remarkable book that Matthew, Mark, Luke, and John must be admitted as competent and true witnesses. Again, no one is justified in claiming that the verdict of "guilty" pronounced by Christ's countrymen was not decisive, since Pilate was the ultimate authority. If the high priest and his henchmen had not conspired to brand Jesus a blasphemer, a criminal, who must be executed, there would have been no Roman trial. Humanly speaking, no Caiaphas, no Calvary; no high-priestly hatred, no high-priestly self-sacrifice by Jesus; no cross-examination after that first hearing by Annas, no cross-bearing after the final hearing by Pilate!

Because Jesus is still on trial before the modern world, every member of this far-flung radio audience, either for Christ or — may God forbid! — against Him, must find comfort or condemnation in this court-room scene. Come, then, as we proceed in our Lenten meditation from the Garden of Gethsemane to the palace of Caiaphas! Behold with us for our warning and our comfort

JESUS CHRIST — CROSS-EXAMINED!

We take our text from Saint Matthew's account (chapter 26, verses 62-64): *"The high priest arose and said unto Him, Answerest Thou nothing? What is it which these witness*

against Thee?   But Jesus held His peace.   And the high
priest answered and said unto Him, I adjure Thee by the
living God that Thou tell us whether Thou be the Christ,
the Son of God.   Jesus saith unto him, Thou hast said."

I

THE CROSS-EXAMINERS

You may recall that it was about two o'clock on Friday
morning when the Jewish Council was hastily convened at
Caiaphas' palace, where the Savior was to be reexamined,
after the private hearing before the ex-high priest, Annas.
Who constituted the court which was to pronounce the
verdict that finally meant life or death for Jesus?   If you
picture this Council as a group of godless men, sworn
enemies of religion, a "kangaroo court" impaneled by
politicians and from city gangs, revise your opinion!   This
was a blue-ribbon jury, an assembly of Jerusalem's noteworthy citizens: teachers, merchants, and professional men.
Every one of the seventy who voted in that Sanhedrin was
a respected community leader; and the seventy-first ballot
was cast by the pinnacle of Jewish society, the high priest
himself!

Nineteen centuries of Gospel history have not drastically changed the spirit of those who today sit in judgment
on our Lord.   The charge has always been raised that the
Church's roster contains *"not many wise men after the*
flesh, not many mighty, not many noble."   While we can
never sufficiently thank God that among the public de-
fenders of our Lord Jesus in this country we number some
of the nation's foremost physicians, business men, scientists,
statesmen, industrialists, artists, the rank and file of Christian membership comes from the middle and lower classes.
Write that down, you agitators who label the Church an
institution for the wealthy!   It is the ever-repeated tragedy
that too many of the rich forget God and destroy them-

selves with their own money. No wonder Martin Luther thanked God that he had been born poor! Most men, basking in the warm rays of fame, begin to worship their own bloated bigness, despise the Almighty, and neglect their fellow-men. Only few show a humility like the Duke of Wellington's. At a Communion service it happened that a poor old man knelt beside him to receive the Sacrament. When one of the church officers hastily urged the shabbily dressed communicant to move away from the Duke, the alert eye of the strategist who had defeated Napoleon at Waterloo immediately grasped the situation, and in an undertone Wellington whispered: "Do not move! We are all equal here." Most men when they have climbed the highest rungs in the ladder of power, are poisoned by the same pride that in the end made Nebuchadnezzar crawl on his hands and feet to eat grass. True, one or two members of the Sanhedrin, Nicodemus and Joseph of Arimathea, were at least secret disciples of Jesus; but why were they not heard in this special session? In charity we may assume with most commentators that they were elsewhere. What tragic absence! Had their voices been raised in our Lord's defense, they would be honored as brave witnesses for the crucified Savior.

Who conducted the cross-examination after the previous, private trial? Again, do not think of a heartless, corrupt lawyer, who would sell his own soul if the price offered were high enough. As utterly incredible as this may seem, the prosecuting lawyer and at the same time the judge in this life-and-death case was supposed to be of the most blameless character, the most exemplary life in Israel, God's high priest, the privileged mediator between Jehovah and His people, the chosen servant of the Most High who supervised the Temple, its sacrifices and treasures, the one priest who was permitted to enter the Holy of Holies. Yet this Caiaphas, who wore a triple crown of gold, bearing the inscription, *"Holiness to Jehovah,"* was anything but holy. It was he who, long before this trial, had foreshadowed his plan to kill Jesus by declaring publicly, *"It is expedient for us that one man should die for the people and that the whole nation perish not."* He, together with many ordinary priests, Sadducees, most of them, were the Modernists of that day, who denied not only the resurrection of the body and the life everlasting but also the sinfulness of man and his need of salvation. Well might the trial of Jesus before Caiaphas have borne the title, "Jesus Christ versus the Hierarchy," "Christ against the Church Leaders."

The hardest struggle in the Savior's cause today is not the Church's battle with the American Association for the Advancement of Atheism, not the counter-attack against the Communist blasphemy, not the campaign of street-corner anarchists and parlor radicals, but the conflict within the churches themselves. The word "Christian" has become one of the most misused terms in the English language. Give a preacher a building with stained-glass windows, an organ, and perhaps an altar; let him, garbed in clerical robes, step into a pulpit, and no matter what he says or does, he can pass as a Christian. He may deny every fundamental truth and even hold Scriptural promises up to public ridicule, but in the minds of the masses he is a Christian. What is of more serious consequence, Modernists lay strenuous claim to this title. If the United States Government takes definite measures to copyright trade names and prohibit their abuse, it is certainly proper that the Biblical forces of this country should protest against the deceptive use of their Savior's name.

What a deadly parallel often exists between the leading churchmen of the Savior's time and the powers that be in some denominations today! Christ's enemies rejected God's Word; in our time ministers write imposing books to disprove Bible truth. The first-century Sadducees denied the Judgment and the life to come; our twentieth-century Sadducees teach the same delusion and try to hide its hopelessness under catch phrases of double meaning. The Savior's opponents were the Jewish church-leaders; and now, too, it seems that the way to commanding positions in certain religious sectors is to put a question-mark behind every promise of God. Caiaphas was appointed high priest by the Roman governor who preceded Pontius Pilate; the 1940 Sadducees are often put into strategic positions by American wealth and *élite* society. The Council which examined Jesus enjoyed the support of public influence. Look at your daily newspapers to see whose sermons receive publicity, those of the consecrated pastor who preaches the cross and the blood and the new life, or of the Modernist who extols the goodness and greatness of man. That Jewish Council was so intolerant that it provided no attorney for Christ's defense; and the same brand of bigotry is betrayed by certain present-day church councils which take deliberate steps to bar programs like ours from the air and to stifle the testimony to the saving Blood. These seventy Sanhedrists conspired to destroy Christ; there are seven times seventy with imposing official authority dedicated to the unholy task of substituting a counterfeit message for the Gospel of golden hope.

Consider also the despicable tactics employed by the Savior's murderers and the complete violation of the legal codes that marked their hatred. *"Thou shalt not bear false witness,"* the Law of their God demands; but the priests, the very men who were to uphold truth, planned the perjury of bribed witnesses. "Be not a sole judge!" the Talmud declares; yet Christ was examined before Annas alone. "Let a capital offense be tried during the

day but suspended at night!" — these are the very words
of Jewish law; but so viciously did they hate Jesus that
it was about two o'clock in the morning when He was summoned before His persecutors. "Thou shalt not judge on
the eve of the Sabbath nor on that of any festival!" the
Talmudic regulations require; yet Jesus was tried on a day
that was both festival and pre-Sabbath. "If a sentence
of death is to be pronounced, it cannot be concluded
before the following day" — thus, literally, does Jewish
procedure prohibit haste; but within hardly twelve hours
Jesus was tried and crucified. "There must be at least
two witnesses for the conviction of a crime," Maimonides,
Jewish authority, stipulates; but, as the Scripture reports,
"though many bore false witness against Him, . . . their
witness agreed not together." The Old Testament prohibits the high priest from tearing his garment; but in
his hatred of Christ, Caiaphas breaks this injunction and
rips his own clothes. The Talmud asks judges to weigh
each case "in the sincerity of their conscience"; but there
was nothing sincere nor any voice of conscience expressed
by that Council which, as other illegalities show, assailed
Jesus by deliberate connivance. We talk of corruption in
our courts, and God knows we have too much; yet with
all this, how careful magistrates usually are to see that the
prisoner receives full consideration! Do you remember
the so-called "trial of the century," when a New York
politician was charged with receiving "protection" money
from gangsters and gambling interests? One single sentence spoken by the district attorney caused the judge to
declare a mistrial; but here, before Caiaphas, every
utterance of magistrate, witnesses, jury, is a hate-filled
attempt to convict Christ.

The same malice marks the modern trial of Jesus.
Some of you condemn Christ without ever giving Him

a chance to explain His blessed promise. You do not show Jesus the fairness ordinary courtesy demands even for your fellow-men. With a fatal prejudice that can send your soul to hell you sentence Jesus on the basis of perjured testimony found in the filthy writings of unbelievers or in the subtle lies of Christ-denying Modernists.

We cannot overlook the sequel to this fatal verdict. When that Council shouted its unanimous sentence, *"He is guilty of death!"* it really pronounced its own doom. Some of the seventy probably lived until the year 70, when the arm of divine justice gripped godless Jerusalem. In that year Titus placed his siege engines around the city walls, and the beleaguered city became an inferno of torture and death. Our age must likewise take heed lest the rejection of the Cross weaken our spiritual foundations. Americans dare not minimize this warning stressed by past history: No nation can prosper through rebellion against God, disregard of His Word, and wilful rejection of Jesus. The present war, despite all the flag-waving, is a visitation from God for the repudiation of Christ. Do you think that the holiness and justice of the Almighty can see a nation like Germany prosper indefinitely when that country has thrust on the world so many gifted but destructive Bible critics and enemies of our Lord? Do you believe that a God who hates evil will continue to shower His rich blessings on an empire like the British where haughty churchmen publicly deny Scripture truth and reject the Savior's atonement? Do you suppose His divine favor can rest forever on France, the nation that helped to start the hostile Bible criticism and that produced notorious infidels? Above all, how long can we in the United States expect continued divine benediction on our land when hundreds of churches have turned from the crucified Christ, some of the largest theological schools disavowed the redemption, and many colleges ridiculed faith in the saving blood?

You may have a score of different answers to the question, "What do the people of the United States need today?" And we will gratefully accept any reply that offers sound economic, industrial, social help. But much more than this, millions in our nation need repentant sorrow over their sins. The country must have the spirit of humility and contrition. The individual citizens — and now, with the Spirit's help, I speak to the hearts of those who oppose the Lord Jesus — should learn from this cross-examination of Christ how tragic it is to see that suffering Savior faced by the fury of hate-filled men and to cry out, *"He is guilty of death!"* Caiaphas did not continue long as high priest after he helped send Jesus to His death. Others who rejected Christ — Pontius Pilate, Herod — were likewise doomed; for no matter how self-confident a man may be, if he allies himself with Jesus' enemies, the time will come when he will shriek in terror; when not our Lord but he is cross-examined; when the court-room is no earthly palace but the bar of eternity; when the judge is not Caiaphas, but the everlasting High Priest! Laugh at this truth if you will; some day you will weep the bitterest tears you ever have shed. While there is still time, as long as Christ's mercy and His forgiveness are extended to you, turn from these cross-examiners to Him who for your sake was cross-examined, and pray that you may find in Him pardon, peace, and eternal blessing!

II

THE CROSS-EXAMINED

How impressively Jesus faces His accusers! Innocent of any charges malice can invent, He listens in silence as perjury follows perjury and old falsehoods give way to new. In His unbroken composure the bound Savior towers so infinitely above His persecutors that Caiaphas rises from his imposing seat in the center of that inquisition chamber to demand, *"Answerest Thou nothing? What is it which these witness against Thee?"* Still no reply comes over Jesus' lips. Does He refuse to speak because He thinks words are useless and nothing can deter His bloodthirsty enemies? Or does He refuse to raise His voice in His own defense because something that He says may help to set Him free? We hardly know, but it has always seemed to me that Christ's silence shows His complete innocence. He needs no lengthy, voluble defense against these accursed lies; He has the divine conviction that the truth of His cause and the fulfilment of His mission must eventually triumph over the worst that earth and hell together can devise against Him.

Behold that silent Savior once more! Turn back to the golden prophecies of Isaiah's fifty-third chapter, where twice we read, *"He opened not His mouth,"* and where for the first time in the entire Scriptures Jesus is directly called the *"Lamb"* — sin-bearing, yet uncomplaining in His suffering. Turn forward from Calvary to the unfolding chapters of the Church's growth, and you will see that in every dark age when the cause of Christ was attacked men have turned to Jesus, repeating the question of Caiaphas, *"Answerest Thou nothing?"* In these latter days it often appears to us, too, that Jesus never answers swaggering unbelief and boasting blasphemy. How is it, we ask ourselves, that Christ permits the foes of our faith, unchallenged and unrebuked, to shake their fists at Him? Why can atheists succeed in crushing Lutheran Finland? Why do Modernists acquire the largest churches, while the humble preacher of grace and truth is often relegated to the backwoods or put on the list of the unemployed?

Why do the godless prosper, despite their adultery and vicious lies, while the godly, trying to walk in Christ's footsteps, meet almost endless reverses?

God's ways are not ours, for our heavenly Father is much more merciful and long-suffering than we are. If a soul can be saved, even a soul weighted down by terrifying sins, He often lets mercy prevail instead of justice. But Christ does hear, and finally He must answer. He may delay; He may postpone; but though His retribution is sometimes slow, it never fails. That inevitable reckoning may come in this life; but no matter how emphasized the prosperity of the wicked and their easy existence may be in this world, Christ always answers in the next world. Don't speak lightly of sin because in your own eyes you may have escaped judgment. Don't think for a moment that because you have emerged undetected from a series of secret transgressions, you can keep on safely pursuing your lusts. The Savior is too close to every life not to know the private vices that you like to believe concealed forever. When Lafayette, friend of Washington and our American Republic, was once imprisoned, a small hole was bored into the door of his gloomy cell; and through that opening a soldier ceaselessly watched Lafayette. Morning, noon, evening, night, midnight — it was terrifying, he recalled, to be confronted by that eye. The eye of God, which penetrates deeper than any X-ray, sees farther than any telescope, magnifies more times than any microscope, is even more relentlessly focused on our lives; and woe to us if, when God delays in punishing our wrongdoings, we think that He cannot see us and will not rebuke us!

What source of strength those of you who are Christ's can find in His silence! When it seems that Jesus does not answer you as afflictions turn your joy into bitter

ashes, take courage in knowing that your Savior's voice
was not perpetually hushed! God's promise to you in
Christ is, *"Call unto Me, and I will answer thee!"* Leave
the hour and minute to the Father, for His time of help
is always the best. Take steel prematurely from the molten
furnace, and it is easily broken. Sometimes the longer
God lets us wait for His relief, the more strengthening the
trial, the more helpful the patience we learn in trusting
Him completely.

It seems that Caiaphas, fearing His whole plan against
Jesus might collapse if the Savior maintained His remarkable silence, quickly changed his tactics. In one pointed
question, for which he dramatically put the Savior under
special oath, he brought the trial to its climax. *"I adjure
Thee by the living God,"* he cries, *"that Thou tell us
whether Thou be the Christ, the Son of God."* Had the
world stood still in that moment, we should hardly be
surprised; for this was the question of the ages. Had Jesus
been silent then, He probably would have been acquitted,
but we should have been surrendered to doubt. If there
were any question about Christ's being God, any uncertainty attached to the fact that, as more than man, yes, as
God Himself, He can do what He pledged, the Christian
faith would hardly offer a better foundation than the
uncertain delusions heathen call their religion.

In that tense moment Jesus, confronted by the world
He loved, perishing in its sins, breaks His silence. Glorious
Lord of all truth that He is, He answered, *"Thou hast
said!"* — the striking way of replying with a firm and unconditional "Yes!"

Thank God for this testimony! The captive, cross-
examined Christ is your God! Let me repeat, so that no
suggestion of doubt remains in your heart: this broadcast
and every one whose voice is heard in our "Bringing-Christ-

to-the-Nation" mission proclaims, and we pray that you believe, just as this Concordia Seminary, from the campus of which I broadcast, has for a century taught, and with blessing from above will continue to teach, that Jesus Christ is not merely a man nor the most noble and exalted of men; not an angel, even the most powerful of cherubim and seraphim; He is — O highest of all holy truths! — nothing less than the almighty God Himself!

Now, it were overflowing grace if Jesus had been only our God and if He had come into the world to show us some way, however hard, long, and exhausting it might be, on which we could return to the Father. But besides being our God, Jesus, as He solemnly testified before the high priest, is our *"Christ."* Do you know the blessed import of this name *"Christ"*? It means the Messiah, the long-predicted Savior, our anointed Prophet, the King of our souls, and our everlasting High Priest, who with the dripping cross of Calvary as His altar and His own sinless body the sacrifice, gave Himself into the death that has atoned for all our sins and assures us eternal life. That pale Captive before Caiaphas loved every one of us with a soul devotion so divine and all-embracing; loved us — listen closely, my fellow-sinners and fellow-redeemed! — despite our sins, our rebellion against God, our continued ingratitude, loved us into that death by which He suffered the punishment we should have endured, paid the whole amount of our indebtedness to God, so that in His name we can offer every burdened soul complete redemption and the promise of heaven, through faith, and faith alone.

Are you a Christian according to the dictionary's definition of the term, "one who believes in Jesus Christ . . . and the truth taught by Him"? Do you accept these two foundation facts emphasized in the cross-examination of Jesus, His deity and His atoning death on the cross? Give up everything in life that keeps you from this radiant conviction! Break down all resistance that blocks your way to Christ! Stifle each suggestion of self-righteousness and of earning heaven by your own merits or some one else's virtues! Come, just as you are in your sins, to your Christ and your God, just as He is in all His mercy; and the same Savior who told the high priest, *"Hereafter shall ye see the Son of Man sitting on the right hand of Power and coming in the clouds of heaven,"* will grant you the pardon and peace by which you can look beyond Calvary to the opened heaven and acclaim Christ, no longer bound by the malice of His enemies, but now victoriously enthroned, your Redeemer and Helper, ready to deliver you in every hour of need. You have in Christ's own testimony the assurance that He is *"coming in the clouds of heaven,"* not only for judgment on those who have rejected Him, but also to bring them who believe Him to their blood-bought and love-prepared places in the *"many mansions."* O come, Lord Jesus, come to every one of us with Thy love! Come to this sin-darkened, unbelieving age with Thy light! Come to the churches with Thy strength! Come to our homes and our hearts with Thy grace! O Jesus, our Christ and our God, come now! Amen.

"SUFFERED
UNDER PONTIUS PILATE"

*"They led Him away, and delivered Him to
Pontius Pilate, the governor. . . . And when he
had scourged Jesus, he delivered Him to be
crucified."* — Saint Matthew 27:2 and 26.

Lord Jesus, our all-sufficient Redeemer:

*We need Thy Spirit's help, beholding Thy cross, to find in Thee
not only an innocent Victim of furious hatred, an unselfish Sufferer, a noble Martyr, but, above all, our Redeemer from sin,
our God agonized for us, our Sovereign and King. By Thy
victory over death Thou canst grant us all we need for this life
and bless us with eternal joy. Help us, therefore, ever to repent
of our wrong, to trust Thee with unquestioning faith, and to find
in Thy presence strength for each day's sorrows and peace for our
war-saddened age! Oh, give Thyself richly to us and to the millions
who need Thee, our Savior of the cross, more than all else! Bless
us with heaven by the promise of Thy love! Amen.*

WE start by asking you a personal favor, which will
cost only a little exertion, but by which you may
help to direct some lost soul to heaven. If, as you hear
this broadcast, there are in your own home relatives and
friends who have not yet found their salvation in Christ,
will you not now urgently invite them to sit down with you
before the radio and listen to God's counsel for their eternal
redemption? If you have acquaintances living without the
Savior, will you not now ask them by telephone to dial the
station that carries this message? Your phone call will
bring them Christ's call. If you yourself have made the
mistake of refusing to acknowledge Jesus as your own
Redeemer and God's marvelous ways have led you to select
this station out of eight hundred others in the United

[248]

States, then this broadcast is meant particularly for you, as though these words were winging their miraculous way over the two or three miles or the two or three thousand that may separate us, to bring you the claims of Jesus Christ on your soul!

What a difference a few minutes can sometimes make! Oil gushes from an impoverished farm, and paupers become men of wealth overnight. A governor signs pardon papers, and convicts suddenly leave the penitentiary — free men. The next half hour can completely change your life and enrich you with Heaven's eternal treasures that neither reverse nor time can destroy. Stay with us during this broadcast. Help others join in this worship!

How we rejoiced at our headquarters last week when almost 12,000 letters were received, the largest number in our past radio history! Twelve thousand letters in five days means that millions are tuned to the 160 stations of our "Bringing-Christ-to-the-Nation" broadcasting system. Thank God for that; and then pray that we can reach the untouched masses in this country who have not yet said to Jesus, "O Christ, Thou art the Savior of my soul, the Substitute for my sins!" Help us speak to some of them this afternoon! They all need Christ. Many of them, as multitudes in this audience, resemble the man of whom our text treats, Pontius Pilate, the Roman governor of Judea, who, face to face with Jesus and convinced of that Savior's innocence, sought to save Him from death but finally delivered Him to be crucified.

It is not by accident that Pontius Pilate is the only man mentioned by name in the Apostles' Creed, the three articles of our faith all Christians accept, whether they be Protestant or Catholic, Lutheran or Reformed. This morning, in the Second Article and climax of the Creed, millions over the earth declared in hundreds of languages, "I believe in Jesus Christ," God's "only Son, our Lord, who was conceived by the Holy Ghost, born of the Virgin Mary," and then not, "suffered under Caiaphas, the high priest"; not, "suffered under Herod, the tetrarch"; not, "suffered under the betrayal of Judas," or "the denial of Peter," but, "suffered under Pontius Pilate." The weaknesses and dishonesties of Pilate are more common to the race, and that means more easily found in my life and yours, than the sins of many other figures in the Lenten tragedy. Therefore with prayer in our hearts and praise for Christ on our lips we shall study the lessons taught by these striking words of the Christian creed,

"SUFFERED UNDER PONTIUS PILATE"

as we find this suffering described in the twenty-seventh chapter of Saint Matthew and summarized (verses 2 and 26) in these words: *"They led Him away and delivered Him to Pontius Pilate, the governor. . . . And when he had scourged Jesus, he delivered Him to be crucified."*

I

THE SCREAMING INJUSTICE OF THAT SUFFERING

When that mockery of injustice, called the "trial" of Jesus before the council of His own countrymen, ended, the Savior was imprisoned at the high priest's palace; and there, under the roof of that Old Testament church-leader, the Savior was subjected to the agony of indescribable torture. During these after-midnight hours the enmity and jealousy pent up during the three years of the Lord's ministry were let loose against Him. The high priest's servants, perhaps even some of the highly respected Sanhedrists, who had just condemned Jesus, began to spit on the Savior. With heavy rods they rained blow after blow on His defenseless body. While His own hands were tied, they amused themselves in hellish glee by striking Jesus with clenched fists or slapping His face with their open hands. They blindfolded Him, and one servant after the other brutally beat Him, demanding, *"Prophesy, who is it that smote Thee?"* If we did not know that according to the plan of divine mercy Jesus should be made the perfect Savior *"through suffering,"* we would wonder, reviewing the silent suffering of that first derision, why the heavens did not collapse on these fiendish torturers and the earth swallow them.

Christ was kept at the high priest's palace until sunrise, for it was illegal to conduct a capital trial at night. Hardly had the earliest rays of that day of destiny, the first Good Friday, broken the darkness, when the Council reconvened to ratify its earlier verdict. This time the priests, the scribes, the Sadducees, the men of affairs in Jerusalem, made quick work of their unholy task. When Jesus once more acknowledged Himself the Son of God and the promised Redeemer, His doom was sealed; as one man the great Council shrieked its impassioned verdict, *"He is guilty of death!"*

For some undefined reason, perhaps because they had no power to execute the death-sentence, the priests led Jesus to the highest authority in Judea, the Roman governor, Pontius Pilate. We know something of this Roman official, from both the Bible and secular history. These sources agree in portraying him as a shrewd, scheming politician, to whom truth and justice could mean but little if they implied personal danger. That spirit of Pontius Pilate has not entirely disappeared from our officialdom. No party platform will admit it, but corruption in Federal, State, and local circles, with politicians swayed by mobs and the desire for votes, is a major menace to our American way of living. Before we think of entering Europe's war to clean up sins across the seas, let us put our own political and official houses in order.

It was about six o'clock in the morning when the mob accompanying the priests, probably to impress the governor, stormed the gates of Pilate's palace and demanded a hearing. Because Pilate was a Gentile and contact with his residence would have made them unclean, the leaders refused to enter but voiced their charges against Christ in the open. They indicted Him on three counts: perverting the nation, forbidding to give tribute to Caesar, and making Himself a rival king. Need I tell you that each one of these accusations was an utter falsehood? When nationalistic fervor sought to make Jesus king of Israel, He spurned that proposal. Instead of leading a rebellion against the Roman rule or refusing to pay tribute, He firmly told the Pharisees, *"Render to Caesar the things that are Caesar's."*

Christians have repeatedly been accused of perverting their fellow-men and of showing disloyalty to their governments. Why did streams of martyr blood flow through the first centuries? Because a Nero claimed that the Christians had burned Rome; because a dozen imperial fiends branded as traitors and state's enemies all Christians who would not worship a pagan ruler. Why have Gospel missionaries been beheaded, burned at the stake, boiled alive, stoned to death? Because these men of God were charged with changing the old order and combating national interests. In our country, too, atheists and other radicals claim that Christianity must be banished from our shores because it is a brake on progress. But true disciples of Jesus are the strongest elements in the support of the nation's welfare. If we were a real Christian nation; if the teachings of our Lord could impel and direct the actions of all our

130,000,000 Americans, we would witness an outpouring
of unparalleled blessings. If trust in Christ instead of the
craving for power were the watchword in modern Europe,
this terrifying conflict, with millions sworn to exterminate
their fellow-men, might never have started.

Perhaps because Pilate immediately saw through the
priests' scheming designs, or perhaps because there was
about this Galilean Prisoner something utterly unusual and
personally compelling, the Roman governor retired with
Christ to the judgment-hall, only to return after a brief
examination and tell the churchmen and the Jewish leaders,
"I find in Him no fault at all!" What an amazing statement for this shrewd, worldly-wise Roman official! Fabulous
amounts have been spent since that fatal Friday to find
some mistake in Christ's career. Men have devoted their
misdirected lives to discover and publicize a single misstep
on Jesus' pathway. Every word our Lord spoke, every
counsel He gave disquieted souls, every denunciation He
hurled at impenitent unbelievers — all have been subjected,
as in the case of no other man living or dead, to a minute
examination and placed under the microscope of hostile
criticism to find a single flaw.

Christ's challenge, however, still rings in our modern
world, *"Which of you convinceth Me of sin?"* We repeat
this question to every unbelieving mind. We will not offer
you $1,000 for any mistake you can discover in Jesus;
for recent events have illustrated that such proposals may
produce much harm. We will, however, make an even
more startling challenge: If any of you infidels or skeptics
who write us uncouth letters can produce from our Lord's
entire life one sinful word or action, we shall publicly tell
the nation of your discovery in our broadcast. Unbelievers
with intellects far deeper than yours have been honest
enough, though refusing to accept Christ as their Savior, to

acclaim His infinite holiness. Rousseau, the French philosopher, whose conduct and writings were a steady denial of Bible truth, had to admit, "The life and death of Jesus are those of a God!" The German unbeliever Strauss, notorious opponent of Christ's atoning love, confessed: Jesus is "the highest object we can possibly imagine with respect to religion." The skeptical historian Renan conceded, "The Christ of the gospels is the most beautiful incarnation of God in the most beautiful of forms." As one tribute follows the other, each wrung from the unwilling lips of those who have attacked the Christian faith, you, too, should at least agree with Pilate, *"I find no fault in Him at all!"*

To picture the full Christ, however, we must know that He was more than sinless and stainless. The decisive question is this: "Is He our God and Savior?" Because only a few hours before He had emphatically declared that He was both Lord and Savior of the race, the churchmen refused to accept the government's verdict of innocence. Pilate, weakening, sought to shift the responsibility of a decision regarding Christ. Because the Savior had lived in Galilee, he sent Him to Herod, the wretched prince, whose reign was marked by debauch and bloodshed; but Herod, in Jerusalem for the Passover, failing to take Christ seriously, returned Him to Pilate. Next, the governor proposed to release Christ by the customary pardon granted certain criminals during the high holidays; but bloodthirsty protests rent the air: *"Away with Him!"* *"Give us Barabbas!"* Resorting to compromise, Pilate offered to scourge Jesus publicly.

Then follow the worst agonies Jesus suffered except in the crucifixion itself: The Savior of mankind is stripped, tied to a pillar, and then subjected to a punishment so merciless that a modern world has barred its excruciating torture. No ordinary whip, but a scourge of rawhide, its thongs tipped with bone or lead, cuts its way into that quivering back and leaves its deep crimson furrows. Often, as the Roman soldiers, heartless rabble most of them, knew too well, the victims of that inhuman brutality soon fell into a dead faint or died before the scourging could be completed. But Jesus did not lose His consciousness even for a moment; it was as though He were to feel the pain of every agony that degenerate men could inflict.

This spirit of Pilate's persecution has remained the heritage of our race. When the average American thinks of antireligious hatred and stifled consciences, he pictures to himself brave Pastor Niemoeller imprisoned in Germany or the closed Russian churches. Most people, however, are not aware that intolerance has spread far more widely over the globe. Haile Selassie, emperor of Ethiopia, granted liberal permission to Protestant missions to carry out their evangelization programs in Ethiopia; but when the Italian Fascist troops stole the country, this work was all but wiped out. Protestant missions flourished in Albania under King Zog, a Mohammedan; but when Mussolini's regiments drove him into exile, Protestant work in Albania stopped. During the bloody revolution in Spain the Reds permitted Protestants to worship unmolested; but now that General Franco is firmly intrenched, non-Catholic worship has been severely restricted.

When the last blow had descended and Pilate saw Jesus still gasping and trembling under the impact of the lash, he felt that the hatred of the priests and the populace would vanish at the sight of such suffering. Expecting an answer of sympathy that even savages sometimes show, he cried, *"Behold the Man!"* — as though he would say, "O look closely at this poor, beaten, bleeding Victim of your jealousy and stop this inhuman torture! What more

do you want?" But the crowd was incited by priests —
and how often have men with holy robes brought a curse
on themselves and their followers when, as the brains of
sinister plots, they made the common people the dupes in
their unholy destruction! The only answer Pilate's appeal
for sympathy receives is the snarling, *"Crucify Him!
Crucify Him!"*; and now at last the charge for which they
demand death is urged: *"He ought to die because He
made Himself the Son of God."* That claim startles the
calloused governor, and once more he retreats with Jesus
to the quiet of the judgment-hall.

You recognize here the decisive issue in the modern
trial of the Savior. No intelligent person will quarrel with
you if you say that Jesus was a great man; but call Him
the Son of God, insist on the fact that He is infinitely more
than man ever was or ever can be, and you will find yourself in a minority, opposed not only by those who boast
that they do not need Christ, but also by many representative leaders of churches who call themselves Christians.
The modern pulpit has much to say about Christ as a just
man, about God dwelling in our Lord, about Jesus as the
incarnation of heaven's virtues; when pressed, they will
admit that to a certain degree other men can be described
by the same deceptive words and phrases. Be clear on this
point: Deny the deity of our Lord Jesus Christ, and you
have pulled the corner-stone from our Christian faith and
reduced it to shapeless ruins resembling the failure and
despair of every man-made religion.

One more thought flashed through Pilate's mind: Try
ridicule, the strategy that has laughed many a case out of
court! Jesus had called Himself a king. Well, let Him
be a king! Who in all the world, he concluded, as the
Savior faced him the last time, would ever seriously believe
that this blanched and bleeding Galilean prisoner could

rival the Roman rule? Still moved by the desire to save Jesus, he hushed the turmoil in the courtyard long enough to say, *"Behold your king!"* That sarcasm was the spark to explode new charges. *"We have no king but Caesar!"* the thunderous cry came back as in mock loyalty the unfortunate nation disavowed its true Messianic King. *"If thou let this man go,"* the mob threatened, *"thou art not Caesar's friend."* They knew Pilate's weak spot, these worldly-minded priests. His administration had repeatedly been marked by questionable procedures and unnecessary cruelties. There had been too many uprisings against Rome, and Pilate could not run the political risk of being reported to Emperor Tiberius as an official who had not crushed every suggestion of rebellion. So the decision was reached. Christ, it was evident, could not be acquitted. Yet Pilate's conscience, whatever was left of it, still uttered one feeble gasp. He ordered a basin of water, and there, before the sullen mob that had been milling and muttering for three hours, he went through a ceremonial act. He washed his hands, protesting, *"I am innocent of the blood of this just person. See ye to it!"* And they did! In blood-hungry protest the rumble of hell itself sounded throughout Pilate's palace, the most shocking curse men have ever wished upon themselves, the scream of Satan himself, *"His blood be on us and on our children!"* Then it was that Pilate, according to our text, *"delivered Him to be crucified."*

Roman law, as later codified, definitely asserted, "The vain clamors of the people are not to be heeded." Pilate, however, yielded to mob threats and transgressed his own empire's basic law. How differently other judges, eminent Christians, have acted when threatened by force! Some authorities call Sir Edward Coke the greatest of all English jurists. He refused to shade the law even for King James.

While his colleagues among England's high justices cowered before the king, Sir Edward, asked to disregard the common law in the king's interest, removed his judicial mantle and, with a gesture of contempt, hurled it in James's face. With an unconcern over the truth that hardly seems possible, Pilate, not made of such loyalty to the law, condemned Jesus to the cross.

If we cast excuses aside and face truth, must we not admit that similar indifference to Christ has gripped masses in this country? Is there not in every one of us, even those who are Christ's, a willingness to compromise and deny the Savior when an open confession of our faith would mean cutting opposition?

Remember the fate of Pilate! He was soon recalled to Rome on serious charges, and he never returned to Judea. Tradition differs concerning the rest of his life. Pious writers claim that before his death he sought escape from despair on Mount Pilatus in Switzerland, but that after wandering restlessly up and down its stony slopes, he finally plunged into Lake Lucerne — a suicide. To this day superstitious natives believe that periodically a gloomy form arises from the waters, washes its hands, and then disappears, only a few hours before a furious storm lashes the lake and the countryside.

This is pure legend, of course, but there is nothing fictitious in the assertion that all who see Christ as Pilate beheld Him — and that means every one in this audience — can never find peace and heaven by following Pilate's pathway. To meet the suffering Savior as you have in these moments; to hear Him say that He is come from God to testify to the truth; to have the conviction that He is blameless; to listen as Jesus says that He is a king, though His kingdom, holy and heavenly, is not of this

earth, and then to turn away from Christ, deliver Him to
His enemies, and finally consign Him to the cross, — and
you do that in principle when you refuse to acknowledge
Him your God and your Christ, — this is the surest way
of bringing unspeakable sorrow eternally on your own soul!

II

THE MATCHLESS BLESSING OF THAT SUFFERING

On the other hand, innumerable blessings come to you
if you behold with the eyes of faith Christ's agony under
Pontius Pilate. Everything he lost by rejecting Jesus you
can gain by accepting Him. Believe the Savior when He
says that He has come to testify to the truth! Kneel down
before Him, not in mockery and derision, as the Roman
legionaries did, but in a faith that says, "O Jesus, suffering
Savior, I know that Thou art the Truth, that every promise
Thou didst make and every warning Thy lips spoke is
the divine and unchanging truth!" Little enough in this
world remains unchanged. From the fastness of the Ant-
arctic Admiral Byrd reports that the South Magnetic Pole
has shifted its position; but here is the immovable spiritual
lodestone of the ages, Jesus, the Christ of God, with His
arms stretched wide over a world disfigured by horrifying
sin. When He says, *"Come unto Me, all ye that labor
and are heavy laden, and I will give you rest,"* take Him
at His word! Let His unchanging grace draw you to Him.

Beholding the suffering Christ, repeat Pilate's question,
"What hast Thou done?" But say it in faith and love!
Put it this way, "O Lord Jesus, *'what hast Thou done'*
for me? Why does the blood stream from Thy furrowed
back and trickle down Thy bleeding head and wounded?"
When you know the true Christ, — and now I take you
into the holy of holies, the heart of our Christian faith, —
you can hear Christ, above His anguish and groaning,

above the jeering rabble and the plotting priests, speak this grace to your soul, "I endured this for you. I stand here mocked and derided, scourged and beaten, in your stead."

Despite our thanklessness, our worship of self, our service to fleshly lusts, lost as we were in trespasses, this ever-blessed Savior offered Himself, His own guiltless body, His own stainless mind, His own spotless soul, as a living sacrifice, to atone — not for some of the world's iniquity or for a selected group of the morally respectable people — but to give Himself into death for the sins of all mankind, — first of all — each of us must say — "for my iniquities and the transgressions of my own heart and lips and hands."

Ask the agonized Christ once more, "'What hast Thou done,' O precious Savior?" and, believing Him, you will find that Jesus did even more than give Himself for you. He not only puts salvation within your reach, He also gives you heaven as your assured blessing, since it is the gift of faith, not the reward of works. Beholding the Christ of the beaten back, we should never be in doubt as to the complete salvation granted by His atonement. A few days ago a couple came to me with the problem of their mixed marriage. (Again I saw the open danger of such unions, and again I warn you against a marriage in which husband and wife cannot worship in the same church and with the same spirit and truth.) Before they left my office, I asked the husband, an unusually intelligent man, how he hoped to be saved, and he answered, "By leading a moral life, fulfilling the Ten Commandments, and doing the will of God." That sounds reverent and uplifting; but how many people lead a completely moral life? Have any of you fulfilled the Ten Commandments? Can any one truthfully say, "I have always done God's will"?

My fellow-redeemed, when you see Jesus before Pilate, suffering the hatred of Jew and Gentile, deserted by His disciples, almost breaking down under the weight of His agony, do not think how good you are! Rather kneel before Christ with this one plea: "O Jesus, be merciful to me with all my sins! Break my stubborn pride! Take away my self-glorification! Show me my human heart with all its sinful cravings and its forbidden lusts! Then, blessed Savior, lead me by Thy promise to Thy pardon! Wash me, cleanse me, make me pure in Thy Father's sight!" And in His name we promise you the redemption that has given myriads the new birth. Through faith in Christ a glorious life in grace will be yours.

How can any one refuse Christ's mercy? Do not make the fatal mistake of thinking that you can wash your hands of Christ, as Pilate did. You cannot push Jesus aside as easily as that. Do not lull yourself into the soul-destroying error of thinking that you can escape making a decision for or against Christ. You cannot remain neutral before the suffering Savior. You either damn yourself with the *"Crucify Him! Crucify Him!"* or you bow before Him to say, "My Lord, my God, my Savior!" Do not think that any one else can answer for you. Pilate tried to have Herod, the Jewish rabble, the priests, even Jesus Himself, remove the necessity of his accepting or rejecting Christ; but this is a matter of personal faith. Strive as you will, you must repeat Pilate's pointed question, *"What shall I do, then, with Jesus?"* Because God is waiting for your reply, answer the Spirit's pleading by praying with us now: "O Christ, Thou Lamb of God, that takest away the sin of the world, have mercy upon me! Grant me Thy peace!" Write us, and we will tell you how Jesus can direct your life and give you the promise of heaven. Will you not, together with the multitudes of Christians in this vast audience, dedicating these closing moments now to Christ, join us in this prayer, "O Christ, before Pontius Pilate Thou wast wounded for my transgressions, Thou wast bruised for my iniquities, the chastisement of my peace was upon Thee, and by Thy stripes I am healed!"?

Heavenly Father, give this trust to Thy children now before Thee! Strengthen this faith in weak, wavering hearts and preserve it in us, our mighty God, until we stand with the redeemed before Thy throne! Hear us for the suffering Savior's sake! Amen.

———

THE THREE CUPS AT CALVARY

"When they were come unto a place called Gol-gotha, . . . they gave Him vinegar to drink mingled with gall; and when He had tasted thereof, He would not drink." — Saint Matthew 27:33, 34.

"The soldiers also mocked Him, coming to Him and offering Him vinegar and saying, If Thou be the King of the Jews, save Thyself." — Saint Luke 23:36, 37.

"After this, Jesus, knowing that all things were now accomplished, that the scripture might be fulfilled, saith, I thirst. Now, there was set a vessel full of vinegar; and they filled a sponge with vinegar and put it upon hyssop and put it to His mouth. When Jesus, therefore, had received the vinegar, He said, It is finished." — Saint John 19:28-30.

O Jesus, our crucified Savior:

How can we ever thank Thee sufficiently that in the depths of Thy Passion Thou didst drink the cup of agony to the last bitter drop, dying to free us from eternal death? By Thy Holy Spirit direct us, every day we live, to examine ourselves by the standard of Thy Word, to acknowledge contritely, unreservedly, the repeated wrong that stains our souls, and to find in Thee forgiveness, strength for every weak moment, courage for all afflictions! Give us thankful hearts that are not content to show their gratitude for Thy suffering only during a brief hour on Sunday, but bring us daily to our knees in prayer for a sin-driven world! Lead us to speak and act, O blessed Savior, so that under Thy grace sinners may be converted to Thee from their evil ways, the sorrowing comforted, the unbelieving rebuked, and the glorious light of Thine atonement brought into many darkened hearts! The cross at Calvary assures us that Thou wilt hear us! Amen.

WHAT a stark-mad, blood-crazed world this is! Events of the week-end seem to forbode that peace is far distant in the European conflict. Both sides appear sworn to a war of extermination, which will not cease until one of the belligerents, exhausted, begs mercy, but receives none. When the grass turns green again, unless God Almighty intervenes and peace endeavors succeed, we shall probably witness mass slaughter and brutal destruction that exceed the worst hitherto known.

The call to arms may resound far beyond the German-French border and the Baltic country, where the Russian giant's fingers are slowly closing around Finland's throat, and beyond China, where invading armies press irresistibly forward. We now read that India's 350,000,000 seethe in unrest as a disobedience campaign plans independence of British rule. Ominous signs point to uprisings in the Arab world. Japanese writers are quoted as predicting that their country may be forced to fight the United States. How completely sin rules the world today! How savagely the lust for power seeks to destroy men's lives and happiness!

If you have never prayed for peace, begin to implore God now; and if you have petitioned the Almighty to stop the horrors of warfare, if it be His will, redouble your appeals! Christians know that intercessory prayer can succeed if diplomats fail, that only Christ holds permanent hope for our age. George Bernard Shaw, England's most noteworthy man of letters, has been outspoken in his unbelief; yet even before the present crisis he was quoted as admitting: "I am not a Christian any more than Pilate was. . . . But I am ready to admit, after studying the world of human misery for more than sixty years, that I see no way out of the world's troubles but the way which Jesus would have found." If scoffers concede that Christ's truth alone can extricate us from the maze of our own mistakes, how much more should we who love the Lord Jesus look to Him for soul help and spiritual guidance! How constantly we should follow Him to Calvary and there at the most sacred spot on the whole earth, in the holiest love men can witness, find through the crucified Savior, peace, perfect peace of soul, for a strife-torn age!

Not only do the seven words spoken by the Savior from the cross testify to His divine compassion for you and me, but even the apparently insignificant events on that Hill of the Skull emphasize the blessed Savior's love for the world that had nailed Him to the cross. To learn that at Golgotha God grants overflowing heavenly grace, consider

THE THREE CUPS AT CALVARY

which the Lenten chapters of the gospels describe in these words: *"When they were come unto a place called Golgotha, . . . they gave Him vinegar to drink mingled with gall; and when He had tasted thereof, He would not drink."* (Saint Matthew 27:33, 34.) *"The soldiers also mocked Him, coming to Him and offering Him vinegar and saying, If Thou be the King of the Jews, save Thyself."* (Saint Luke 23:36, 37.) *"After this, Jesus, knowing that all things were now accomplished, that the scripture might be fulfilled, saith, I thirst. Now, there was set a vessel full of vinegar; and they filled a sponge with vinegar and put it upon hyssop and put it to His mouth. When Jesus, therefore, had received the vinegar, He said, It is finished."* (Saint John 19:28-30.)

I

THE CUP OF COMA

Last Sunday we left Jesus doomed to the cross through Pontius Pilate's indifference and cowardice. Hardly had the Roman governor pronounced the sentence, when the soldiers tore the crown of thorns from Jesus' bleeding head, removed the mocking robe of scarlet from His scourged back, and dressed Him in His own crimson-stained garments. In a few moments the cross was prepared; staggering under its burden and its curse, Jesus, His soul weary unto death, His body aching and bleeding, was forced to bear the rough timbers that soon would bear His broken body. Today much is done to lighten the suffering of criminals before their execution. Special meals are provided; all reasonable requests are fulfilled; death itself is made as quick as the advance of modern science permits. These final favors are willingly granted to degenerate murderers, fiendish killers, ruthless kidnapers; but the enemies of the sinless Christ, not satisfied with repeated torture and derision, crowded the hours before the crucifixion with piercing pain and deepened humiliation.

The death-march begins its winding course toward Golgotha: in front the calloused Roman soldiers, eager to be through with this bothersome duty; a small group of sympathizers, close to the Savior; a crowd of morbid spectators, following. Tradition has embellished these last miles. Stations have been invented at which Jesus is said to have stopped or performed a miracle. The Scriptures know nothing of this. The only events in that death journey which the New Testament recounts are the Savior's collapse under the weight of the cross, the drafting of Simon of Cyrene as cross-bearer, and the last sermon Jesus preached, a warning addressed particularly to the women who lined the road or followed the procession: *"Daughters of Jerusalem, weep not for Me, but weep for yourselves and for your children."*

Finally — and how endless the way of sorrows must have seemed to Jesus! — the cortege of the cross reached Calvary. Today no one can definitely identify the scene of the Savior's crucifixion. Perhaps God has kept the location of earth's holiest sanctuary unknown; for if the site of Golgotha were common knowledge, how the hostility to Christ would seek to desecrate its ground! With equal insistence many so-called Christians would glorify the place of the cross instead of the Savior's love. No last-hour pardon was granted, and no reprieve postponed the execution of Pilate's sentence; but before the nails were hammered through Christ's quivering flesh, we are told, *"They gave Him vinegar to drink mingled with gall."*

This is the first cup at Calvary. We do not know whose hand reached out with that draught, a sedative, or narcotic, to ease pain and make death less excruciating. It may have been the last service of a friend or an ancient Jewish custom. Perhaps the soldiers offered Jesus this cup since it would make the work of crucifying smoother and easier. Whatever the motive, when we stop to behold the cross and its immeasurable anguish, the four wounds and their agony, the loss of blood and the sinking weakness, the tension of the body and the aching muscles, the racing fever and the raging thirst, we feel that, if we had been at Calvary, we would have cried: "O Jesus, drink this cup! Hast Thou not suffered enough? Why prolong this harrowing terror? O Jesus, drink this cup!" But the suffering Savior would have spurned that plea, for we read, *"When He had tasted thereof, He would not drink."* His suffering was no accident. He was to be nailed to the cross by divine direction, and no prospect of relief from crushing pain nor the hope that consciousness would gradually become numbed could move Him to escape the full force of that penalty.

Men have sometimes taken on themselves the punishment that others have deserved. Near Palmyra, Missouri, one can find in a lonely cemetery a modest marble tablet on which is chiseled, "This monument is dedicated to the memory of Hiram Smith, who was shot at Palmyra, October 18, 1862, as a substitute for William T. Humphrey, my father." During the Civil War William Humphrey and nine other Southern sympathizers from Palmyra were to be executed for the abduction of a Northern farmer. For some reason Humphrey was spared on condition that a substitute die for him. Hiram Smith, a young man of twenty-two, was shot in Humphrey's stead. But there was no compulsion or last-minute selection in Christ's taking our place. Only His indescribable love led Him to the cross; and because of that mercy Jesus was unwilling to die without full consciousness, without suffering completely the entire anguish for our sins.

Have you ever wondered what would have happened if Jesus had accepted that first cup? Had His spirit been deadened into insensibility, He would never have spoken that most magnificent of all prayers for pardon, "*Father, forgive them, for they know not what they do.*" Had He been unconscious, He would not have given us the holy example of concern for His mother which lives forever in these words from the cross, "*Woman, behold thy son!*" "*Behold thy mother!*" If He had drunk that cup of coma, perishing sinners would never have heard this merciful pledge to the penitent thief promising heaven immediately after death, without any intermediate purging, "*Verily I say unto thee, Today shalt thou be with Me in Paradise.*" If Jesus had left the world while under the influence of a narcotic, men would have asked, "Did Christ actually know what He was doing when He died?" But because He suffered "*unto the end,*" because in the depths of that ordeal Jesus did not lose His consciousness, even momentarily, we are convinced that He faced death for us knowingly, willingly.

We, too, must meet the miseries of life awake. Pampered minds will find it difficult to endure the reverses which the future may hold in store for them. We hear much of better days and a higher standard of living. Two expositions, one on each coast, will again portray for millions of summer visitors the World of Tomorrow with the breath-taking advances that present-day inventions promise. But what guarantee have we that tomorrow will bring the ease and comfort these world's fairs exhibit? During certain eras in modern history all progress has been retarded, and we may be facing far-reaching readjustment in which America will be called on to suffer as millions in Europe and Asia have. If it be God's will that we be subjected to undreamed-of hardship; if in our homes defeat and disaster should leave their devastating, deep-grooved marks; if our personal ambitions are to be dashed to pieces, let us not shriek in protest but learn of Jesus how to face afflictions. Last week we buried a beautiful child, scarcely a year and a half old, the only daughter of a pastor. Unexpectedly and too quickly death claimed the baby girl. Although sorrow cut deeply into her parents' hearts and tears flowed freely as the little casket closed, the resignation and trust in God's higher wisdom evidenced at this funeral showed that Jesus can teach us how to suffer.

What gave Jesus the strength to refuse the cup of coma and *"endure unto the end"*? At the beginning of His Gethsemane sufferings Christ had entrusted Himself to His Father's love and guidance, and now, on Calvary, He steadfastly set His heart and mind on God. He would not take the easier way and drink the vinegar mixed with gall, for His actions repeat the resolution of Gethsemane, *"The cup that My Father hath given Me, shall I not drink it?"* If you want to face your sorrows courageously, turn away from human theories of self-trust that can drug you into forgetfulness, indifference, false hope, but which eventually lead you to despair! Rather cling to the truth of God!

Fix your thoughts, your prayers, your desires, on your heavenly Father through Christ! Submit to His direction, resign yourself to His plan for life! Say, as Jesus did, *"Not my will, but Thine be done,"* and the Holy Spirit will sustain you in the hardest, cruelest, blackest moments.

Particularly do we ask you to avoid the sin of drunkenness, by which cowards habitually try to drown their sorrows in alcohol. The wide advertising of whisky, hard liquor displays in drug stores and restaurants, the constant cocktail-drinking, the increasing intoxication — all of which, we believe, will provoke the largest temperance movement the United States has ever seen, if the nation is finally awakened — are leading misguided people to think they can get rid of their difficulties by getting drunk. What about the aftermath — debauch, self-respect sacrificed, homes broken, good name and reputation lost? Above all, what about God's sentence pronounced upon impenitent drunkards? As unnumbered tear-stained wives and mothers, uncounted suffering children, plead with us, we ask you whose sins have just been scored to fight the evil of drunkenness by looking steadfastly to God, by praying especially in moments of temptation for the constant presence of Christ.

Always keep a definite, unbridgeable distance from the narcotics, which play a hideous role in modern society: opium, morphine, cocaine, marihuana, the ancient drug our age has revived, particularly to destroy the purity and the conscience of our high-school boys and girls. It is a blot on our nation that at least a million Americans are drug addicts. While the Government has taken commendable steps in checking this vicious evil, we ask you to help any unfortunate victims you may know by directing them to the forgiving, sustaining Savior. He refused that stupefying cup; and through trusting faith even the most inveterate drug addict can find strength and hope.

II

THE CUP OF MOCKERY

The second cup offered Jesus at Calvary after He had been nailed to the cross was the cup of mockery. It seems that the Roman soldiers detailed to supervise the crucifixion had sat down to eat the noonday meal. Some of them, joining the cruel carnival beneath the cross, began to mock Jesus, *"coming to Him,"* as the text states, *"and offering Him vinegar and saying, If Thou be the King of the Jews, save Thyself."* How gladly Jesus would have taken that sour wine! The last time any cup touched the Savior's lips was probably Thursday night in the quiet of the upper chamber; and after hours of torture, exposed as He was, to the sun and the force of the elements, our Lord would have welcomed refreshment. Yet it was offered only in mockery, and He had to continue enduring His thirst.

The age of mockery has not passed. Today, in the press and on the radio, one meets repeated attacks on Christ and His sacred Word. A leading automobile company features an advertisement burlesquing God's holy angels. The editorial page of a large Detroit newspaper brazenly calls one of the Bible-stories "a nursery tale." An educational gathering in St. Louis is entertained with a joke centering about Peter and the pearly gates. Yet those who call themselves Christians often accept this mockery without protest. Now, you and I may belong to different church groups, and I would be the last to minimize the importance of doctrinal differences; but if we cannot work together, we can at least work toward the same end. Those who believe with us that Christ, Son of God and Son of man, the Savior of a world perishing in its sins, is the only Hope of the age and those who with us acclaim the Bible as God's full and errorless revelation must protest every time a blasphemous voice is raised in public or private to speak that damnable "if" of the soldiers, "*if Thou be the King of the Jews,*" "*if Thou be the Son of God.*" The tragic truth that the Christian faith is often thus ridiculed and that unbelief is securely enthroned in American public life, must be explained by the grievous fact that many American churches, either through fear or disinterestedness or inability, have not protested against this derision. Give us your help in dashing that cup of sarcasm to pieces! By open, repeated, determined statements refute every utterance in the press, over the air, on the stage, and from the public platform that sneeringly refers to Christ and says, "'*If*' Thou be the King, the Savior, the almighty God."

Even churches have joined in questioning Christ's Word, denying His miraculous power, rejecting His deity. A radio friend sends an extract copied from a Sunday-school quarterly issued by a large Protestant denomination. The section dealt with our Lord's miraculous feeding of the five thousand, that stupendous wonder which should mean more in the United States today, with its relief rolls and destitution, than in any previous age. Instead of acknowledging Christ's divine power in multiplying the loaves and the fishes, this is how that paper — not a rationalistic sheet from the last century, not an atheistic publication, but an official church organ — explains away the miracle: Many among the five thousand in the desert had secretly brought food along, but were too selfish to share it with others. However, when they saw the lad open his lunch and distribute his store of food among those around him, they immediately concluded, "Well, if that boy can share his lunch, we can, too." So they brought forth their secret provisions, apportioned them among those who had nothing, and, lo and behold, there was plenty for every one! — How long, do you suppose, would the busi-

ness world tolerate such disloyalty? Yet churches endorse
that unbelief by printing it in their Sunday-school leaflets!
Do you not agree that we cannot continue to witness without stinging rebuke the blasphemy by which the hands of
churchmen raise the cup of sarcasm before the crucified
Savior, and taunt, " '*If*' Thou be the King, the Christ, the
Savior"? Can you not see that in your own life problems
you must turn your head, as the Savior did, away from
every one who suggests the ease of life but has the ridicule
of your God on his lips?

III

THE CUP OF COMPLETION

The third cup at Calvary was only a sponge. We are
told, "*Jesus, knowing that all things were accomplished,
that the scripture might be fulfilled, saith, I thirst.*" This
word from the cross is the shortest of the seven sacred
utterances of Jesus, the only reference to His own physical
suffering. Now "*that all things were accomplished,*" the
divine plan for salvation was closing its deliberate, God-
controlled program, the Savior found time to think of
Himself. The burning fever, the inflamed wounds, the
torment of thirst, one of the most terrifying agonies, made
His parched lips speak this short pleading sentence,
"*I thirst!*"

What stark reality rings from this cry at Calvary!
Many people today teach and try to believe that pain,
sickness, and suffering are imaginary; but when on the
cross the perfect Son of God moans, "*I thirst!*" that delusion must vanish. We are confronted here with truth,
emphasizing the real human nature of our Lord and Savior.
When we behold the Lenten tragedy and witness Christ's
majestic serenity amid the never-to-be-measured torture
and the hellish derision; when we hear His love pleading
for sinners and promising Paradise to a murderer; when

the sun is darkened before our eyes and the earth quakes beneath our feet, it is not hard to believe in the deity of Jesus, nor to confess with the centurion, "*Truly, this was the Son of God!*" At Calvary we may wonder more about the Savior's humanity. How can any man endure what He did? How can any mortal show the mercy and forbearance He revealed? But as we hear that hoarse, pitiful, pleading "*I thirst!*" we know, though we cannot understand this mystery, that Jesus was a true man. He felt to the fullest Golgotha's pain and thirst so that He could sympathize with our griefs and sorrows. Whenever the torment of life becomes unbearable, you can turn to the crucified Christ and say: "O Jesus, You suffered all this and much more for me! You know the torture of my body and the pangs of my mind." How blessed to have this echo of sympathy come from the cross, "Yes, My beloved, I know your anguish, for I have felt in My own body every pain that can disturb you."

Yet that cry, "*I thirst!*" pledges more than sympathy. It reveals Christ's compassion in suffering for your atonement. Sir James Young Simpson, famous British physician, whose testimony is particularly significant this Sunday since he introduced the use of chloroform to alleviate human pain, described his faith in these words: "I looked and saw Jesus, my Substitute, scourged in my stead and dying on the cross for me. I looked, believed, and was forgiven." If you, too, in the blessed all-inclusiveness of the Savior's Gospel will behold the parched and thirsting Christ who once invited, "*If any man thirst, let him come unto Me, and drink,*" but who now, instead of exerting His divine power, receives refreshment from a Roman soldier; if you believe in your heart and confess with your mouth that Jesus is tortured by thirst so that you never need thirst in hell or plead as the rich man did, "*Father*

Abraham, have mercy on me and send Lazarus that he may dip the tip of his finger in water and cool my tongue"; if that Savior suspended in mid-air between the world that crucified Him and the heavens that forsook Him, is enshrined in your heart as your personal Savior, how blessed His thirst, how charged with eternity's highest love every racked moment at Calvary!

That sponge filled with sour wine becomes the cup of completion; we are told, *"When Jesus, therefore, had received the vinegar, He said, It is finished!"* In a few moments the suffering which changed the world and opened heaven would be over. His divine heart would cease beating, His pulse stop throbbing, His eyes close, and all the screaming horror would cease. The crowds would trickle back to Jerusalem; His dead body would be removed from the cross; darkness would fall over the scene; and His sorrows would have passed forever.

More than anguish was finished. The truth of God, foretold by ancient prophecy, had gone into fulfilment. The predictions of this parched thirst recorded in the Twenty-second and the Sixty-ninth Psalms, together with a dozen other Old Testament previsions of His agony and His atoning death, had become reality at Golgotha.

Chiefly, however, the last chapter in the plan of salvation was fulfilled. Every demand that even the holy God made for the payment of our sins was satisfied by the Savior's self-sacrifice. When Jesus bowed His head in death, so far as our salvation was concerned, nothing remained for us to complete. He left no mistakes to be corrected, no uncertainties to be adjusted, no insufficiencies to be supplied. Everything that any soul in this audience needs for heaven is granted on the altar of the cross at Calvary. All else in life may be incomplete. A hundred tasks loom before us as unfinished. But when Jesus drank the third cup the end was at hand and with it completion — victory!

Three cups at Calvary! The first two, the cup of coma and the cup of mockery, Jesus did not drink. But the third, the sponge saturated with sour wine, the cup of completion, He drank and then cried, *"It is finished!"* Since the cups of our lives are filled from the overflow of His, may we spurn every act of spiritual cowardice and disloyalty, grasp the salvation concluded at the cross, and confidently exult: *"I know whom I have believed." "For I am persuaded that neither death nor life nor angels nor principalities nor powers nor things present nor things to come nor height nor depth nor any other creature shall be able to separate us from the love of God which is in Christ Jesus, our Lord!"* Amen.

THE HOLY OF HOLIES — OPEN
TO ALL!

"The veil of the Temple was rent in twain from the top to the bottom." — Saint Mark 15:38.

Ever-blessed Lord Jesus:

Let not the holy blood which on Thy cross flowed for our sins be shed in vain for any one of us! Bring us all to faith in Thee and trust in Thy death-bought mercies! To this end, O Savior of our souls, remove completely from us every thought of our own worthiness and help us, as we stand at Calvary, to know that we are lost without Thee but saved eternally with Thee! In this wide-spread worship send Thy Spirit into our hearts, particularly to those who once acclaimed Thee their Savior but who have since denied Thee! Plead with them, through Thy convincing power, to realize that, if they persist in rejecting Thy mercies, they have no hope! Mightily endow our broadcasts with power from on high, strengthen all those who have prayed for our mission of the air to continue their intercession, comfort the sorrowing, and lead us all, O wounded, bleeding, dying Savior, ever closer to Thy matchless grace! Hear us as Thou hast promised! Amen.

S ELDOM has the human hatred of Jesus Christ shown itself more vicious than in the repeated assaults on church-buildings dedicated to the Savior. In the year 303 the Roman Emperor Diolectian began the bloodiest campaign against Christ the world has known. He concentrated his efforts on demolishing every place in which our Lord was worshiped; and so sure was he of complete victory over the despised Son of God that he had a triumphal column erected with this inscription, "The name of the Christians has been destroyed." That boast was soon disproved, however; for by an exhibition of divine power that should strengthen our modern defense of Jesus, only twenty-two years later, in 325, Constantine the Great, his successor, exalted the Bible throughout the Roman

Empire as the supreme source of saving truth; and the ruined, desecrated churches were rebuilt and rededicated to Jesus.

During the French Revolution an actress of notorious morals was elevated to the high altar of Notre Dame Cathedral in Paris and introduced as the Goddess of Reason. Boastfully the leader of this blasphemy declared: "Mortals, cease to tremble before the powerless thunders of a god whom your fears have created! There is no god! Henceforth worship none but reason!" With enthusiastic approval that congregation of atheists bowed in adoration. But experience soon showed that a nation of godless citizens could not long continue; and within a few months the French National Assembly, the same men who had prostrated themselves before the Goddess of Reason, formally voted that belief in the existence of God was necessary. The actress stepped down from the altar; later she died amid poverty and filth. The cathedral was cleansed.

During our War of Independence British troops established a riding-school in the Old South Church at Boston and transformed it into a circus. Pulpit and pews were torn out and burned; hundreds of loads of gravel were spread over the floors; a bar was set up for alcoholic refreshment. The walls that had reechoed with God's Word now rang with profanity and carousal. After only a few weeks, however, the British were forced to evacuate Boston, and the Old South Church was restored.

Often when men thus try to profane God's house, they are mocked by their own defeat, just as the church-closing enemies of Christ will finally be set to naught in Europe. But when God Himself visits His righteous anger on any church, that building remains disavowed. Strikingly is this truth illustrated in an electrifying occurrence which marked the Savior's crucifixion. The Temple curtain was suddenly ripped through its entire length — symbolical per-haps of the complete devastation that would soon raze the whole structure. Because this startling incident con-veys much vital instruction and blessed assurance, we shall stand in spirit before that torn veil to exclaim,

THE HOLY OF HOLIES — OPEN TO ALL!

devoting our thoughts to Saint Mark's inspired record (chapter 15:38), *"The veil of the Temple was rent in twain from the top to the bottom."*

I

THE OPENED SANCTUARY — A WARNING

Before we visit the Temple, let us linger a few moments under our Savior's cross. Soon the Son of God, suspended on that accursed tree for six hours, suffering not only the agonizing pains that are racking His body but enduring infinitely more as He bears our sins, will breathe His last. The sun has darkened as though it would enshroud the whole earth in mourning; a hush begins to fall on the noisy, morbid crowd beneath the cross. Slowly the head of Jesus drops, and His face, a few hours before blanched white by the suffering for our sins and still streaked by the blood that flowed from His crown of thorns, suddenly seems lighted with new love. As His death-marked lips speak their farewell, listen closely! The apex of the ages has arrived! The climax of all the centuries is to be revealed in this moment! The divine plan for our redemption is being completed forever and the prophetic promises fulfilled to the letter as Jesus Christ bows His head into death, crying, *"Father, into Thy hands I commend My spirit!"*

We can hardly be surprised that nature itself began a mighty protest when on the cross God died for man. An ominous, foreboding rumble was heard and felt, the tremors of an earth quaking in reproach. Men feared that the world's foundations would collapse as granite rocks and boulders were irresistibly split. Even the dead were shaken from their graves.

These startling tremors were felt in the Jerusalem Temple. No sooner had Jesus breathed His last than the sound of ripping and tearing such as men had never heard before filled the place of worship. The costly curtain that completely veiled the Holy of Holies, the sanctuary's most sacred part, was torn in the middle from top to bottom! No accident could suddenly cut that covering in two. Nor can unbelievers intelligently laugh this story out of the Bible; for Josephus, the Jewish historian, tells us that forty years before the Temple was destroyed (approximately the year of the crucifixion), mysterious occurrences were noted in the sanctuary. At that time, he reports, the chief light in the golden candlestick was suddenly extinguished. The Talmud joins him in revealing that the great Temple-gates, kept tightly closed, were abruptly jerked wide open. Even tradition preserves a recollection of disaster and tragedy which struck when Jesus died.

That torn drapery was evidence of divine displeasure. Century after century our Savior's fellow-countrymen, the chosen people, had enjoyed close contact with their God. Of all nations they alone had the sacred Scriptures; to no other people did Jehovah delegate His prophets; to none other did He reveal Himself as He had in that Holy of Holies. As the crowning climax of His love for Israel He sent His own Son to be born of a Jewish mother in a Palestinian hamlet. Despite these unparalleled distinctions, Israel proved itself ungrateful, rebellious, unbelieving. It stoned the prophets, spurned the light-giving Scriptures; it rejected and now crucified the Son of God Himself. The Almighty's patience is not without end nor His long-suffering without limit; and with the dead body of Christ nailed to the cross, the hands on Heaven's clock marked the hour for destruction. God's wrath now ripped this curtain into two separated parts and would soon strike the entire sanctuary with such devastating force that not one stone would be left standing on the other.

What a direct, unmistakable warning we can find for our country and ourselves in this torn veil overhanging the Holy of Holies! Many people regard as absurd the mere suggestion that our spiritual blessings can be restricted. They forget that God's Word is not bound to one place, that His presence and mercy will finally depart from any people who wilfully spurn His grace. The main course of Christianity has always been westward. As Eastern nations have fallen into spiritual lethargy, the path of the Gospel has steadily been toward the setting sun. If in America we are found wanting when weighed in future emergencies, who knows but what the Gospel's vanguard may cross the Pacific to the unevangelized half of humanity in India and China, there to build up new churches, new and molding world forces?

Do you think that, as our great Lord looks at this land, rich, powerful, lavishly endowed, blessed in a hundred ways as no other nation, He sees wide-spread reverence for Christ, deep love of His Word, and complete trust in His mercy? More than half of our people belong to no church. More than two thirds did not attend services this morning. More than three fourths are not concerned about working for the Savior. Examine our literary tastes, and you will be shocked to hear that a best seller is almost smothered with profanity and saturated with crude immorality! Study our home-life, and you will learn that divorce, assuming an accepted role in our leading families, is regarded by some as a social asset, a fashionable experience. The papers print as a bit of entertaining news the report that a group of women pledged themselves to marry only once. Survey the studied assault on childhood, and you will find one illegitimacy or abortion to almost every two normal births. When the Federal Bureau of Investigation releases figures to show that every three minutes an automobile is stolen and every two minutes a burglary committed, that one of every eighty-eight citizens is a major criminal, do you not agree that we could not complain should our heavenly Father withdraw the spiritual blessings that this nation as none other enjoys?

That question becomes the more pointed when we survey American church-life. What mighty things God could permit our people to accomplish if there were more courageous faith! Suppose we had the family altar in each Christian home, with children brought up in the nurture of the Lord and all churches seriously concerned about youth education. (Some one sent me a Sunday-school sheet for children of kindergarten age. The cover shows a picture of "Our Cat's Supper." The other pages deal with birds, bunnies, dogs, pussies, donkeys, and chickens. But in the whole pamphlet, published as a part of the graded course in the International Sunday-school System, the precious name of Jesus Christ is found not once.) Suppose we could keep our college-age young men and women from being subjected to the antimoral teachings of titled foreigners (like the leader of the away-from-Christian-marriage movement, invited to lecture at New York City College) and instead give these young folks Christ's basis for home happiness! Suppose every one of the quarter million American churches would preach sin and its damning consequences, grace and its cross-gained forgiveness, banishing all modernist, Scripture-questioning, Christ-rejecting preachers, and removing politics, theat-ricals, dances, raffles, illegal money-making schemes, from their activities! — Do you not feel that a better day would then dawn on our country? However, the trend is not in this constructive direction; and because the churches are not growing closer to Christ nor the pulpit testimony becoming more loyal to the Cross nor the zeal of the home more definitely directed toward the Savior nor the fervor for soul-winning notably increased, we must be prepared for the tragic possibility that, unless God's mercy prevails, many congregations will feel the wrath of God as the Jerusalem Temple did at the crucifixion. We are told that men of public affairs and international experience, like the late Ramsay MacDonald, signed a manifesto declaring: "It is our conviction that statesmanship will fail and that political programs will prove futile . . . until they embody the spirit and the practice of Christ. . . . We proclaim our faith in the Gospel of Christ as the final truth concerning the relationships of one man with another"; but it is equally true that this same Christ and His Gospel are assailed ruthlessly in American pulpits, by radio chains and religious publications. We must, therefore, have a penitent back-to-the-cross movement in the nation, so that, please God, our country's blessings and the Christian Church's glory may not be taken from us and our children!

There is, however, a personal, individual message in the rent veil which, we pray, may penetrate particularly into the hearts of those who have rejected Jesus and who, like the enemies of Christ on that Good Friday, are crucifying Him anew with ungodly living. It is tragic enough, God knows, that millions of people in this country have never been Christians; but it is doubly tragic that vast multitudes of others who once belonged to the Savior have renounced Him for the world. As surely as that sanctuary was desecrated and later destroyed, so, you backsliders, no matter how prominent you have become since you left

Jesus, your life will be desecrated and your hopes of a blessed eternity destroyed if you persist in opposing, denying, betraying Christ. That Redeemer, whose loving glance restored perfidious Peter, pleads with you from the cross, "O My poor, wayward, unfaithful followers, come back to Me! Regain the joy of faith that once was yours! Recapture the inner happiness you knew with your God-fearing parents, your Christian husband or wife; the calm you have lost now that you have turned away from Me to serve sin! O come back to the cross and by the holy blood you see dripping from these wounds I truly promise to forgive, restore, strengthen, and bless you even more than ever!" Answer that love! Follow that invitation! Professor Henry Drummond, a notable figure of the last generation, falsely sacrificed his faith in Christ to the interest of science. He made the mistake some of you have made. He believed that men know more than God, that the laboratory, not the Bible, is the decisive means of establishing the truth; but he was never satisfied with his unbelief, and during his last illness he confessed to Sir William Dawson, the Christian geologist: "I am going back to the Book to believe it and receive it as I did at first. I can no longer live on uncertainties. I am going back to the faith in the Word of God."

May you go back, too! As your crucified Savior looks down from the cross to plead for your return, answer with repentance, faith, and trust! Follow Him now, without excuse or delay, knowing that, if you persist in disavowing Jesus, God's hand that tore the Temple veil will finally tear into shreds any hope you may have of earning heaven by yourself! For, fight against this truth as you may, even though your consciences whisper, "He's right! That's the truth!" here is Christ's final verdict, *"He that believeth and is baptized shall be saved; but he that believeth not shall be damned."*

II

THE OPENED SANCTUARY — A BLESSING
AND A PROMISE!

The torn veil, however, presents a marvelous promise of mercy. On that Friday, in the mid-afternoon when the priest arrived to prepare the evening sacrifice on the altar before the Holy of Holies and found the sacred drapery torn apart, he may not have realized that Jesus, whose lifeless body was being removed from the cross, had come to end all this Old Testament temple worship and to bring a New Testament in His blood. Many people today are similarly ignorant. They hear of the rent veil, but they fail to understand that on the death day of Jesus, God tore down that entire Old Covenant ceremonial. They speak of the Sabbath as though we were still under Old Testament dispensation. They mention the tithe as though it were still a rigorous command of God Himself. But they forget that these ancient sacrifices and rituals pointed to the Savior Himself; that the Sabbaths and festivals, the food laws and the fasting customs, were, as the Apostle puts it, only *"a shadow of things to come."* When Jesus died His atoning death, these Mosaic ceremonies died with Him; for here is the clear verdict of His Word, *"Christ is the end of the Law."* In the face of mistaken tendencies to put the Old Testament yoke on the Christian Church, we ought to think clearly and in harmony with the Scripture concerning blue-laws for Sabbath observance; we must protest against the preaching that makes people uncertain of their salvation if they do not give 10 per cent of their income or that leads them to feel they must still pay their way through the gates of eternity. The cross at Calvary and the torn veil at Jerusalem combine to repeat the Apostle's urgent plea, *"Stand fast ... in the liberty wherewith Christ hath made us free."*

The severed curtain permitted light to penetrate into the Holy of Holies and remove the mystery that lay behind the heavy drapery. So it is with Christ and His Gospel. He told His enemies, *"In secret have I said nothing"*; and true Christian churches have no hidden shrines, no mystic oaths, no clandestine rites, no private initiations, no cryptic rituals. Cults and sects multiply and bring to our shores the pagan mysteries of India, Persia, the Far Orient and the Near East; and the spirit of our age regards membership in secret societies as business distinctions and social advantages; but as the parted curtain reveals the hidden sanctuary, we remind ourselves: "There is nothing in our entire Christian faith that cannot be seen by every one, young and old; nothing that even the most childlike mind cannot believe in this message from the cross, *"God so loved the world that He gave His only-begotten Son, that whosoever believeth in Him should not perish but have everlasting life."*

Especially, however, does the rent veil assure us of our free approach to God in Christ. The entire Temple area at Jerusalem was a forbidden place for many. In 1871 archeologists found an inscription with these words: "Let no Gentile enter inside the barrier gate and the fence around the sanctuary! Any one trespassing will bring death on himself as the penalty." If it meant death for Gentiles to set foot in the Temple grounds, what would penetrating into the far more sacred Holy of Holies mean? Only one human being, God's high priest, could enter that hallowed place, and that only once annually, the solemn Day of Atonement, when the nation's sins were removed. Only in one way, by bringing the blood of animals slain as expiatory sacrifices, could he enter on that *Yom Kippur*. For every other person, even for Herod, the king, and Pontius Pilate, the Roman governor; on every one of the remaining 364 days in the year, including the momentous Passover and joyful Purim, the Holy of Holies was closed, dark, soundless. Through no other offering besides the purifying blood, not even gold and silver, could the threshold of this sacred spot be safely crossed. If these plain instructions were violated, the punishment was immediate death. With such fear did the high priest later regard that supersacred place that he never entered without having a cord tied to his foot, so that, if he perished in that innermost sanctuary, his corpse could be dragged out. That Holy of Holies, as far as history shows, was the most exclusive and restricted spot in the whole world, and rightly so; for here the almighty God, with His perfect sinlessness, condescended to meet sinful man. No wonder a heavy, closely woven curtain completely separated that sacrosanct enclosure from the rest of the Temple! No wonder darkness pervaded the place; for human eyes were not to witness the awe-filled mystery that man in his iniquity is permitted to approach his Maker in His holiness.

Good Friday, the Christians' Day of Atonement, forever made all earthly priests' sacrifices superfluous. Christ's blood had a cleansing power which the blood of no rams or bullocks could ever exert. At Calvary He finished our salvation, and that completion made an earthly temple with an exclusive sanctuary unnecessary. We build no holy of holies into our church structures, because through Christ we can meet God anywhere we wish to approach Him in His Word. We can come before our Father any time we seek communion with Him in Jesus' name. Through trusting faith your home, poor and shabby though it be, can have a holy of holies just as sacred as the mysteries in that inner Temple shrine! It is often difficult, sometimes impossible, to meet earthly rulers and men of affairs in business or politics. Do you remember how official society in Washington was thrown into turmoil by the failure of a large number to receive invitations for meeting the king and queen of England? But the King of kings is accessible to every one of you through faith. God has no favorites. The temple of heaven is open to all, regardless of race, color, position, who approach the Father in Christ's name. With the world-moving events that receive God's attention, He has time and love for, and takes interest in, your problems. How blessed to know that in every sorrow this invitation of solace reaches all who are Christ's:

> Come, ye disconsolate, where'er ye languish,
>   Come to the mercy-seat, fervently kneel;
> Here bring your wounded hearts, here tell your anguish;
>   Earth has no sorrow that Heaven cannot heal.

How reassuring to believe that you can approach Jesus yourself, without any minister or priest to introduce you! For as the high priest entered the Holy of Holies with the blood of slain animals, so you enter heaven, not trusting in your own understanding or emotions, but relying on God's love, finding your credentials in nothing less than Jesus' cleansing, atoning, life-giving blood!

That faith — and here we have a magnificent New Testament declaration — makes every believer a priest of the Most High. "*Ye are a chosen generation, a royal priesthood,*" the apostle exults, "*that ye should show forth the praises of Him who hath called you out of darkness into His marvelous light.*" In the practice of this universal priesthood we must find challenge and hope for Christ's cause. Churches must outstrip Communism and reach the masses with the message of the Cross before they are poisoned by the appeal of Red destruction. "*He died for all!*" should be more than a pulpit platitude. It must be the impulse to an energetic program of an evangelizing

Christianity. Too many of you will agree with everything I have said and affirm that Christ is the only Hope for sinful men and women; yet you do little to spread the glorious message that the Holy of Holies of heaven is not closed, but that there is full, free, and final salvation for every penitent, believing heart in the blood of the Lord Jesus Christ. May God in His mercy give us the deep-souled devotion to Christ and the red-blooded courage required to exercise the privileges of our priesthood!

Mightily has our Savior blessed this radio testimony to the open heavens. Thousands of letters, more each week than ever before! New stations continually added! The latest is in the frozen Hudson Bay district, not far from the Arctic Circle, and will, we hope, reach many Eskimos and isolated souls. Mightily will God bless you, too, if you, a priest and prince in the eternal kingdom, testify publicly and boldly to Christ, the crucified Savior!

The Book of Acts tells us that soon after Pentecost there was a momentous conversion of the Temple priests. God, whose hand ripped that curtain, touched their souls and taught them the meaning of this miracle. As we return for a last glance at the dying Christ and the torn veil, may the Father's Spirit so guide our hearts that, convicted of our sins but also of Christ's sin-destroying grace, we follow the Apostle in having *"boldness to enter into the Holiest by the blood of Jesus."* Let us here and now affirm our faith in the crucified Savior, resolving to meet sin, temptation, sorrow, reverses, with the inner, immovable confidence that joy of life and peace in death itself are granted us through the Cross and the free entrance into the eternal Holy of Holies which Christ promises those who are His!

Father, give every one of us this assurance for Jesus' sake! Amen.

"CHRIST IS RISEN! HE IS RISEN INDEED!"

> *"As Christ was raised up from the dead by the glory of the Father, even so we also should walk in newness of life."* — Romans 6:4.

O Christ, our risen Redeemer:

Eternal, unbroken thanks to Thee that on the first, glorious Easter Thou didst mightily prove Thyself the Lord of life and of death itself! Help us all to stand gratefully before the empty tomb, there to acclaim Thee our mighty God, our merciful Savior! Grant us, through trusting faith, to know that, because Thou livest, we, too, shall live and that Thy resurrection is our pledge of life eternal! O Jesus, on this glorious Easter let us rise with Thee to the heights of soul happiness, casting off all gloom of despondency, conquering our sorrows and pains, defeating the fear of death, overcoming all doubt, and, beholding Thee as our resurrected Lord, find new faith, new courage, new holiness of living! Enrich us with this Easter gift, our risen Christ; for we pray these petitions in Thy holy name! Amen.

THE United States is one of the few countries in which the customary Easter-greetings contain no reference to the resurrection of Jesus Christ. Throughout the Greek-speaking world, for example, Christians address one another in the same Easter salutation that rang through the early Church, *"Christos anestee!"* "Christ is risen!" and with the ancient response, *"Aleethoos anestee,"* "He is truly risen!" In the Latin Church of the first centuries the Easter-greeting was, *"Vivit!"* "He lives!" and the reply, *"Vere vivit!"* "He lives indeed!" In Spanish lands Christians say, *"Cristo vive!"* In Germany believers, no matter to which church they may belong, salute one another with exultant joy: *"Der HErr ist auferstanden!"* and the reply,

"Er ist wahrhaftig auferstanden!"   Even in Russia, where Communist slogans have not altogether banished the reverence for God's truth, loyal followers of Christ, meeting their kindred in the faith, say, *"Christos Voskres!"* and receive the reply, *"Voistinu Voskres!"*   All these expressions serve one thought and purpose: they glorify the risen Savior.

In our country, however, we say, "Happy Easter!" forgetting that the word "Easter" may have no connection with the open grave and in no way testifies to the resurrection miracle.   Because the Savior's triumph over the tomb, together with the crucifixion, which preceded it, are the most blessed of all truths, and Christians should follow the angel's command, *"Go quickly and tell His disciples!"* instead of limiting their Easter conversation to the subjects of new clothes, spring hats, festive food, holiday programs, post-Lenten parties, we ask you who are the Lord's to help inaugurate and maintain a Christ-exalting movement by which believers in all churches greet one another on this day with the salutation, "Christ is risen!" and respond, "He is risen indeed!"

On the first Easter only a few followers of the Savior could sound that triumphant note; but on this 1940 Easter, when over the 171 stations in our "Bringing-Christ-to-the-Nation" broadcasting system millions can hear the message of our Lord's victory over death, multitudes should heed the plea to keep Jesus in Easter by greeting every one whom they meet before the close of this day with the faith-born declaration, "Christ is risen!"   May God give every one of you the resolution to proclaim, "He is risen indeed!"

To strengthen our faith in the resurrection reality, let us — and I include especially the doubtful and uncertain, even the scoffers and atheists in this audience — stand once more in spirit before the rock-hewn grave in Joseph's garden, where the broken seal, the removed stone, the prostrate Roman guard, the empty tomb, the discarded burial shroud, the white-robed angel with his announcement, *"He is not here but is risen!"* all combine to impress us with the holy, heavenly truth that Jesus, God's Son and the world's Savior, has eternally defeated death for Himself and for all men. With the Easter cry,

"CHRIST IS RISEN!   HE IS RISEN INDEED!"

we invite you, rather, we urgently plead with you, to study and believe the inspired resurrection message of Saint Paul (Romans 6:4), *"As Christ was raised up from the dead by the glory of the Father, even so we also should walk in newness of life,"* and by the Spirit's guidance to find the Easter truth and the Easter newness.

I

THE EASTER TRUTH

When the Apostle summarizes the triumph of this sacred day in the seven short words *"Christ was raised up from the dead!"* he regards the mysterious but magnificent bursting of the grave as an unquestionable, supreme truth. In the entire New Testament record the resurrection victory is never debated; no lengthy defenses of its facts are offered; no attempts are made to vindicate the details in the Easter narratives. Throughout the Scriptures and the early Church the declaration that "on the third day He rose again from the dead" is uncompromisingly accepted as the great climax truth of our faith, the necessary keystone in the arch of our hope. No resurrection, no redemption! No open grave, no opened heaven! No risen Christ, no risen Christians! This is the unavoidable alternative: *"If Christ be not risen, then is our preaching vain. Yea,*

*and we are found false witnesses of God. . . . If Christ
be not raised, your faith is vain, ye are yet in your sins.
Then they also which are fallen asleep in Christ are
perished."* Yet, as Paul triumphed, *"Now is Christ
risen,"* so I want your faith to ring, clear and unhesitating.
Some of you doubt or deny the angelic proclamation, *"He is
risen!"* because you have never taken the time to behold the
Easter evangel with open eyes. You have had your mind
poisoned by a destructive teacher, an atheist agitator or an
applauded skeptic. Will you not be fair enough to read
through the New Testament evidence for the Savior's
restoration to life?

If you submit to the Spirit's guidance, you will experience the same startling reverse that challenged the
life of Gilbert West. He thought that he had found confusion and contradiction in the four gospel accounts, and
his exposure, he boasted, would reveal the complete im-
possibility of the open grave. When he had finished his
investigations, however, he penned this remarkable confession: "As I have studied the evidence for the resurrection of Jesus Christ from the dead and have weighed it
according to the laws of evidence, I have become satisfied
that Jesus really rose from the dead, as recorded in the
gospels, and I have written my book" (the book that was
to destroy all faith in the resurrection) "on that side" —
the side of Christ and His truth.

More recently we have witnessed a similar challenging
change from wavering doubt to convicted faith. Frank
Morison, acclaimed for his recent book on Pontius Pilate,
tells us that, when as a young man he began seriously to
study Christ's life, he had the definite feeling that the
New Testament Scriptures rested on very insecure foundation. Higher critics and professional enemies of the
Bible had given him the impression that God's Word was

unreliable. The few things that these destructionists left standing the physical science courses in which he was enrolled proceeded to undermine. Scientific thought was obstinately opposed to every miracle. He had read the great Huxley's verdict, "Miracles do not happen!" and had come to the conclusion that the laws of the universe could never be suspended. He could not, however, entirely subdue a reverent regard for our Lord acquired during his childhood; and in order to find peace of mind, he decided to study the Savior's suffering and resurrection. He proposed to strip the Scriptural record "of its overgrowth of primitive beliefs and dogmatic suppositions." He would see Jesus as He really was, not as the Christians believed Him to be. Hardly, however, had he plunged into the eternal Word, when his thoughts concerning Christ were revolutionized. What he calls "the irresistible logic" of the gospel narrative gripped his heart; he found that he could not write a book attacking the Savior's death and resurrection; instead, he published a volume on the first Easter, a reverent defense of Bible truth.

You, too, will be able to overcome doubt and to exult with the Apostle, *"Christ was raised up from the dead,"* if you prayerfully approach the Easter-story, asking for the Spirit's strength and light as you study its statements. The trouble with most people who reject the Easter Gospel is not to be found in any insurmountable opposition by their brain processes, but in their stubborn unwillingness to concede the truth. A brilliant New York attorney is quoted as admitting, "I am convinced that Jesus really did rise from the dead, but I am no nearer being a Christian than I was before. I thought that the difficulty was with my head. I find that it really is with my heart."

How convincing, however, the Easter evidence is when both the head and the heart accept Christ! Thomas

Arnold, beloved headmaster at Rugby, asserted that no fact of history is so well attested as the Savior's resurrection; and assuredly an imposing array of witnesses declares its complete, eternal verity! Listen to their testimony! Mary Magdalene, who hastened to the tomb even before daybreak, the first in all the world to meet the resurrected Savior, asserted, *"I have seen the Lord!"* The other women who lingered long at the cross on Good Friday and who likewise came early on that Sunday morning to embalm the Savior's body, found the stone rolled away and an angel of the Lord, clothed with raiment white as dazzling snow. *"He is not here, He is risen,"* was the cry that greeted them. They could explain how as they left the empty tomb they met Jesus, heard Him speak joy to their hearts, fell at His feet and worshiped Him. Simon Peter, restored by a glance of his Savior's grace, knelt before his resurrected Lord, and though the Scriptures give us no details of the meeting, we may well believe Peter could testify that Jesus raised nail-scarred hands in benediction on him who was to become the rock disciple. James, one of our Lord's brethren, who at first did not accept Him as God's Son and the world's Savior, likewise stood face to face with Jesus; and if he could give his testimony to our radio audience, he would assert that his whole life was rebuilt and purified through this contact. Thomas, the doubting, who would not believe unless he saw the print of the nails and put his own fingers into those scars, mounts the witness stand in behalf of Jesus to announce that he did behold the wounded hands and feet, the riven side, and that we shall be blessed if we believe even though we do not see. The two disciples on the Emmaus road who were filled with unspeakable joy when Christ *"went in to tarry with them";* the entire company of disciples, who had hid themselves behind shut doors and suddenly saw that the glorified Savior was in their midst to declare, *"Peace be unto you!"* the seven followers who went fishing with the resurrected Christ and with Him ate breakfast on the shore; the five hundred believers who in one manifestation beheld the Lord, perhaps on Mount Tabor in Galilee; and the Eleven who were with Christ on Mount Olivet at His ascension — all these, together with the mighty missionary Saint Paul, who actually saw his glorified Savior on the Damascus road and then went out to start the conquest of the world for Him, are personal, competent witnesses to this miracle of the ages. If their testimony, combined and detailed as it is, does not convince the most skeptical of Christ's resurrection, the difficulty lies not in the Easter truth but in the refusal to bow before that truth.

So convincing is the evidence that, when submitted to careful scrutiny by legal experts, it has been thoroughly vindicated. In a remarkable book by Simon Greenleaf a special section is devoted to the Resurrection, with the result that the Gospel narratives are completely endorsed. Some of you say, however, "Who is this Simon Greenleaf? Is his opinion recognized?" Let me answer not only that he was professor of law at Harvard and perhaps the most distinguished jurist ever connected with that eminent university, but also that the *London Law Magazine* called him one of the most highly esteemed legal authorities of his century, asserting that he has shed more light on the laws of evidence than all lawyers who adorn the courts of Europe. Now, if that distinguished authority unreservedly endorses the Resurrection, why does any one in this audience hesitate to subscribe to its complete truth?

Every Sunday, the day of worship selected by the early Church because Christ rose on Sunday; every baptism, the sacred Christian rite instituted by the risen Christ; every church and mission preaching the glorious message that

Jesus has conquered death for all men — these are the incontestable proofs of the Easter fact, proofs, however, which those who are Christ's do not need, since they have the Spirit's testimony in their hearts.

You see, Jesus had to rise from the grave. It was clearly foretold in the Old Testament and plainly predicted by the Savior Himself; and before God's holy Word can be broken, — remember this, my discouraged friends who need a firm foundation for your hope, — everything on, under, and over this world will collapse into dust. The Scriptures cannot fail; and God's guaranty for the Bible's every promise of comfort and sustaining love is to be found at the open grave. — "Christ is risen! He is risen indeed!"

Jesus had to be resurrected from the dead to prove that He is no mere mortal leader or human theorist but God Almighty, with power over life and death. No man can master the grave and defeat decay. During recent weeks world-wide attention has been focused on a remarkable discovery in Egypt. After years of plodding search scientists uncovered a secret, concealed tomb. When the debris of centuries was removed and the door, solemnly sealed 3,000 years ago, was opened with appropriate ceremonies, there, in an imposing burial chamber, amid gold ornaments and almost priceless jewels, lay a mysterious mummy case of granite. Beneath it was a second sarcophagus of silver and below that another covering of solid gold. Within lay the remains of Pharaoh Psou-Sennes. A thousand years before Christ he ruled Upper and Lower Egypt with an iron hand. Princes, priests, and people bowed abjectly before him, but finally he bowed before death. Despite his money and men he could not escape from the tomb; and within that mummy case, which will soon be a museum exhibit, his shriveled, blackened corpse testifies to the relentless grip of the grave. — How our hallelujahs should ring out today when the open grave testifies that Jesus Christ was very God of very God, the Ruler of life and of death itself! — "The Lord is risen! He is risen indeed!"

No other explanation for the open tomb has ever been able to satisfy the human mind. Unbelievers used to say that Jesus had merely swooned when taken from the cross; only apparently dead, He was later revived in the grave. But the Roman soldiers knew better; they were so positive that He had breathed His last that they did not follow the usual custom of breaking His legs. Skeptics used to assert, repeating a first-century falsehood, that the Roman guards slept at their posts and Christ's disciples, under the cover of darkness, stole His body. Yet even the bribery of the priests could not make this story plausible. It meant death for a Roman soldier to fall asleep on duty. Besides, it would tax any one's imagination to believe that the great stone could be rolled away, the official seal broken, and a company of men go in and out the grave to remove a corpse without being heard or seen. Infidels used to claim that the Resurrection rests on the fantasy of hallucinated women and suggestible followers; but even open critics have rejected this absurd theory. Thus you can bring one attempt after the other to take the supernatural out of the Easter miracle and to account for it on purely human premises, but each endeavor is doomed to abject failure. Only one explanation remains: Christ rose from the dead because He was the all-powerful God, with the divine omnipotence required to destroy death! "Christ is risen! He is risen indeed!"

Christ had to rise from the dead because His resurrection was the crowning climax of His love. Had He stayed in the grave, not only would His promises of new life have been unfulfilled and His claims for divine power disproved, but His entire suffering, the agony of the cross, the God-forsakenness, and the never-to-be-fathomed sorrow that crushed His soul, would have been in vain. The entire purpose of His incarnation would have remained unaccomplished. When, however, on that bright Easter morning, the power of earth and hell, the priestly craftiness, and the official guard, the rock-hewn grave and the impressive seal at its entrance, the winding linen and the burial shrouds, could not keep Jesus in the tomb, it was Heaven's highest proof that Calvary's one sacrifice for the sins of all ages had been accepted, that Jesus' blood had not been shed in vain, that as Christ *"was delivered for our offenses,"* so He *"was raised again for our justification."*

This trust is indicated in our text when it declares *"Christ was raised up from the dead* BY THE GLORY OF THE FATHER." Easter is Heaven's glorious seal, God's glorious endorsement, the Father's glorious acceptance of His Son's self-sacrifice for the world's sins. Easter is the promise of peace and pardon to every one who believes. Therefore, in the name of the risen Christ, I ask you, whoever you are, do you subscribe to the seven simple words of our text, *"Christ was raised up from the dead"?* It matters little what your opinion may be on a thousand other issues, past, present, and future; but for the sake of your soul, believe the resurrection miracle! Stifle gainsaying doubts that demand, "How could Christ return to life?" Turn away from skeptical, sneering men of affairs to the resolute faith of the mighty leaders in science, culture, and progress who have joyfully accepted the Easter miracle! Today with unquestioning trust take God at His word! Ask Him for strength to overcome every uncertainty, and if you follow the promptings of the Spirit that now asks you to acclaim Christ, you, too, will be led, as doubting Thomas was, to behold the Savior with a confidence that says, "My Lord, my God, my ever-living Savior!" You, too, will gladly tell all whom you meet, "Christ is risen! He is risen indeed!"

II

EASTER NEWNESS

Without this radiant joy, life must lose its beauty and blessing. Herbert Spencer, England's learned philosopher, did not accept the Easter victory; yet in his last hours he asked that only one word be chiseled on his tombstone, the Latin *Infelicissimus,* meaning "The most unhappy one." The rejection of the Easter victory always leaves men without hope, while humble confidence in this truth bestows new assurance.

It is this newness for which our text appeals when it says, *"As Christ was raised from the dead, . . .* EVEN SO WE ALSO SHOULD WALK IN NEWNESS OF LIFE." When Jesus rose from the tomb, an entirely new era dawned on the world; a New Testament was offered to men in which the most persistent and overpowering terror, the cringing before the grave, was removed for all who acclaim Jesus their Savior. What trembling the thoughts of death often provoke! Classify the fears and phobias of men in any way you will; add up the fright caused by sickness, age, loss, imprisonment, dishonor, and the sum total will be far below the heart-sinking despondency, the cold sweat of terror, the hysterical surrender to despair, which often marks life's end.

Ask a soldier who has seen godless scoffers go over the top and face death in No Man's Land how they chatter and quake; ask a sailor who has stood with infidels on the decks of a doomed ship how they fell on their knees in ghastly consternation; ask a doctor to describe the last moments of blasphemers, when the terrors of hell are written on their faces as shuddering curses leap from their lips, and you will understand that the most crushing of earth's other burdens is not to be compared with what men often fear in their last moments. We hear of exceptions, it is true; a disillusioned woman writing "Exit smiling!" on the walls of her hotel room and then plunging from her high window to a splattering death on the sidewalk below; a convicted murderer approaching the gallows with swaggering unconcern; highly emotional sufferers wishing themselves dead. But unless the conscience is altogether destroyed, every one who is without Christ shrinks from death. Men know, although they may glibly deny the existence of God and ridicule the mention of heaven and hell, that there is a judgment, a retribution, a punishment beyond the grave. We need not argue this fact with any one in our audience; the solemn warning voice tells you that you cannot live in sin and hope to escape punishment. But I do need to show many what Christ and the Easter resurrection can mean to them; for ignorance and superstition concerning the future existence are blighting the lives of millions. If the census enumerators, whose activities have been widely discussed in our newspapers, should ask the 130,000,000 Americans to express their hopes for the hereafter, the answers would be bewildering and contradictory; but on Easter, if we ask Christ concerning eternity, He points us both to the open grave and the open heaven to say: *"Because I live, ye shall live also!"* *"I am the Resurrection and the Life: he that believeth in Me, though he were dead, yet shall he live!"* *"In My Father's house are many mansions: . . . I go to prepare a place for you."*

As you read these and scores of other passages promising a blessed eternity with Jesus, thank God that no

hesitation or uncertainty lingers behind His pledges. They
are the highest truths that even Heaven knows. With the
Easter faith in your heart, you need not grovel in despair
to ask, "What will become of me when life stops?" You,
the mortally sick, the invalids whose existence hangs on
a thin, shortened thread; you in the prime and strength of
life who may be cut down by the sudden accidents that
lurk closely and loom frequently on the pathways of our
modern life — believe that Christ's resurrection guarantees
your resurrection! Easter is the divine warrant that God
has forgiven the sins which bring eternal death as their
wages. This holy day offers the surety that God has accepted the suffering and dying of His own Son as the
payment for your sins and the ransom for their punishment. Knowing that your transgressions are nailed to
the cross and that Christ is the living, divine Savior and not
a dead deceiver, you can confidently believe that the grave
does not end all; that you can escape the terrors of hell
and be blessed in heaven, before the presence of Jesus.
For here is that plain but powerful promise of life, *"God
so loved the world that He gave His only-begotten Son,
that whosoever believeth in Him should not perish but
have everlasting life."*

It is true that temporal death comes to every one of us,
as it came to Christ; but it is only a passing instantaneous
change from our earthly existence to that incomparably
more blessed heavenly life. For at the open grave we learn
through faith that we are more than creatures of accident,
controlled by a cold, cruel fate, directed toward everlasting
discard and decay; rather, that we are God's children of
holy destiny, who come from God and, through His Son,
will return to Him.

With the fear of death removed — and how confidently Christians can long for eternity! — with heavenly

bliss positively promised all believers, you can understand why our text beseeches us to *"walk in newness of life."* Easter tells us that old fears, old weaknesses, old sorrows, old doubts, are all passed away in the newness of the Savior's resurrection. Does anything keep you from this blessed newness? Do old, heavy problems lurk in your soul beneath new Easter garments? Analyze them in this day's radiance, and their darkness will disappear. Are your troubles money difficulties, family quarrels, questions of health? Are you the victim of malicious plotting, crooked politics, and hateful revenge? Stand before the empty tomb to realize that the Christ who has the power over death can control these smaller issues in your life and turn your crosses to advantages, as the Good Friday defeat gave way to the Easter victory. Whatever your personal problems may be, the tragedy that your husband has lost his God and his love for you; the cutting blow that after years of faithful, unselfish service you have been cast aside; especially the recurrence of private sins, repeated concessions to wrong, worry over your salvation and spiritual condition — look to the heavens reopened by the resurrection and know that *"the sufferings of this present time are not worthy to be compared with the glory which shall be revealed in us"!* Trust Christ implicitly! Trust Him even though it seems that He permits you to be crushed under the weight of affliction! For finally, in God's good time and in His blessed way, the dawn of deliverance will break, and the new day will find you stronger because of your night of anguish.

Has the deepest sorrow, bereavement, darkened your home? Does it seem to you that the last glimmering joy of your life has disappeared with the death of a beloved one? Instead of questioning the Father's love and goodness in allowing your husband, the mainstay of your home, or an only child, the center of your affections, to be snatched away by death, dry your tears, strengthen your heart through Christ, and remember that Easter proves that God's way with His children is always the road to redemption and victory! Behold Jesus emerging from the tomb and take heart in the Easter comfort that all God's beloved, through Christ, will come forth to life eternal!

Commit yourselves wholly to the risen Christ on Easter, the day especially appropriate for dedication to the Savior! Take your sins and weaknesses, lay them at the foot of the cross, hasten to the open grave, and there you will find newness of life, forgiveness of your transgressions, a fortifying of your faith, and the joy of assured salvation! For Easter, blessed Easter, is yours for life and death, with this triumph of trust: "Christ is risen! He is risen indeed!" Amen.

THE WHITE-ROBED IN HEAVEN

"These are they which came out of great tribulation and have washed their robes and made them white in the blood of the Lamb. . . . And God shall wipe away all tears from their eyes." — Revelation 7:14-17.

Holy, hallowing Spirit of God:

*P*urify our souls by removing doubt, distraction, worldliness, and making us, through faith, temples of the risen, living Christ! Show us that, since our Lord's resurrection is the seal of forgiven sins, the defeat of hell, and the conquest of death, faith in His mercies grants us eternal life and the pledge of heaven! Oh, lift up our eyes constantly to that painless, blissful Paradise which, once promised to the penitent on the cross, has been prepared for every one who trusts in Christ's atoning death and His Easter triumph! Help us to believe humbly as we confess all the wrong in our hearts and on our hands, to believe trustingly as we bring all our needs and sorrows to Christ, to believe victoriously, since we know that the grave has been conquered and heaven opened for us! Hear us and guide us until we reach that heavenly home, for Jesus' sake. Amen.

DURING a chilly afternoon a few weeks ago casual visitors in a Chicago park would have noticed an unusual group gathered on a lagoon bridge. They would have seen that the leader, after a few preliminary remarks, asked those with him, witnesses and newspaper reporters, to join in the Lord's Prayer. Then as he dramatically stretched out his hand, clutching a hymn-book, he cried: "Clarence Darrow, I am here in fulfilment of the pact we made with each other. If you can manifest your spirit to me, do so now!" For a full minute he stood in rigid silence. The wind blew; birds twittered on a near-by limb; the subdued drone of the city's traffic played its monotone background; a reporter coughed — but nothing happened. Turning to the witnesses, the leader declared,

"No manifestation!" Clarence Darrow, widely publicized atheist attorney, had promised that after death he would try to establish contact with his friends and, if possible, explain some facts concerning eternity. To show the presence of his spirit, Darrow had agreed that he would shake the hymnal from his friend's hand; but in two annual attempts the result was identical — "No manifestation!" The Chicago lawyer did not return to reveal the hereafter.

Probably Clarence Darrow placed little stock in spiritism. He refused to debate even the Biblical resurrection, declaring: "As well might one discuss the question of . . . whether a soap-bubble is still a soap-bubble after it has been burst into a million fragments." It may be that he changed his mind on this point, however; for a member of our radio audience who visited Darrow less than a year before his death reports that this leader of unbelievers, Christianity's Public Enemy Number One in this country, confessed: "You know, sometimes I think that there actually is a Supreme Being; and if there is anything to the doctrine of the Holy Trinity, the Holy Ghost has been working on me, because I unconsciously pray to God every night after I am in bed."

Whatever he thought of the hereafter and the possibility of the dead communicating with the living, we unhesitatingly assert that no spiritist can bring back a departed soul. No medium can put you in contact with your dead relatives. No *séance* can correctly answer questions concerning the life beyond the grave. How we thank God that a Fort Wayne medium turned to our broadcast one Sunday and was moved to reject spiritism and accept the Lord Jesus! Pray God that others may follow her! For spiritism is fraudulent, anti-Scriptural, and destructive. We challenge all mediums to produce one so-called manifestation of spirits that cannot be duplicated by sleight of hand and tricks of parlor magic. So much intense suffering, groundless suspicion, unhappiness in the home, and especially distrust of Christ have been created by those who claim to receive guidance from the dead that the wise laws banishing this unsavory practice should be drastically enforced.

As Christians, we reject all table-tilting, slate-writing, wall-rapping demonstrations. Nor do we find the pledge of our resurrection in modern cults whose founders claim that they were ecstatically lifted up to heaven or in any vague after-life promises of human philosophy. Our Bibles offer us an assured revelation of eternity written by one whom God permitted to behold the heavens' unspeakable marvels, Saint John, author of the last New Testament book with its many pictures of the New Jerusalem. In one of these magnificent previsions, our text for today, John shows us the everlastingly redeemed in their glory and blessing. With the Easter truth still ringing in our souls, "The Lord is risen. He is risen indeed!" let us find joy and strength in this foregleam of Paradise as we behold

THE WHITE-ROBED IN HEAVEN

described in Revelation 7:14-17: *"These are they which came out of great tribulation and have washed their robes and made them white in the blood of the Lamb. . . . And God shall wipe away all tears from their eyes."*

I
WHO ARE THESE WHITE-ROBED?

If Saint John were alive today and would assert, as he does in these words, that there is a heaven in which he beheld men and women, bodily resurrected and glorified, he would be barred from some of our wealthiest churches. Despite the fact that the New Testament uses the word "heaven" and related terms many times, present-day pulpiteers often seek to convince their hearers that the Biblical heaven is merely childish fantasy and the resurrection of the body absurd, impossible.   These ecclesiastical Liberals are contributing heavily to moral decline and rising crime waves; for whenever the clergy buries the truth of retribution after death under a discussion of governmental and political problems, people may lose their sense of right and wrong.

How far this unbelief has gone may be seen in the last book by the late Dr. Richard C. Cabot.   Discussing honesty in church-work, the renowned Boston physician and Harvard medical-school lecturer openly declared that, though every Sunday hundreds of thousands, members of a well-known Protestant denomination, repeat the words of the Apostles' Creed "I believe in the resurrection of the body and the life everlasting," he has yet to meet the first person in that entire church — and this includes the clergy — who believes in the bodily resurrection!   So deep has been the descent from Christ's truth!

That church-body, however, is not alone in this rejection.   Last Sunday, on the glorious Easter Festival, when Christian pulpits should have rung with God's pledge of our own resurrection, a pastor in an imposing New York church, officially committed to the defense of the Bible, told his congregation, "The lingering hope which surrounds us this Easter is the abiding hope not that we as individuals might live beyond the grave but that our world might be saved from the death of evil and hate."   At the same time 4,000 people crowded in a frequently headlined place of worship overlooking the Hudson River to be told that "the message of Easter is not to be identified with . . .

a physical resurrection. . . . The important thing in the Easter festival is the . . . philosophy of life that the spiritual is real." Will you find any comfort in this when you face eternity?

Modernists may smile, skeptics question, infidels ridicule, spiritists counterfeit, philosophers speculate; but human quibbling and quarreling with the everlasting verities cannot change Scriptural truth; there is a heaven where, before God's throne, Saint John beheld the ransomed of Christ. Our Lord, — and are you keenly conscious of the fact that, if you deny the resurrection, you charge Jesus with misrepresentation? — our blessed Savior Himself, not only assured us that there are many mansions in His Father's house and that through His death He would prepare a place for us; He not only repeatedly mentioned the kingdom of heaven, with its incorruptible treasures, its angels, its blessing and glory; the whole purpose of His life, death, and resurrection, He constantly restated, was to give us that endless radiance. When His apostles, the writers of the epistles, preached the risen and ascended Christ, they emphatically asserted that, as Christ had been raised from the dead, so all who bow penitently and trustingly before Him would be resurrected unto glory. The human body, worn, broken, disease-ridden, laid to rest in the grave, drowned in the ocean depths, reduced to ashes by disastrous conflagration, or blown into a thousand pieces by an exploding shell in Europe's suicidal war — that earthly frame is destined to decay. No process men have ever devised can stop that. The lost art of the Egyptian embalmers could not prevent the shriveling and final destruction of mummies. It is reported from the Russian capital that even the mysterious processes by which the corpse of Lenin was to be eternally preserved have not restrained an unmistakable blackening of his remains. It is the everlasting pledge of Christ's truth, however, that the body which is sown in corruption *"is raised in incorruption. . . . It is sown in weakness; it is raised in power. It is sown a natural body; it is raised a spiritual body."* Our lifeless, decomposed remains, so the Scriptures specifically promise, will be fashioned *"like unto His"* (Christ's) *"glorious body."* Indeed, Saint John says, in heaven *"we shall be like Him"*!

In His risen glory Jesus could pass through bolted doors, miraculously transport Himself from Jerusalem to Galilee without cumbersome travel, and in general throw off many limitations of space and time. His resurrection body is, as ours also will be, perfect, without mark or blemish.

What sustaining comfort we can find in this promise! Some of you have lost your limbs; others suffer from a treacherous cancer, which eats living tissues so fast that even radium can hardly stop its rapid destruction. In hospitals for shell-shocked, horribly disfigured faces are still covered with veils or heavy bandages. Through Christ, in the resurrection, all these deficiencies will be supplied. Many of you are deformed, crippled, stunted, paralyzed. Lift up your hearts to Jesus, because in heaven none of these weaknesses burden the redeemed! In the United States alone 100,000 people are blind, but in the New Jerusalem those who believed shall see far more than the clearest human vision ever beheld — colors and beauties far in excess of earthly shades. Another 100,000 in this country are said to be deaf or to have lost the faculty of speaking; but when through faith they have become saints above, their sound range will be in vast excess of our limited hearing; their silence will be broken as they join in the celestial hallelujahs with tones no human vocal cords have ever formed.

We make no attempt to conceal the fact that the resurrection of the body and the Paradise blessings are truths which we cannot analyze with our poor powers of understanding. It is far beyond the reach of our senses and too glorious for earthly analysis. But do not think that you are scientifically logical if you make the fatal conclusion, "I will not believe in heaven because I cannot understand it." That is the worst of all illogical mistakes. You cannot understand how in these pulsating spring days the grass, the shrubs, the flowers, withered and dead in winter, can bloom forth in new life; but no one with the average quota of common sense denies that spring is here. Dr. George Moore, director of the world-famous Missouri Botanical Gardens, writes us that lotus seeds may survive three or four hundred years and, when planted, still will sprout. Why should we not concede that our bodies after the few years or centuries they may repose in the grave, can break forth in newness of life? Even if illustrations like this do not move you, then believe the Bible when it pictures the redeemed of God before the celestial throne. In his *Story of Mankind,* Hendrik van Loon, beginning his chapter on the Middle Ages, specifically says: "I do not expect you to catch the meaning of what I write without rereading this chapter a number of times." Do you expect to catch the meaning of the heavenly ages without rereading God's Word again and again? When you study it, may the Holy Spirit remove all apparent conflicts, as He did in the case of Max Mueller, world-famous Orientalist and philologist, who is quoted as confessing: "How shall I describe to you what I found in the New Testament? I had not read it for many years and was prejudiced against it before I took it in hand. The light which struck Paul with blindness on his way to Damascus was not more strange [than that which fell on me] when

I suddenly discovered the fulfilment of all hopes, the highest perfection of philosophy, the key to all seeming contradictions of the physical and moral world."

One of the most frequent questions asked in your welcome letters — and I cannot thank God sufficiently that He has given us the privilege of helping so many thousands of you — centers about recognition in the next life. Death comes to a family, as it entered thousands of your homes during the past week, and immediately you ask: "Will my beloved husband, whom I have just laid to rest in the cemetery, greet me in heaven?" "Will Mother know her children?" "Will brothers and sisters be reunited in the resurrection?" While other creeds have mistaken ideas of a vague impersonal existence, the Bible leads us to assume that those who are saved for eternity will preserve their identity. It is true, you find no detailed argument for this recognition in the Bible; but that, we believe, is because the Scriptures accept this as a fact in consequence of the bodily resurrection. People now know us by our earthly form; and in the endless Easter we shall be known by the features of our spiritual body, just as Christ was recognized by His post-Easter body. In the change from time to eternity our personalities will not be lost. Therefore the Bible mentions individuals in heaven — Abraham, Isaac, Jacob, the elders, the disciples, the many redeemed who come from the East and the West, and the martyrs of many lands and ages.

In that radiance we shall see and meet and know faith's mighty heroes and brilliant minds. There, too, some of you will be reunited with a Christian mother who died soon after your birth, or a Christian father who twenty-three years ago was drafted for war across the seas but who never returned. If your wife died believing in Christ and you, too, are *"faithful unto death,"* you can be sure that she will be waiting for you in heaven. If your little boy, snatched from life all too suddenly, loved the Lord Jesus, what a blessed reunion can be yours in eternity!

How important it is, then, that our family relationships are hallowed by Christ, so that we may appear together before the everlasting throne? Christian young folks who think that love is the only thing that counts, realize of what surpassing importance it is to avoid every thought of marriage with an unbeliever! A union like that is always overcast with the dark cloud foreboding separation in heaven. Experience combines with the Word of God in asking you to build your homes only with a true believer, so that you can worship together here and hereafter, avoiding even on earth the tragedies that usually come to the home divided against itself through the acceptance and the rejection of the Lord Jesus. Keep Christ in your family!

II

WHENCE CAME THESE WHITE-ROBED SAINTS?

Our text not only assures us that there is a heaven with bodily resurrection and recognition; it also identifies these white-robed saints as those who "*came out of great tribulation.*" The word "tribulation" is interesting. It comes from a term denoting the process by which wheat and grain are put through the threshing-machine to separate the kernel from the straw. The redeemed whom the apostle beholds have been pounded and beaten in life, but only to remove the worthless chaff of sin and save their precious souls. They are the Christian martyrs persecuted for their faith. Some may also have endured slander as gossip maliciously burdened their lives. But God permitted these visitations so that their suffering would bring them closer to Him. They may have spent almost all their lives on sick-beds; but that affliction drove them to their divine Physician. They may have been forced to eke out a poor existence, fighting against poverty, when accident, dishonesty, fraud, made them paupers; but all that happened so they could acquire the faith of the apostle and rejoice, *"I count all things but loss for the excellency of the knowledge of Christ Jesus, my Lord."* These white-robed eternally redeemed may have come from loveless, broken, sin-blasted homes, where adultery destroyed the love of husband and wife or where selfishness separated parents and children; yet from that evil within their own walls they came forth purified and strengthened. They may have been surrounded by constant fear and mental depression, but that trial came upon them so that they would learn the rich blessing of turning away from themselves and trusting God completely. They may have cried through bitter, lonely nights and sustained new pains during long, heartless days; they may have wept until the tears could flow no longer, cried until their voices broke, or lived in stunned silence as one bereavement followed the other; yet through Christ their sorrows were disguised blessings, and from these tribulations they were transferred to a blessed eternity.

If you, too, have the heavenward vision and, being risen with Christ, *"seek those things which are above,"* you have found the only satisfying solution to the problem of your suffering. Need I tell you that our age gropes for that answer? A few weeks ago a member of the House of Representatives refused to run for reelection because he was overtaxed by pleas for help from the people of his district. He said: "I get no rest. I cannot step from my front porch without being asked for assistance. People are always writing for help. Why, there is no peace of mind for me even when I sit down to a meal. My thoughts turn to the pleas of those who are hungry and need the help I cannot give." But God will never resign His position as Provider for His children. He can always help and often does through the refining strength of affliction.

Every day your letters ask that everlasting "Why?" — "Why must I stagger under the weight of adversity?" From Massachusetts a friend writes: "I have loved my Savior for over fifty years, but at times I wonder why. For the past six months I have had a terrible trial. I have tried to be a shining light, but it seems to me that I am a stumbling-block. Why, when I tried so hard all my life?" A Nebraska mother confides: "We met with great tragedy last October. Our son lost his wife in an automobile accident. They had just established a Christian home. Often the question comes to us, Why did God take her away when they were both so happy and both serving the Lord?" Here is the plea of a distracted Michigan woman: "My mind is becoming more and more a jumble over unsolved problems. I can't get rid of the feeling that some day I may become insane, and the terror of such a thing is unutterable agony. Is there no help for me? I've prayed for eighteen years. Why is God apparently deaf to my cries?" From California a listener asks: "I had a business worth over a million dollars, but I lost it all, even though I tried to serve the Lord. Why must I be driven to poverty when, although able to work, I am rejected as too old?"

No satisfying explanation can be given to these and the almost endless similar problems except that all Christians can view life as a school in which they are being trained for eternity, where they will have a thousand unspeakable joys for every sad moment on earth, heavenly blessing for the curse of past agony, celestial beauty for all that was hideous in life. It is hard for some of you

constantly to be battered by adversity's blows and to believe
that through Christ, the oftener you are brought to your
knees in human helplessness but with sacred trust in His
mercy, the closer you come to heaven. But some blessed
day, in the fuller knowledge, you will realize how completely true is the promise of Scripture *"The sufferings
of this present time are not worthy to be compared with
the glory which shall be revealed in us,"* when you, too,
purified through your afflictions, stand face to face with
Jesus before heaven's throne.

There, in that better land, we know that God, approaching the white-robed saints, *"shall wipe away all tears from
their eyes."* In Christ's heaven the cause for grief will
disappear forever; the sin that now fills our hearts with
fear and burdens our consciousness with terror will vanish.
No dread of change nor concern about a hereafter will
disturb us, for heaven will be the eternal homeland, where
every question will be answered, every desire fulfilled.

True, we cannot picture to ourselves a new life without any sorrow. If we measure heaven by our human
understanding, it may seem to us that eternity would be
full of regrets; the sorrow of a wife whose husband has
been doomed to eternal death; the grief of a great American like George Washington looking down on a nation
that has so ungratefully sinned and forgotten its sacred
obligations; the pain of Martin Luther, beholding forces
allied in the attempt to destroy the work of the Reformation and bring men back to the old delusion of a self-
earned salvation. These tragedies on earth, some people
think, must provoke remorse even in heaven. Yet here
is the text, *"God shall wipe away all tears from their eyes,"*
or, as the second-last chapter of the Bible has it, *"There
shall be ... neither sorrow nor crying, neither shall there be
any more pain."* Our new existence will be so glorious

and superhuman that not one of earth's sorrows can reduce
its complete joy and happiness. Peace, perfect peace; love,
heavenly love; joy, unspeakable joy; rest, unbroken rest —
that endless blessing Christ has prepared for you!

III

WHY ARE THEIR ROBES WHITE AND CLEANSED?

Who in this wide assembly of the air is not moved with
heart-felt longing for these blessings? But how many of
you know beyond question the one way to this eternal
glory? The easy, convenient preaching of universal deliverance, which holds that all men are going to heaven,
no matter how they have lived or believed, and that, since
God is the Lord of love, there can be no hell — this open
denial knows neither God and His justice nor sin and its
destruction.

To be assured of heaven, we must have the faith which
these eternally redeemed had, of whom our text says,"*They
have washed their robes and made them white in the blood
of the Lamb.*" They were not always saints but, as you
and I, they were marked by sin. They may have been
grievous transgressors on earth, their iniquity shocking
and terrifying; yet, however deep their sin, through faith
in Christ they found forgiveness. They washed their
soiled and stained robes in "*the blood of the Lamb,*" Jesus
Christ, "*the Lamb of God, which taketh away the sin of
the world.*" That holy blood did what all human cleansing
processes can never do: it removed the grime, purged the
stains, took away the spots, and their garments became
glistening, white, spotless, radiant.

This is a picture, but it clearly promises that, if we
believe, "*the blood of Jesus Christ, His Son, cleanseth us
from all sin.*" If we are not ashamed of this emphasis on
the blood but know, with deep penance over our sins, that

this sacred crimson fluid washes away the wickedness of our hands, lips, hearts, so that in the sight of the holy God we are actually without sin; and if we remain loyal to that atoning Christ, then — O praise be to God's eternal mercy! — heaven will be ours.

The saints of God came from tribulation to heaven only through Christ. The absurd, anti-Scriptural teaching that souls must lie dormant or unconscious for millions of years; the cruel, anti-Biblical doctrine that even those who have died in the faith must be cleansed and purged in a third place besides heaven and hell (of which the entire Scriptures know nothing) that, since the blood of Jesus Christ is not enough to cleanse us from our sins, His atonement must be supplemented by the good works of saints and that we can pray to have others help us into heaven — this terrorizing teaching attempts to undo what the holy Christ has done for every one of us. Page through your Bibles — and take the verdict of the Scriptures before you take the verdict of any man or any Church! — and you will seek in vain for one promise of heaven that is not built wholly on Christ's redemption.

If we love Jesus, let us make *"the blood of the Lamb"* the appeal and promise of more active, more consecrated, more Christ-exalting churches! *"The blood of the Lamb,"* — I can see some of my modernist friends and other self-enlightened listeners making mental reservations and wondering how we can still believe the old Gospel — *"the blood of the Lamb,"* let that be the mark on the door-posts of your home, to keep your dwelling as a Christ-centered haven of rest! *"The blood of the Lamb,"* let that be the faith of our children as we teach them to pray:

> Jesus, Thy blood and righteousness
> My beauty are, my glorious dress.
> Therewith before my God I'll stand
> When I shall reach the heavenly land.

"*The blood of the Lamb,*" let that be the watchword on earth, the victory song in heaven!

That puts many of you squarely before a decision. From today on, having listened to this broadcast, you can never say, "I do not know the path to heaven." After you have heard that Christ is the Way, Jesus looks for a response. Will you be washed in His blood, made holy and cleansed in God's sight? Don't say that it is too late, for this is the promise even for the last hour, "*Him that cometh to Me I will in no wise cast out.*" Don't push this plea aside, declaring that you have tried Christianity and it has failed. We are not asking you to try Christianity; we are asking you to believe it, to throw yourself wholly on God's mercy in Christ and experience what a blessed Savior He is. If you argue that God is the Father of love and there is no danger of His condemnation, listen to this warning from Christ Himself, "*Except ye repent, ye shall . . . perish.*" You may object, "It will cost me too much to accept Christ." What will it cost to reject Him? Eternal darkness, death, and despair in hell! You may not be ready to leave favorite sins or part with old companions in wickedness. But which is better: life with God or death with sin and its associates? You may be persecuted when you confess Christ, but think of the white-robed martyrs who have come out of tribulation into heavenly glory! Without delay or excuse, without any minimizing of your sins, say to Christ, "Wash me! Cleanse me! Purify me by Thy holy blood! Then shall I be cleansed for heaven."

As for you tried and true Christians, ask God for the strength and the courage required to proclaim pardon in the Savior's blood! Pray that our broadcasts may increasingly swing the gates of heaven wide to many helpless souls! Think of it! Within the past two weeks openings have come to us for broadcasting in Porto Rico, Panama, Colombia, and Venezuela — besides the work already started in Ecuador. Pray for blessing on our radio mission and a mighty outpouring of the Spirit in our country! Plead for our part in the evangelization of South America! Help us meet the unusually heavy financial responsibilities that this remarkable expansion has placed on us, knowing, as most of you do, that we pay for every moment of our chain broadcasts at full station rates. With that faith and love you, too, after life's tribulations, your robes washed white in *"the blood of the Lamb,"* will stand before heaven's throne with your fellow-redeemed from all these countries, there to join in the never-ending hallelujahs to the Father, who created us; the Son, who redeemed us by His blood; and the Holy Spirit, who keeps us in the faith! May the holy, Triune God grant all this for Jesus' sake! Amen.

REDEMPTION IN THE RISEN CHRIST

"Jesus saith to Simon Peter, Simon, son of Jonas, lovest thou Me more than these? He saith unto Him, Yea, Lord; Thou knowest that I love Thee. He saith unto him, Feed My lambs." — Saint John 21:15.

Jesus, Savior of our souls:

As we ask ourselves whether we really love Thee who on the cross didst love us unto that end of shame and anguish, we find so much of indifference, even denial of our faith, that we hardly dare lift up our eyes to behold Thee and beseech Thy merciful forgiveness. Remember not our sinful unconcern, we entreat Thee, and by Thine everlasting grace lay not this coldness of heart against us! Show every one who has turned traitorously from Thee that it is never too late to return and that Thy mercies are renewed every morning, even for the faithless, the backsliders, the betrayers! Send Thy Spirit to touch many hearts with the fire of a fervent faith and draw us closer to Thee, our never-changing, ever-blessed, all-victorious Lord and God! Amen.

"WHAT, in your opinion, is the most fundamental need in the lives of the young people of America today?" Last week this question was put to President Roosevelt, and his answer may surprise you. "No greater thing could come to our land today," he declared, "than a revival of the spirit of religion — a revival that would sweep through the homes of the nation. . . . I doubt whether there is any problem, social, political, or economic, that would not melt away before the fire of such a spiritual awakening."

Most of us will agree: America needs a mighty revival; for all human attempts to solve our problems have failed. Our almost endless multiplying of laws has swollen Federal, State, and local statute books to unparalleled proportions; but crime marches on in wider and lengthier procession. We have spent an astonishing total of many billions for education; yet too often our schools have failed in building character and in preparing youth for life's responsibilities. Our diplomacy is dedicated to keeping the United States out of war, but with startling similarity to events twenty-five years ago our ambassadors make inflammatory speeches and are charged with committing this country to war long before the bloodshed started. American scientists record stupendous advances. They have given us faster automobiles, larger airplanes, deadlier poisons, more destructive munitions. Modern science has made life easier and speedier; but has it made our existence better and purer? Economists have devised intricate financial and commercial systems; however, does any one honestly maintain that they have removed our difficulties? It is only a few weeks since a White House committee reported: "More than one half and closer to two thirds of American children in cities live in families where the income is too low to maintain a decent standard of living. . . . The situation of farm children is at least as bad." In short, we ought to recognize that this country faces critical days, with inflation, debt repudiation, or national bankruptcy in one form or another, social upheaval, Communistic conquests no mere theoretical possibilities. Even if we escape war, a terrifying readjustment will follow when peace is declared. Prepare for that now, if you can! Should these money-mad war-mongers succeed in drawing the United States into oversea hostilities, make ready for poverty, industrial stagnation, internal conflict far worse than we have ever witnessed!

There can be no doubt, we need a revival of religion, and we agree further that it must start in the homes, where the foundation for permanent improvement must be laid. — But what sort of religious revival? The last census showed over 200 different religious groups in this country, and if the present census lists all the cults and sects within our borders, this number will be vastly increased. Do we need an upswing of the modernist religion, which rejects Jesus, denies Bible truth, and removes the certainty of faith? The last twenty-five years, with their systematic revolt against Christian hope, have brought us only increased misery, and modernist leaders themselves have repeatedly confessed their failure. Do we want a revival of the creed which tells distracted men and women that they must earn heaven by their own personal penance and good works? God forbid! No matter under how much pomp and ritual that worship is disguised or in what magnificent churches it may be housed, it remains the age-old delusion of salvation by character, achievement, payment — not by Christ's blood and righteousness. Only in the confidence that takes us before the crucified and resurrected Savior have we a religion which offers hope for our daily problems and — this is vastly more important — penetrates into our souls with the promise of eternal salvation.

This

REDEMPTION IN THE RISEN CHRIST,

the assurance that can restore the unfaithful and help win America's youth for Jesus, is impressively shown in our text, Saint John 21:15: *"Jesus saith to Simon Peter, Simon, son of Jonas, lovest thou Me more than these? He saith unto Him, Yea, Lord; Thou knowest that I love Thee. He saith unto him, Feed My lambs."*

I
FAITH IN HIS REDEMPTION WILL RESTORE THE FAITHLESS

These words take us to a memorable post-Easter day, when early in the morning Jesus appeared to a group of His disciples on Galilee's shore, ate breakfast with them —

and then turned to Peter for a momentous conversation. What love that reveals! Peter, who had made the most clear-cut confession of Christ the gospels contain, but, excepting Judas, had become guilty of the most dastardly disavowal; the fire-breathing follower of Jesus who at the beginning of the Savior's suffering promised, *"Though I should die with Thee, yet will I not deny Thee!"* — only soon to reject his Lord shamefully — that disciple with his despicable denial is made the particular object of our Lord's loving concern! Had a soldier been guilty of this disloyalty toward his country, he would have been executed. Had any man otherwise shown the same treachery toward a friend and benefactor, he would have been rejected forever as one unworthy of all consideration. How utterly different the Savior's endless mercy! That discredited traitor is close to Christ's heart, so close that immediately after His resurrection Jesus instructs the women, *"Go your way, tell His disciples* AND PETER!" So intent is the risen Redeemer on restoring His outcast follower that here on the lake shore he calls Simon Peter aside for a blessed conference and a sacred commission.

Our twentieth century has produced many perfidious Peters, who were once close to Christ, active in His service, but who like the impulsive disciple have turned completely from grace. Some of you in our radio assembly know this denial from your own experience. You have come from Christian homes; a godly mother daily prayed for your salvation and tirelessly worked to keep you with God; a believing father, week after week, brought you to Sunday-school and church. You solemnly promised at the altar rather to suffer the pain of death than deny Christ. You took an active part in the Lord's work as members of the choir, Bible-class teachers, congregational officers — but something happened. You met the world, as did Peter, and associated with Christ's enemies. Unwilling to endure the opposition, you, too, said, if not in words, then in actions that speak louder than any formal utterance, *"I know Him not!"* Instead of having Christ's peace in your hearts; instead of working for the holiest purpose that can engage human attention and effort, you are outside the Church, opposed to the Savior, on the sure road to hell.

Should you see your own sin mirrored in Peter's faithlessness, then find the same Jesus who approached that disciple now drawing close to you. Blessed Savior that He is, He does not wait for you to come to Him; if He did, you would never find the shelter of His protecting arms. With His overflowing grace He loves all men, especially those who, once fervent and enthusiastic in the faith, have permitted their trust to become lukewarm and finally cold. Is not He, the Good Shepherd who leaves the flock of nine and ninety to find the one stray lamb, the same divine Redeemer, who, while cherishing all His redeemed, extends His particular care to the deserters? Don't remain in the crushing despair that almost daily finds expression in your letters, when you think you have fallen too low and become guilty of such treacherous disloyalty that even Jesus will not forgive and restore you. Here, pleading with Peter, is the same Savior who in this moment would speak pardon and peace to your heart.

See how gently our Lord deals with Peter! He does not denounce him with the scorn of withering anger: "Peter, how damnable your treachery was! You denied Me, and now I will deny you." Not a syllable of reproach crosses the Savior's lips. With a magnificence of mercy that our age hardly knows and even many churches fail to employ, Jesus says: *"Simon, son of Jonas, lovest thou Me more than these?"* — recalling Peter's boast on the night of the betrayal that his faithfulness to Christ was greater than that of other men. Jesus asks, as it were: "O Peter, you saw Me suffering. You beheld Me dying on the cross. You knew that I was laid cold and lifeless into Joseph's grave. In this moment you, Peter, see Me resurrected with power and in glory. Now, do you love Me more than all others?" Three times the Lord asks Peter, *"Lovest thou Me?"*; and we may discern a blessed purpose in this repetition. Three times on that fateful Friday night Peter had asserted his affection; three times he was now asked to proclaim his true devotion to Christ. Thrice in the early hours of that black Friday he had renounced his Savior; thrice on this glorious day of the resurrection cycle he is to acclaim the Lord Jesus!

Today this immortal *"Lovest thou Me?"* cannot be repeated too frequently. These three words form the question of all ages; they contain the one basic issue on which every hope for revival must ultimately rest. It is not enough to ask, "Do you love God?" for men have had a thousand contradictory pictures of the Almighty; the issue must be, "Do you love the Lord Jesus?" It is not sufficient to inquire, "Do you love Christ as He has been reconstructed by our modern unbelief — Jesus, the great Leader, the mighty Teacher, the magnificent Example, the courageous Pioneer, the Trail-blazer for a new era, the misunderstood Martyr, the noblest Figure of all centuries, the mighty Molder of all history"? Peter's question — and yours — is: "Do you love the Lord Jesus, the Christ of Gethsemane with its sinking weakness, the Christ of Calvary with its blood, its torture, its agony, its God-forsakenness, and its death of shame — the Christ of resurrected glory, whose triumph over the grave proved that He is the mighty God, the eternal Father's only Son? Do you love the Lord Jesus, above all, as your Savior? Do you confess that, when He hung on the cross, He suffered as your Substitute; that, when He died on Golgotha, His death granted you life? Have you testified before men that the red blood which flowed from His wounds can accomplish the otherwise utterly impossible, remove your scarlet sins? Is your love for Jesus a deep, genuine devotion that means far more than merely knowing Christ, respecting Him, admiring Him, offering Him a few spare moments, incidental thoughts, and superfluous pennies"? — Or must you admit: "Yes, I love Jesus — as I love any great man"; or: "I love the Lord — on Sunday and in church"; or: "I love Christ, but I also love the lure of the flesh"; or again: "I love my money, I love life, I love myself far more than Jesus"? With the personal appeal of these words we ask: "Do you yourself love the Lord Jesus?" The faith of the fathers will not save the children; there has to be a personal acclaim of Christ in each heart. Thank God if your wife's name is written in the Book of Life, but be sure that your name is recorded there!

May God grant you His cleansing, strengthening Spirit so that, however grievously you may have denied the Savior, you make Peter's answer yours, *"Lord, Thou knowest that I love Thee."* As the resurrection was proof sufficient for the erring disciple that Jesus was his God and his Savior, so may that magnificent truth call you back to faith with the confession, *" 'Lord, Thou knowest that I love Thee,'* despite my thanklessness, my treachery, my turning from Thy pardon. I love Thee, Jesus, for Thy compassion on me, poor wretched, sinful, traitorous, as I am. I love Thee for the grace renewed every morning and the restoring that has called me back to Thy mercy. O help me always to love Thee, Jesus, to live my faith through Thee!"

If this is your heartfelt declaration, you have once more the full forgiveness through His love. That confidence strengthened Peter to take up the battle for Christ against the world. That returning to Jesus has given many, once weak and wavering, new courage. Archbishop Cranmer, under the pressure of Bloody Mary, was induced to deny his faith and turn Catholic; but he could not lose the sight of his suffering Savior and soon returned to the evangelical creed. That meant death, of course; and when at Bloody Mary's order the flames were kindled around him, he thrust the hand that had once written the denial of Christ into the flames and held it there until it was consumed, often exclaiming, "That unworthy hand!" God will help when you, too, are restored to Christ, by granting new resolution and endurance in facing the worst that life and death combined can offer.

If, then, we are to have a revival in this nation, let it be a Christ-centered awakening in which those who have deserted the Savior, the lukewarm and indifferent, are called back to the blood-bought, resurrection-sealed redemption — a revival not restricted to an emotional upswing, a temporary enthusiasm, a shallow change, but a contrite return to Jesus, a repeated questioning by the Savior, *"Lovest thou Me?"* and the constant answer, *"O Lord, Thou knowest that I love Thee!"*

II

FAITH IN HIS REDEMPTION WILL BLESS OUR YOUTH

How meaningful now to read that, when Peter was restored to discipleship, Jesus gave him the commission *"Feed My lambs,"* the youth to be won and preserved for the Good Shepherd's flock! Throughout His ministry Jesus paid particular attention to the needs of the young. He took the children in His arms and blessed them. He made their faith a pattern of God-pleasing trust. He spoke of their guardian angels in heaven, and gladly He received their hosannas when He entered Jerusalem. Now, shortly

before He returns to His Father, He puts the youth on His restored disciple's conscience.

What divine prudence He displayed! If there is to be a revived Christianity in America, particular attention must be paid to the nation's youth. Horatius Bonar, whose sacred songs are in almost every hymnal, found that of 250 souls won for Christ under his labors the converts under twenty years numbered 138; between twenty and thirty years, eighty-five; but between fifty and sixty years, three; between sixty and seventy years, one; and over seventy, not a single person. Why have many of you, my elderly friends, close to the grave, so ingrained yourselves against Jesus that, with eternity almost knocking at your door, you have not put your house in order by accepting the Savior?

Without making any unfavorable comparisons with past years, it seems to me that this appeal, *"Feed My lambs,"* was never more necessary than today, when insidious forces are coaxing young people from Christ. A California listener tells us of a local public-school teacher who reported to her sixth-grade class the gains and losses she made at the Santa Anita track. It was easy for her to create enthusiasm for gambling, with radio comedians featuring horse-race betting; and her pupils were soon directed to cut from newspapers the columns listing the horses run each day. To carry out the betting idea, each child brought marbles to pay the classroom wagers and was thus — in the public school — initiated into the vice that causes inestimable distress in many homes.

In the higher brackets of our educational system, the colleges and universities, pronounced antichristian and antimoral tendencies sometimes hold undisputed sway. An Indiana mother confides: Her eighteen-year-old son, enrolled in an engineering course at a notable university in that

State, is obliged, contrary to his religious principles and ideals of decency, to read filthy books. One of these volumes to be read in detail for a passing grade in the course the mother condemns on this sweeping charge: "I run out of adjectives when I undertake to describe it. It sounds like the licentious dream of a marihuana smoker. I am glad that my boy was simply revolted by the book, but I tremble to think of its degrading influence on many a young man who must read it but who has no Christian training and background." Now, his mother did what few of you have done but all should do in such attacks on morality: she addressed an inquiry to university officials, asking why this book was prescribed. The reply, think of it, stated that the book was "broadening." — Broadening to the gutter! we say. It has actually come to this, that a tax-supported school like the City College in New York can seek to employ a man whose writings are unquestionably destructive, who a few years ago was definitely indicted in a magazine on the charge that, "though a married man, when he went to China, he was accompanied by, and lived with, another woman. . . . His wife secured a divorce from him while he was in China, and he continued living with the other woman but did not marry her." Do you want your sons and daughters subjected to this immoral TNT that can blast their happiness and purity to irreparable fragments? Then protest!

These anti-Bible attitudes sometimes start in the elementary schools. Therefore give your boys and girls Christ-centered instruction, such as that which you can obtain free of charge in the hundreds of Christian day-schools that my Church maintains in various sections of the country. If you take our advice and send your child to one of these schools, — and they are open to all children, — you will ever be grateful.

Other dangers outside the educational system confront our youth. Was any previous generation closer to crime than the American boys and girls of today, with the gangster movies, gangster broadcasts, gangster comic strips, gangster big-little books? Last night your children could have heard — and we fear many of them did hear — a broadcast which is teaching young America the details of crime, acquainting them with the language of the underworld, revealing the technique of arson, kidnaping, murder. If you parents who like to listen to that program think that we are bigoted and narrow, then hear this verdict of the chief probation officer in the Saint Louis Juvenile Court, "From my actual contact and experience let me state one contributing factor, where I lay the blame for forty-six cases of crime among boys in 1939, and this is the despicable program over the radio." — If only the broadcasting systems or even some commercial concern were prudent enough to give the nation's youth what it does not receive today, a Bible broadcast with the unparalleled interest and heroism the Scriptural stories contain!

Now, if Christ's lambs are to be fed, that spiritual nourishment must first be given in the home. A distracted mother in the State of Washington asks, "My serious question is, Will God hold us parents responsible for our children and their families' salvation?" If you parents have done what God expects fathers and mothers to do for their own flesh and blood, and your sons and daughters have nevertheless forsaken Christ, He certainly will not blame you; but if you have kept your children from His Church and the Bible; if they have seen sin, indifference, hostility to Jesus in your lives, heard unbelief, cursing, blasphemy, from your lips, God will certainly hold you responsible. You sophisticated, self-satisfied parents, smug in your own conceit, who have never taught your little ones to pray, never led them to Sunday-school, never brought them to church, remember that on the day of Judgment your child can come before you and demand: "Father, why didn't you bring me to Christ?" "O mother, why didn't you take me to church?" Think of that here-after — now! Ask yourselves, even in your own unbelief, if what I say may not be true! We want to help you! Let us send you some Christian literature!

If we are to bring our children to Christ in the homes, we must have Scripture-reading, prayer, and the worship of God in our family circles. A revived Christianity must start with a rebuilt altar. Not long ago a Canadian aviator told of visiting General and Madame Chiang Kai-shek, China's Nationalist leaders. A few moments after he had arrived for dinner, Japanese airplanes zoomed down on the city, trying to destroy the Generalissimo and his wife, since their death would be worth more than the capture of an entire army. Less than a quarter of a mile away bombs destroyed a city block; yet after that raid was over and the business transacted, General Chiang Kai-shek in-vited his visitor to join in the evening devotion. The man who has been called to lead China's four hundred millions spent thirty minutes in Scripture-reading and prayer as he pleaded for guidance and, with amazing charity, asked God to help him and China not to hate the Japanese people. He even prayed for the enemy aviators who had just dropped their bombs. In Jesus' name he consecrated him-self and his home to God's service and asked that the divine will be done. — As we hear this account of a convert's prayer in war-torn China, the contrast with many Amer-ican church-members is inevitable; despite all their bless-ings even church-members are often indifferent to prayer and neglectful of God Almighty.

Thank God for the Christian parents who bring up their children in *"the nurture and admonition of the Lord."* You will pardon this personal remark when I share with you the joy that today my own dear mother observes her eightieth birthday, having devoted year after year to her Savior, with self-denying service to her children and all whom she could help. My mother, your Christian mother, our God-fearing fathers, whether they are alive now or whether God has taken them to heaven, have given us the faith that alone offers the pledge for stronger, better churches and a more devout nation. Should our most determined efforts not be directed to guard that heritage and promote faith in the Lord Jesus?

A woman once asked Francis Whalen Parker how early she could begin the education of her child. The eminent Chicago educator replied: "When will your baby be born?" "Born?" the woman gasped, "Why, he's five years old now!" "My dear lady," he cried, "don't stand here talking to me! Hurry home! You've already lost the five best years." Fathers and mothers of America, the early years are the most important. Have you brought your boys and girls to Christ in response to His appeal, *"Suffer the little children to come unto Me and forbid them not; for of such is the kingdom of heaven"?* Are they baptized? Have you taught them their prayers? Does your family ask God's blessing at every meal? Do you read the Scriptures with them? Are your children enrolled in Sunday-school or a church-school? — These are vital issues. Let us help you answer them in a God-pleasing way. If your sons and daughters are not prepared for eternity and you doubt your own ability to do what God expects of you, thousands of pastors associated with me are eager to suggest practical, Bible-centered direction. Give us the spiritual direction of your child! Let us furnish a plan for Christian instruction and training in the highest ideals of life and assurance for eternity. We can show you what it means to fulfil Christ's command *"Feed My lambs!"* — and what blessings that obedience brings.

Before us lie problematical years in which not you older folks but your sons and daughters will feel the brunt of many problems. Bring our youth to Christ! If everything else gives way in their lives, Jesus will not. His love will remain unclouded for all who trust in Him. As these words are spoken, a solar eclipse is covering the sun and darkening the earth; but Christ is the Light that never fails, the Sun that never loses its brightness. Come back to that Light, you who are wandering in darkness, as Peter returned to his Lord! Bring into that brilliancy the youth of our country, the fathers and mothers of tomorrow! With an active, militant Christianity, trusting only in the Cross and the blood, knowing no other Savior than Christ, no other book than the Bible, no other hope than the trust of faith, we can have a revival in spirit and in truth that will shake this country to its foundation. God, shake us soon, for Jesus' sake! Amen.

"ALL HAIL THE POWER OF JESUS' NAME!"

"All power is given unto Me in heaven and in earth. Go ye, therefore, and teach all nations, baptizing them in the name of the Father and of the Son and of the Holy Ghost, teaching them to observe all things whatsoever I have commanded you." — Saint Matthew 28:18-20.

O Christ, Lord of all power in heaven and on earth:

Reveal Thy strength to us in these moments of worship! Show us Thy mighty sin-canceling grace! Lead us to believe unquestioningly in the potency of faith by which life and salvation, the gifts of Thy blood-bought mercies, are ours! We need to trust Thee more completely, Lord Jesus, to know confidently that in every trial, in the agony of pain or the hour of death, Thou, Sovereign of our souls, canst save to the uttermost. We can live the truly abundant life which Thou wouldst give us only when we rely on Thy mighty love. Therefore strengthen our weak faith, increase our wavering trust, and help us, no matter how hopeless our future may seem, to look only to Thee, the Father, and the Spirit for divine guidance from earth's sorrows to heaven's glory! We are Thine, for Thou hast redeemed us by Thy blood. Hear us and bless us for Thy truth's sake! Amen.

WITH what shock and swiftness the terror of war has spread since last I spoke to you! In a confidential bulletin to American business executives, dated April 6, a Washington financial agency calmly predicted that for the next months we should see only slow-speed war with no intensified hostilities. This announcement was hardly off the press when, on April 8, the world was stunned by the conflict in Scandinavia. If these experts cannot foretell even by a few days the invasion of two entire countries, how can we have any certainty for the future, any assurance that this mad war will not provoke the most horrifying destruction humanity has ever witnessed? Who knows whether by next Sunday other nations will not have been irresistibly drawn into this disaster? Who can say positively that the sinister, profit-seeking forces of propaganda may not succeed in sending our youth across the seas? God prevent that!

One thing we should know, however: the hundred millions of dollars spent for this annihilating conflict will impoverish nations already tottering on the narrow edge of bankruptcy and help throw the whole world into financial chaos. The longer the war lasts, the farther it extends, the deeper the poverty and the wider the upheaval our age will suffer. The launching of every new battleship, air bomber, and submarine means higher taxes for the common people, who in the final analysis must pay for every war. Certain it is, therefore, that atheistic Communism will receive powerful support and that the churches' cause will meet with increased opposition, both abroad and at home.

Where, then, are we to find the help and the hope required safely to face this future and solve our personal problems? In money? This generation has seen people pay millions of paper marks for a sandwich. In Government aid? Who knows the size of national treasuries after the war? Besides, many of your worries, the questions of a tortured soul, difficulties in the home, the anguish of incurable disease, are too deep to be removed by a PWA grant. Can we find the pledge of inner peace in culture or by a studied plan of meeting misfortune? Too many Masters of Arts and Doctors of Philosophy roam through the land, their lives complete failures. Last week again the newspapers brought the usual toll of college crime and intellectual suicide.

In these critical days, with our own perplexities added to international strain and threats of even deeper sorrows, we should take refuge in Christ, our Savior, and, repeating the acclaim of the immortal hymn,

"ALL HAIL THE POWER OF JESUS' NAME!"

find strength and joy in our Lord's declaration (Saint Matthew 28:18-20): *"All power is given unto Me in heaven and in earth. Go ye, therefore, and teach all nations, baptizing them in the name of the Father and of the Son and of the Holy Ghost, teaching them to observe all things whatsoever I have commanded you."*

I

HAIL JESUS AS THE GOD OF ALL POWER!

In these words, addressed to His disciples before His glorious ascension, Jesus plainly asserts that He is God. If *"all power"* is given Him; if He controls the forces of nature, the strength of men, the rule of the entire universe, even the might and majesty of the glorious, eternal heaven, He must be the Almighty and All-powerful.

Some of you, however, like to believe that Christ was only a man. The trouble is this: You have not fully and reverently studied His life. You have permitted your mind to be restricted by reason, poisoned by a polished skeptic's unbelief. Will you not be as fair to Christ as you are to any human being and answer these questions? When Jesus defied hurricanes and with one sentence quieted a storm-tossed lake, was not that evidence of divine power? When He cured all manner of sickness, healed deformities, restored sight, hearing, speech, were not these demonstrations of superhuman might? His repeated feeding of famished multitudes, His reading the unspoken thoughts of the disciples, His majestic glance that sent enemies prostrate — could men or angels of themselves perform these miracles? When He restored cold corpses to pulsating life; above all, when the rock-hewn sepulcher, the official seal and the guard of Pilate's troops could not keep Him in the grave, who can reasonably doubt that Jesus exercised powers found only in God Himself?

Of course, you may object that these wonders never occurred; but that denial contradicts the clear-cut statements of trustworthy witnesses. Saint John says that his *"testimony is true"*; Saint Luke speaks of *"many infallible proofs"*; Saint Paul declares, *"I know whom I have believed"*; and you, too, will know if you let the Spirit of God work in your heart and bring His decisive proof.

Listen also to the voice of history. Sometimes it has seemed that Jesus was defeated, that His truth was sentenced to the scaffold, while unbelief remained securely enthroned; but in every conflict Christ, the divine Conqueror, has ultimately prevailed. They crucified Jesus, but He rose again. His followers were murdered; but martyr blood was the seed from which great spiritual harvests were reaped. Within the churches selfish unbelief disguised and disfigured the Savior, but our Lord threw off every man-made restriction, reformed and restored His Church. A hundred times it appeared to human eyes that Christianity had gasped its last breath. Bible critics boasted that our faith is *passé;* infidels calmly announced the number of years that the Christian "superstition," as they called it, would survive; but that Gospel, often ground to the dust, has always risen with new strength and authority.

Forget history for a moment to see how Christ can prove Himself God in your life! When He says, *"All power is given unto Me,"* He includes, as He once specifically said, all power over sin. Because He paid the penalty for our transgressions, offering His life on the cross for ours, He can cleanse and heal sin-stained hearts, transfuse new energy into sickly souls. A few days ago a New York woman was apparently fatally wounded when a bullet pierced her heart. In a remarkable operation a surgeon cut four ribs from the breast-bone and took the heart into his hand. The punctured left ventricle spouted blood with every beat, but the surgeon took a stitch every time the heart quieted and finally sewed the wound. Meanwhile, however, the woman was seriously weakened by the loss of blood, and an intern climbed on an operating table to have a quart of his blood pumped into her veins. Now hospital officials predict the woman will recover completely. These surgical triumphs well deserve the newspaper publicity they receive; but why do people pay so little attention to Christ's spiritual healing, which completely restores the human heart? Why do men think so lightly of the Savior's blood with its eternal cleansing? Mighty minds have blessed God for that grace. T. Sidney Cooper, whose paintings have attracted world-wide attention, was asked for his opinion of the Bible; he answered: "It brought me to see that I was lost in sin and had no power to save myself. It showed me how I must get God's forgiveness for all my iniquity. It told me the door of mercy was open and that salvation was freely to be had. It showed me the wonderful sacrifice of Jesus Christ, and through His precious blood all my sins are washed away. For *'He hath made Him to be sin for us who knew no sin, that we might be made the righteousness of God in Him.'* I read the Bible daily." May we, too, immersing ourselves in these Scriptures, come to Christ in the faith which triumphs, " 'All hail the power of Jesus' name!' because He has broken the dominion of sin in our lives, freed us from the tyranny of hell as from the darkness of eternal death, and granted us life, light, and never-ending happiness."

More than this pardon comes from Christ. His omnipotence is exhibited in the protection He extends to His believers. Once you crown Jesus Lord of all in your life, a mighty but invisible wall surrounds your whole existence to keep you safe and unharmed for God's blessed purposes. Nothing else can protect you in that way. Years ago, in India, Edward Payson Scott planned to begin work among the Naga, a dangerous hill tribe, whose language he had studied. Refusing military escort, Scott set out alone with his Bible and his violin. Apprised of his approach, the natives ambushed him, and Scott suddenly found himself surrounded by hostile savages, their spears directed toward his heart. Then the power of Jesus showed itself. The missionary took his violin and played the hymn he had previously translated into their tongue:

> All hail the power of Jesus' name!
> Let angels prostrate fall!

Before the end of one verse the spears were lowered and the Nagas listened attentively to the first Gospel-message they had ever heard. When he had finished the last words,

> Oh, that with yonder sacred throng
> We at His feet may fall,
> Join in the everlasting throng,
> And crown Him Lord of all!

the hostility had vanished; tears could be seen on some faces. Scott, welcomed by those who had planned to kill him, spent many years of blessed missionary activity in their midst.

Perhaps not as dramatically, but with much the same love, Christ's power protects us through faith. Thousands can testify that Jesus helped when earthly support failed, cured when medical science offered no more hope, supplied when money was gone. Trust the Savior! Cast *"all your care upon Him, for He careth for you!"* Bow submissively before Him to say: "O Jesus, Thou hast power to shield and deliver me. I entrust myself wholly to Thee. 'Take Thou my hand and guide me o'er life's rough way!'" While everything else in life may fail, the Savior's love will answer that plea by fulfilling His sacred pledge of guidance.

Some, disillusioned, point out that repeatedly those who are the Lord's seem to suffer most. Why do Christians often pray for progress and receive reverses; for blessing, and meet affliction; for protection, only to suffer disaster on the highway; for the joy of life, only to find racking sorrow? Even that comes from Christ's power. To keep you in grace, your pride must often be checked, your self-confidence destroyed, your reliance on God increased. Sometimes Jesus permits you to lose everything so that the eyes of your faith may be focused only on Him. We may be left alone in life so that during the loneliness of bereavement we turn to the Savior and say, *"Whom have I on earth beside Thee?"* In every affliction, however, in heaped losses, persistent crosses, continued torments, Christ can change defeat to victory. Cling to this comfort in your darkest moments, my sorrowing friends: His purposes toward His own are always for their preservation in the truth. Therefore offer Him heartfelt thanks and exult, "'All hail the power of Jesus' name' for His protecting grace!"

His limitless might reaches its perfect fulness *"in heaven."* At His Father's right hand, worshiped by cherubim and seraphim, adored by the eternally redeemed of all lands and ages, the Lord Jesus awaits those who lived and died in the faith. There, when we stand at the bar of divine justice to give an account of our lives to the holy God, how blessed the confidence that the Savior will plead for His believers and say: "O Father, I have borne their sins. I have fully atoned for every iniquity, sinful thought, hateful word, and evil action. Father, though their sins were scarlet, they are now white as snow; though they were red like crimson, they are white as wool." By that sin-destroying love you and I shall be granted our prepared places in the heavenly mansions, and with celestial joy we shall sing, " 'All hail the power of Jesus' ' eternally hallowed name!"

Fellow-sinners and fellow-redeemed, what a glorious Savior Jesus is! How magnificent His power to save, protect, preserve, for all eternity! Since His grace freely bestows everything you need for the salvation of your soul, peace in a war-torn world, joy amid the sorrows of affliction, spiritual wealth and health in earthly poverty and sickness, should you delay another moment before giving yourself to Him in repentant faith? With Jesus offering you heaven's promise, can you afford to permit any favorite sins, the lure of the flesh and the lust of the eyes, to keep you from declaring, "I crown Thee, O crucified but ever-living Savior, my King, my Lord, my Redeemer"? God bless every one of you with such resolute faith!

II

HAIL CHRIST AS THE SAVIOR OF ALL MEN!

How eagerly, then, should we follow our Lord's command, *"Go ye, therefore, and teach all nations, baptizing them in the name of the Father and of the Son and of the Holy Ghost"!*

"All nations" — what surpassing strength of comfort these words contain! Thousands of census enumerators

will not succeed in listing each inhabitant of the United States; but God's penetrating eye sees every one even in the most remote sections of the globe. *"All nations"* — this is the risen Savior's guarantee that on the cross He died not for a preferred few, a small, selected group, but for men, women, and children of every race and nation, color and condition, with none too exalted for His grace, none too lowly for His mercy. He is the Savior of India's Hindus and China's coolies, Greenland's Eskimos and Africa's Zulus, South America's Indians and Australia's bushmen, Tibet's Mongols and Arabia's Bedouins, Congo's pygmies and Borneo's head-hunters, America's multi-millionaires and the nation's 25,000,000 destitute. Jesus — praise His holy name! — is the one Redeemer for the oppressed, disgraced, downtrodden, forsaken, and helpless; He is the Christ for all men. His Word, translated into a thousand languages and preached in even more tongues, proclaims: *"God so loved* THE WORLD *that He gave His only-begotten Son, that* WHOSOEVER *believeth in Him should not perish but have everlasting life."* Cling to this blessed *"whosoever"!* Richard Baxter, noted Scotch divine, who restored what was regarded as a hopeless church by building the family altar, could never sufficiently thank God for that *"whosoever."* It meant more to him, he wrote, than if the Holy Spirit had put his own name in the Bible. For, he declared: "If God had said that there was mercy for Richard Baxter, I would have thought I was so vile a sinner that He must have meant another Richard Baxter. But when He says 'whosoever,' I know that He means me, the worst of all Richard Baxters." "All hail the power of Jesus' name," for He is the Savior of the world!

Our text emphasizes that *"all nations"* are to be taught, as our Savior specifies, *"to observe all things whatsoever*

I have commanded you." Jesus wants firmly indoctrinated Christians with an intimate understanding of His truth. He is not satisfied with emotional Christianity which makes inner feeling — not God's promises — decisive. He wants more than nominal faith; many of you Christians in name would be seriously confused if called on to explain the Savior's creed. Our Lord asks for more than an inherited faith. Some in this audience belong to a certain Church simply because their parents happened to be members of that communion. Jesus cannot recognize a compromise which approves one part of His doctrine but rejects another. He demands, "Teach 'them to observe all things whatsoever I have commanded you!' "

This complete avowal of the Gospel is the outstanding need in present-day church circles. Modernist leaders say: "We accept Christ's Golden Rule but not His blood atonement. We endorse His social principles but not His plan of salvation. We grant that He was born at Bethlehem but not of a Virgin. We preach that He died on the cross but say nothing about a bodily resurrection." Deny only one truth of the Savior's teaching, and you have weakened the authority of every promise He has ever made. It is either the whole Christ or no Christ!

The only Church that can survive will be the group which believes in doctrinal preaching and teaching. This leads me to make a statement concerning religious union movements in the United States. Every Christian, of course, wants one truly united Church, not several hundred different denominations, subdivisions, and infinitesimally small religious bodies. We regret, for example, that American Lutheranism consists of three or four separate groups, and we pray for one Church, built on absolute unity, with unquestioned acceptance of every Christian doctrine. Indeed, we beseech God to make those who love the Savior one also before the world. But to form an outward union in which Christ's teachings are ignored or compromised ultimately results in doctrinal indifference and must sacrifice saving truth. The call of the hour is for nothing less than full agreement, unrestricted acceptance, entire loyalty to every revealed truth. For that glorious unity all who love the Lord Jesus should systematically consider the differences now separating them and follow the verdict of God's Word in every disputed issue.

Complete loyalty to Christ brings its own reward. Some of you pastors, it is true, will find little compensation for your faithfulness. Do not be discouraged! Rather have less applause, smaller charges, more opposition, with Jesus than without Him a large, fashionable church where the Law is hushed and the Gospel replaced by current topics. If allegiance to our Lord means that you denounce unholy tendencies in your church-bodies; if it demands that you pastors protest against open disloyalty among the higher-ups in your denominations; if obedience to Christ's command involves discrimination and penalties, confess your Savior! If they seek to stop you, come out, be separate, and God will bless you for your testimony!

As an aid to our salvation, a sign of membership in the Church, Christ offers the blessing of Baptism. In His divine compassion He has instituted for every man, woman, and child throughout the world this sacred act of washing, which, when accompanied by faith, cleanses and purifies. Worldly organizations demand high initiation fees; fashionable clubs set exclusive membership requirements; intellectual societies are open only to the learned; but Jesus has a simple, free, universal rite — washing with water. When a sinner is baptized, not by any power inherent in the water, but by faith, he becomes God's child, reborn *"by the water and the Spirit."* Here is Mark's

record, "*He that believeth and is baptized shall be saved.*"
These are Christ's words. You deny or ridicule them
only at the peril of your soul. When Jesus Himself thus
makes this sacramental act a part of every Christian's
life, why do some of you belittle water baptism, seek to
reduce its effect and limit its blessing? Why do you not
stop at the clear text and believe the apostle when he
says, "*Baptism does also now save us*"?

This washing of regeneration is so sacred that it must
be solemnized, according to the Savior's words, "*in the
name of the Father and of the Son and of the Holy
Ghost.*" The glorious, ineffable Trinity itself is involved
in this Sacrament. Blasphemous scoffers in the last century
performed mock baptisms in the name of liberty, equality,
and fraternity. Modern infidels suggest the trinity of
beauty, truth, and love; but take Christ at His word, and
find in Baptism the power of the Father who created us, the
Son who redeemed us, and the Holy Spirit who sanc-
tifies us. We have never asked you to accept baptismal
blessings without having some listeners in various sections
of the country write that they are ready to join the Church
in this way. I pray that today will be no exception and
that God's Spirit will touch many hearts with the desire
to be baptized and through faith saved for eternity. If one
of the thousands of fellow-workers in whose name I speak
can serve you, whoever you are, give us the privilege of
bringing baptismal blessings to your home and your whole
household!

The time for teaching "*all nations*" grows shorter.
How eagerly we should grasp the remarkable missionary
facilities of the radio! For several weeks I have been at
the point of telling you how miraculously our heavenly
Father has blessed our broadcasting. Six years ago we
had only two stations, but Jesus' power was with us.

Today this "Bringing-Christ-to-the-Nation" program has become the largest radio system in the country, with about 175 stations — supported by our Lord and, as far as human help is concerned, by nothing else than your prayers, your interest, your gifts. Opposed by powerful church combinations; attacked by clergymen; for instance, by a Michigan preacher who, after last week's message on the blood of the Lamb, wrote: "Why do you spread this dribble about Christ's red blood making us white? How can you believe that atonement?" assailed by groups who have tried to put us off the air because we insist that there is only one way to salvation, faith in the precious Redeemer — this broadcast has extended in the North to the Hudson Bay district, where isolated trappers, prospectors, and Eskimos can hear the Word. Central America is covered by a powerful station in Panama, with long and short wave. We touch the West Indies through a Porto Rico broadcast. In South America we have Ecuador's "The Voice of the Andes"; and more recently one outlet in Venezuela and three in Colombia have been offered us. A special staff is now engaged in translating our messages into Spanish for these and other foreign stations. To the West, through the instrumentality of a United States Navy chaplain, we have secured in Manila the Orient's most penetrating station.

Visualize the startling spread of our work as depicted in these letters: From Nassau, Bahama Islands: "I tuned in the Lutheran Hour, which I had never heard before. I was really sorry when it ended. My husband listened most attentively to the heart-searching questions." From Christchurch, New Zealand: "We enjoy your straight-out, spiritual messages and the appeal for the people to seek Christ." From Queensland, Australia: "Your Christ-centered program is very timely, of the type which, sad to say, has almost disappeared in these days." From a plantation in New Guinea: "This is the first time we had the pleasure of hearing your broadcast. Our nearest white neighbors are thirty-five miles away across the open ocean." From Wanhsien, in Szechuan Province of war-torn China, one of our missionaries writes: "About a thousand miles west of Shanghai, on the Yangtze River, we heard you speak over the radio. Thanks to God! We thrilled with joy." From Hongkong: "We received your message here on the island of Cheung Chau. The broadcast will by the grace of God open up new missionary possibilities in the Far East." From Manila: "I heard your religious program on Sunday. I am very much interested in the broadcast, as it touches my soul." From San Juan, Rizal, in the Philippines: "Enclosed please find two pesos. I should like to know more about your belief. Do enlighten me further!"

If only there were time to tell you in detail how richly our heavenly Father has blessed us! But we have only begun! My fellow-redeemed, I firmly believe that during the next months God Almighty will open to us a hundred stations in Asia, Africa, and, when the war is over, in Europe. Spanish broadcasters in South America have expressed real joy at the prospect of cooperating with us. However, we need your prayers, and your financial help to make the transcriptions. Ten cents sent to our mission of the air brings Christ's message to 200 people; a dollar, to 2,000. Ten dollars will send the Gospel to a large section of South America. One hundred dollars will cover Central America for several months. One thousand dollars — and what is a thousand dollars if only a single soul be won? — will keep the broadcast Gospel for an entire year in the Philippine Islands and large areas of Formosa, South Japan, China, French Indo-China,

Australia, New Zealand, Cochin-China, Cambodia, the Malay Peninsula, and India. Before God we ask for your small contributions as well as for the $100 and $1,000 gifts that you, the richly blessed, can give back to the Almighty for this quick and inexpensive method of bringing Christ not only to this nation, but also to distant parts of the world. This is the first time we have made this direct appeal. — Yet, O God, Thou who dost hold us responsible for the souls of men whom we can reach, be with us and bless us! O Christ, to whom *"all power"* is given, strengthen the sacrificial love of Thy children! O Holy Spirit, stir us into flame until by Thy grace the redeemed in earth's remotest nation may with us hail the power of Jesus' holy, precious name! Amen.

———

CHRIST EVER WITH US!

*"Lo, I am with you alway, even unto the end
of the world."* — Saint Matthew 28:20.

God, the Father, Son, and Holy Spirit:

With all our hearts we thank Thee, O Triune God, that Thou
hast given us the privilege of broadcasting the promise of full, free
salvation through our Lord Jesus; and we praise Thy power and
love because of the manifold, undeserved blessings with which Thou
hast remembered us. For the remarkable extension of our radio
mission, for every blood-bought soul turned to Christ through these
broadcasts, for the instruction, warning, comfort, extended to multitudes, we give Thee all honor and glory. Strengthen us, we plead,
to face the veiled future with the realization that through faith
Jesus is constantly at our side, ready to raise us when we fall, to
sustain us in the weak moments of temptation, adversity, and doubt!
Keep us in Thy grace, and whatever may befall us, let us always
hear our Redeemer's pledge, "Lo, I am with you alway, even unto
the end of the world"! We ask the Savior's presence in His holy,
saving name. Amen.

IT is with feelings of regret that we have seen this Sunday
approach, for today marks the end of our present radio
season. Until the fall, when, God willing, your prayers
and interest supporting us, we resume this testimony to
Jesus Christ, our broadcasts will rest.

I speak of regret because we ought to be on the air
each Sunday during the entire year. The forces of hell
take no vacation; neither should we. Coast-to-coast
programs that oppose the Lord Jesus continue for twelve
months. Should we be satisfied with six, even though un-
American, discriminatory, and dangerous radio policies
permit Christ-denying agencies to broadcast free, while
we must pay for every moment of our chain programs at
full commercial rates? This is not the time to stop exalt-

ing the Savior's Cross. The world is hastening from Jesus; many churches are turning traitorously from the Almighty, wasting precious time on frivolities while the souls of millions perish, retreating, though our Lord points to the whole world, saying, *"Go ye!"* This is not the hour to leave the air, when men's hearts quake with fear at the thought of wider warfare and longer misery, when from Moscow atheism announces new attacks on Christianity and in our own country a revival of paganism shows itself even in the antichristian education of our children.

This broadcast has stood for the inerrancy of the Scriptures, the substitutionary suffering and the atoning death of the Lord Jesus Christ, for justification by faith and salvation for every repentant sinner. What other message can be as important as this? We have stressed the Christian ideals of marriage and family life, indicted divorce, warned against artificial birth control as it reduces the size of many families, promotes immorality and weakens national strength. We have pleaded with our youth to keep their distance from taverns, dance-halls, lustful motion-pictures, and filthy stories. We have urged marriage of Christians only within the Church, so that Christ can reign in the home, to sustain families during sorrow and sustain true spiritual unity. Is not that the appeal for which this morally loose age cries? We have raised our voice against every attempt to remove the line of demarcation between Church and State, showing how dangerous it is for the United States to recognize a single religious group and what disastrous consequences may arise if certain churches and their leaders continue to influence political life and governmental affairs. Do you not agree that this emphasis is imperative? Yet how many broadcasts plainly proclaim these basic truths? May this be the last "vacation" our "Bringing Christ to the Nation" mission of the air will ever take! When we resume our work in October, may God give us the courage and the support required to make ours a regular, uninterrupted, week-after-week, yearlong warning and appeal in the name of our only Savior!

Yet, though these network broadcasts stop today, we have a promise of joy and strength which can bless us until we meet again in the fall. No one can predict what will happen in these intervening months. Sinister forces endeavor to drag us into the war. God rebuke them and put their devilish plans to naught! After the last two weeks no military authority of whom we have read has predicted anything but enlarged warfare and invasion of other nations. Financial advisers are at a loss to foretell even major trends. Fortune-tellers confess that they are at their wit's end. The *Astrologers' Journal,* London, stopped publication on account of "uncertain conditions." Jesus alone knows the future. Besides, He has given us the assurance that, come what may, clinging to faith's promise, we can exult,

"CHRIST EVER WITH US!"

For among the last words our blessed Savior directed to His disciples there is this pledge to His followers throughout the ages (Saint Matthew 28:20), *"Lo, I am with you alway, even unto the end of the world."*

I

IT IS A PROMISE OF MERCY

When Jesus spoke these words, the time had come for His last will and testament. Shortly before the Eleven had been asking questions concerning the time their Master would establish an earthly kingdom and make them regents in His glory. How some of them must have thrilled when Christ began to speak, declaring, *"All power is given unto*

Me in heaven and in earth"! This sweeping statement showed that our Lord could give them wealth, dominion, honor, worldly triumph. But the Savior knew the lustful, covetous human heart too well. He bequeathed no money, although all silver, gold, hidden and known wealth in the world, are His; for as churches wax rich, they often become carnal, overbearing, forgetful of the poor. Our Lord extends no promise of earthly rule, since His disciples often abuse power and sometimes destroy their fellow-Christians. No pledge of intellectual leadership can be found in these parting instructions; because even churches have arrogantly permitted reason to crowd out divine revelation. No, Jesus' final instruction revealed that His messengers must serve instead of being served. They must leave their homes, break family ties, overcome aversion for the Gentile world, go to all nations and preach, not the pleasing announcements of men's goodness, but their total depravity, the sinfulness of every human heart, and then the pardon, peace, life, through faith in the blood-stained cross.

The disciples soon realized that they had inherited from Jesus a destiny marked with pain and martyrdom. Their own eyes had seen the appalling price Jesus Himself had paid in bringing His fellow-countrymen the Gospel. What suffering would await the apostles as they sought to extend the evangel over the earth! They were unlearned, fishermen, most of them, who had come from despised Galilee; and now they were to preach the message of a Judean Messiah before a world that then as now hated the Jew. They must invade the strongholds of Greek wisdom and Roman power with a creed which the heathen world regarded as foolishness and weakness, since the passions of lust and the craving for power locked that first century in their iron grip. But Jesus had help for the titanic task; and He offered it in the last sentence He addressed to His disciples on earth. Pay attention to it because it may be the last promise of Christ you will ever hear, with reports of railway disasters, tornadoes, and sudden death crowding the daily newspapers! Here is His final pledge, *"Lo, I am with you alway, even unto the end of the world!"* He will be their constant Companion, He promises His redeemed. In every dark, cheerless hour He will walk at their side. They will be obliged to face no battle alone nor to rely on their own strength in any conflict. He, their ascended Lord, will be with every one of them, in every place, at every hour!

What magnificent mercy is revealed in these words! Not only did our Lord's limitless love move Him to leave heaven's glory for earth's sin and sorrow; not only did He live His life of service and self-sacrifice, to die on the cross, weighted down by the world's transgression; but in His glorious mercy and resurrected power He accompanies the believers to bless them with His divine presence. Not satisfied with the fact that His holy angels have charge over us, He, the risen Savior Himself, wants to be with us personally.

Do you, His present-day disciples, realize the radiance of this mercy? His grace, full and free, redeemed you. His love, undeserved and unearned, chose you. His divine devotion, infinitely above understanding, keeps you close to Him in the faith. *"By grace are ye saved, through faith, and that not of yourselves: it is the gift of God."* With that clarion-clear declaration the Apostle asks you to center your faith on the complete grace of the Lord Jesus Christ.

The most heroic Christians have always humbly shown their acknowledgment of the Savior's constant guidance. Some time ago a Saint Louis newspaper stated that John Bunyan, author of *Pilgrim's Progress,* seeing a criminal pass, exclaimed, "There, but for the grace of God, go I."

He confessed that, had God not mercifully intervened, he would have been a degenerate lawbreaker, thief, murderer. One reader of that newspaper wrote, saying that not John Bunyan, but William Bradford, early governor of the Plymouth Colony, had uttered these words. Some one else added that the same statement is credited to John Wesley. The fact that three notable men would speak in the same humility to recognize God's grace in Christ moved me very much, but I soon learned that other eminent Christians had made the same admission. In my own Church Dr. C. F. W. Walther, who a hundred years ago helped bring a band of Saxon immigrants from European oppression to American religious freedom, saw a convict led away in chains. That night the picture of the criminal flashed through his mind, and he wrote in his diary, "But for God's grace I would be that condemned wretch." Did not Saint Paul state that same truth in this meek acknowledgment, *"By the grace of God I am that I am"?*

For you personally, however, the decisive question is not whether others have testified to Christ's sustaining mercy, but whether you have knelt before Jesus to declare that His Spirit has prevented you, with all the heart's lustful longings, from becoming a public disgrace, a perverted fiend, a heartless monster. God grant that you have this humble, cross-centered, Christ-exalting trust!

Hear this warning, however: Jesus will not remain with you, no matter what your church-membership, congregational position, family faith may be, if your continued worldliness and protracted sin against better knowledge pushes the Savior away! There is too much sham Christianity today, and often it is impossible to distinguish a believer from a worldling. Both frequent night clubs and laugh at the same suggestive jokes. Both are found in secret organizations, bound under the same anti-Biblical oath. Both read the same tainted books and magazines, converse on the same scandals, see the same *risqué* plays with all their profanity and godlessness. The chief difference is this, that the unbeliever readily admits he is against Christ, while the churchgoer wants to pose as Christian at least on Sunday. In eternity increased condemnation will await the unfaithful church-members because of the Lord's warning, *"Unto whomsoever much is given, of him shall be much required."* Our parting plea to those who have only the Christian name but no deep conviction in Christ, is: Fall on your knees in penitence and prayer! Believe that the Savior's blood can cleanse you of insincerity, remove your deceit, and give you a new heart and a right spirit!

The promise of His constant companionship should bring many who have lived against Jesus under His protection. This assurance, *"Lo, I am with you alway, even unto the end of the world,"* is not granted regardless of our attitude toward Christ. Today certain classes of ministers desecrate their office by holding flowery funeral orations eulogizing men and women who never had any thought for the Savior except that of hatred; flabby churches label every Jew or Gentile a Christian, promising that all will be saved; one of our transcription stations refuses to accept our broadcast because, as the manager states, we mention "hell," and the better classes in that community do not believe in hell. It is necessary, then, for the holy God has commanded that these warnings must be issued, to remind you that without the Lord Jesus you are forever lost. Unless you acclaim Him your Savior, you cannot approach God; for here is His clear-cut ultimatum, *"No man cometh unto the Father but by Me."* Nor can you have hope for this life if you reject Christ. He will not accompany any one who constantly thrusts

Him away. Do you not want divine help for the sorrows with which God even now punishes many of you, making you pay bitterly for the folly of unbelief? If you remember nothing else of what you have ever heard in this or any other Christian broadcast, may God's Spirit convince you that the Savior loves you, too; that the only barrier which can keep you from walking through life with Him at your side is your own denial!

An Iowa woman writes that her father, for whose conversion she has prayed for twenty-five years, listened to our broadcast one Sunday and cried out: "Oh, I want that blessing! If only there were a chance for me!" God convinced Him that there was a "chance" for him, and now he has confessed Christ as his Savior. Because many others among you, despite your long disregard of Jesus, have had your hearts touched by the Holy Spirit and are asking, *"What must I do to be saved?"* let us give you the answer which the Lord proclaimed in His first recorded sermon, *"Repent ye and believe the Gospel."* Now, the repentance Christ wants is much more than a hazy feeling of sorrow over some wrong you have committed, much more than a resolution to improve your ways. It is a complete change of heart and mind, a contrite confession of all your sins, with no attempt to disguise or excuse them, a pleading guilty to the charges raised by God's Word. Real penitence requires restitution, righting the wrong, paying for the losses you have inflicted. It means, most of all, praying for pardon in Jesus' name through faith in the cleansing power of His blood.

With true contrition and firm trust in the Savior, knowing that you need only believe, since His promise, repeated three times in the Scriptures to give you triple assurance, reads, *"Whosoever shall call on the name of the Lord shall be saved,"* you, no matter how completely you have rejected Christ, how blasphemously you have spoken against His eternal mercies, how cruelly you may have destroyed your own happiness, weakened your body, stultified your mind, and brought the terrors of hell on your soul, can find forgiveness for the most damnable wrong, pardon for secret sins, cleansing for the hidden vices and past iniquities that may bring disgrace through exposure. Here in Christ is your God and Savior, on every unmarked pathway, the Companion who *"sticketh closer than a brother."* His plea is never more direct than when it asks you, "O sinner, come home!" His appeal is never more personal than when He promises you, as He does now, guidance for time and eternity. In His name and in this season's last broadcast, facing all the uncertainties a troubled tomorrow may produce, confronted with this terrifying truth that without Jesus you are lost forever, we plead, Accept Christ now, before it is too late and the Almighty's judgment dawns!

II

IT IS A PROMISE OF POWER

What magnificent power comes from Christ's abiding presence! Human teachers live their short life span, die, and molder in the grave; but Jesus, because He is our Lord and Redeemer, is resurrected and lives with us. War reports tell us that the German government has removed the remains of Charlemagne inland from a frontier city. He was the mightiest monarch Europe has known since the days of the Caesars. He ruled the continent from Constantinople's gates to the bleak Baltic provinces; but he could not rule death. Two hundred years after he had been buried in a tomb of royal proportions and lavish decorations, one of his successors, Otto III, pried his way into Charlemagne's burial-vault; and the flickering torchlight revealed the decayed body of the great emperor seated on a white marble throne-chair, his spectral hand clutching a scepter, his skeletal head tilted under the weight of the imperial crown — a mock ruler, unable to escape the tomb. One hundred and sixty years later even this ironical evidence of his royalty was taken away. Emperor Frederick Barbarossa entered the tomb, removed crown, scepter, marble chair, and transferred the moldering bones of Charlemagne to a near-by chapel. Now his remains have been moved once more. How helpless death has made the monarch of the mighty Holy Roman Empire! How easy to transfer his ashes! But our ever-victorious Christ reigns today with undiminished power, and His influence cannot be "evacuated" from one city to the other.

He lives to prove His promise, *"Lo, I am with you alway,"* in His protecting love. A score of dangers arise by day and twoscore by night; quickly could death overtake us were it not for His shielding hand. In His wisdom our Father has concealed many besetting hazards around us; for if we knew all perils to health and life which crowd into every moment, our hearts would be filled with constant fear. Sometimes, it is true, disaster does overtake God's children as it did not many hours ago, when a crack express train, thundering through the night, roared from the rails and brought injury or death to large numbers. Yet even when those steel cars were crushed, Christ was with His own, unto the end.

No place on earth is too remote for His universal protection. Sir Sven Hedin, famous explorer, who has faced dangers few men ever encounter, declares: "Without a strong and absolute belief in God and His almighty protection I should not have been able to live alone in Asia's wildest regions for twelve years. During all my journeys my Bible has always been my best lecturer and

guide." David Livingstone, confronted by death almost
every day in Africa, assaulted by fever, attacked by whites
and cannibals and slave-traders — that mighty Christian
explorer, who was once crushed by the jaws of a lion,
asserted: "Shall I tell you what has sustained me in my
exiled life, among strangers whose life and language
I could not understand? It was this that comforted me
at all times, *'Lo, I am with you alway, even unto the end
of the world.'* " No matter where your way takes you,
through faith you can have the positive conviction that
Christ is as near to you as He was to His disciples in
Palestine.

Believing the Lord Jesus when He says, *"Lo, I am
with you alway,"* you know that He understands your
needs and can provide for you *"according to His riches
in glory."* These are matters of serious concern to many —
this battle for daily bread, the struggle to keep the home,
the difficulty of finding work; and we see scanty hope
for healthy improvement. Our exports have been sliced
drastically. War industries flourish, but profits in blood
are as dangerous economically as the flushed cheeks are to
a consumptive. A single machine replaces two hundred
workers. Small business often cannot withstand the competition and tactics of some chain stores. The upper age
limit in certain commercial enterprises and in misguided
churches is below forty. Government indebtedness in-
creases. Millions of the poor grow poorer, and the few
rich become richer. Now, what can we offer these discouraged, destitute masses? Social revolution with economic upheaval? That does little more than increase the
misery for the lower classes. We need a sound financial
program, of course, one, we insist, that does not oppose
God's code; but at the same time we must direct men
to Christ and convince them that He is with them to supply

all their needs, if necessary, by miracle. Over in Finland, where, after the spring thaw, survivors are still burying their frozen dead; in Norway, where sufferers wonder what new burden awaits them with the break of each day, it may seem that trust in Jesus has proved futile. Yet Christians in these war-harassed countries, still singing "A Mighty Fortress Is Our God!" will find that even their poverty and suffering ultimately must *"work together for good."* Who knows — divine omnipotence may transform destitution and grieving in these nations to marvelous blessings both for their people and the world!

"Lo, I am with you alway," the Savior repeats to you, the bedridden, the invalids, the victims of dread, deadly diseases, who in moments of weakness may feel surging bitterness arise within you to demand, "How can Christ be with me?" Don't let that resentfulness gain mastery, for such thoughts are not from God! Believe Jesus without any question, and He will help you bear pain. He will grant you patience. He will give you a resigned, consecrated heart. Should it be for your spiritual development, He will restore and strengthen your weak, broken body.

The same promise holds for every sickness of body and mind. A Minnesota mother writes: "I have so many fears and misgivings as to my own unworthiness that I spend many sleepless nights filled with a sense of utmost despair and stark fear. Please help me!" An Indiana listener asks: "Often when I pray or mention God's name, horrifying thoughts and words run through my mind. How can I overcome this frightful thing?" We find the answer by recognizing that as Christians we have no promise of smooth and frictionless existence. On the contrary, we are told we must enter the Kingdom through much tribulation. This frightened wakefulness, this intrusion into your prayers, may be the thorns in your flesh; but God can remove them in His moment, the best and only time. Stay close to Christ in prayer, Scripture-reading, Holy Communion, and He will never forsake you! I once heard a woman scream that she was eternally lost since she had committed the unpardonable sin; but later she died a peaceful, victorious death, committing herself wholly to the Savior. He was with her, even through dark and distracted years. Keep that comfort locked in your hearts, you Christian wives in unhappy marriages; for example, the Ontario mother who writes, "O my God, my God, help me! Pray for me as you have never prayed before! I haven't walked for sixteen years, and my husband curses me and is going to leave me." If every one forsakes you, Jesus will not; for here is the Savior's promise, *"Him that cometh to Me I will in no wise cast out."*

Approach the Lord in childlike faith, all you who have fears in your heart, sorrows in your soul, trouble in your home, and He will hear you, for He is always close at hand. A dispatch from England tells us that last week a stranger knocked at a cottage door in Gosport. Inside, the mother cried happily, "That is Len, my boy!" Hardly had these words been spoken when her son, Leonard, clad in Canadian uniform, entered. Though she had not seen him in thirty-one years, her mother love recognized even that knock. But the Savior love of Jesus, who is constantly at our side, hears us and knows us even before we knock, often granting our requests before we pray.

In such closeness to Christ the churches must find blessing for these challenging years. This generation's hope lies not in any vague, abstract worship of an unknown deity but in Jesus, God's Son and the world's Redeemer, who has promised to be with us. We need a return to the spiritual confidence of the first-century faith. Those early worshipers in the catacombs felt Christ's presence in an unmistakable, personal way and were strengthened for every crisis by this realization of His divine protection. Religious groups in the United States ought to discard all secular, political ambitions and wholly dedicate themselves to the privilege of proclaiming the Savior's nearness. Appeals are made asking the churches to sway the Presidential election. They ought to refuse completely; for if they engage in this mud-slinging battle, they will be enlisted for every campaign; the ministry to men's souls will suffer, and the Gospel's mighty influence will be curtailed. Moreover, when churches enter the political arena, it will not be long before the Government meddles in religious affairs. In these strife-torn days of delusion, let American Christianity have one message and proclaim it in no uncertain, muffled voice: redemption in Jesus Christ, the Savior ever with us!

Our Lord has kept His promise, *"Lo, I am with you alway!"* in our broadcasts, as a demonstration of His truth and power. We started last October with eighty-two stations, and through His guidance that number was more than doubled within less than six months. About 170,000 people in this country and Canada have written us so far this season. As we indicated last Sunday, letters now come from the other side of the globe, even from India. New fields are constantly opening. Last week powerful stations were offered us in Bolivia and Argentina. The work must continue and expand! At least a hundred more stations throughout the world should be enlisted to tell men and women in their own language that once they are Christ's, they have the joyous assurance of His presence. These stations can be secured, if only you will pray and work for the international spread of this broadcasting system which now seeks to bring Christ to the nations. Your letters, prayers, interest, support, under God, will help us establish the mightiest radio system for Jesus history knows.

Until this radio mission for Christ is resumed a few months hence, may our Lord abide with every one of you! Perhaps many now joined in this far-flung worship will be called home by their Savior before our eighth broadcasting season begins. It may be, too, since the signs of the last times are being fulfilled unmistakably as never before, that our Lord will not linger long before He returns. Yet in peace or war, plenty or want, health or sickness, honor or reproach, happiness or suffering, life or death itself, here is His promise to every believer, *"Lo, I am with you alway, even unto the end of the world."* Trust this grace, build your daily hope on its mercy, and no matter how the tide of human affairs may turn, you can cling safely to the Rock of Ages, *"Jesus Christ, the same yesterday and today and forever"!* On that glorious day, when all of us who are Christ's, you whom I can never meet on earth but whom I shall know in heaven, stand before the throne of the Lamb, our robes washed white in His blood, then as the Christ of all power repeats, *"Lo, I am with you alway,"* we can echo, "Blessed Savior, lo, thanks be to Your mercy, we are with You alway!"

Our Lord Jesus Christ be close to you until we meet again! Amen.